"*InterGenerate* is a veritable encyclopedia for those wishing to build capacity for the intergenerational church. These writers blend strong research with inspiring stories, and their solid biblical and theological foundations are embedded within 'ministry-in-the-trenches' experiences. Every church leader will find actionable wisdom in this collection."

—**Sydney Hielema,** PhD, Faith Formation Ministries, Christian Reformed Church, Canada, and author of *Deepening the Colors* and *Vivid*

"Rather than living in isolated, peer ministry paradigms that no longer work, *InterGenerate* offers the church a bold, new vision of spiritual formation from cradle to grave. This book imagines the body of Christ as a series of intimate, joy-filled, intergenerational relationships.

—**James Penner,** Canadian youth sociologist and lead author of *Hemorrhaging Faith*

"*InterGenerate* signals an exciting and important shift in conversations around ministry for youth, children, and congregational care. Many of the authors have been on the front lines, working to shift congregational attention to an intergenerational focus. There is a lot to learn in these pages."

—**Andrew Root,** PhD, Professor of Youth and Family Ministry, Luther Seminary, and author of *Faith Formation in a Secular Age*

"The church is an intergenerational community, but the challenge for twenty-first-century leaders is to enhance it more intentionally. This book will equip you with a theoretical framework and praxis guidelines to become an effectively intergenerational church."

—**Jan Grobbelaar,** PhD, Facilitator of Research and Academic Development, Petra Institute, De Doorns, South Africa

"*InterGenerate* unleashes the potential for authentic, high-impact faith formation for people of all ages. These diverse writers orient our thinking and provide practical strategies to bring intergenerational ministries to life in the everyday relationships of everyday churches."

—**Eugene Roehlkepartain,** PhD, Vice President of Research and Development, Search Institute

"I'm thrilled by *InterGenerate*. It is encouraging that so many academics and practitioners have united to develop and apply intergenerational ministry practices. Here you will find the most up-to-date theory and practice of intergenerationality, written by people who love Christ's church and desire to see all ages thrive together."

—**Christine Lawton,** PhD, Program Director of Institutional Assessment, Concordia University, and coauthor of *Intergenerational Christian Formation*

"The balance of academic ideas, theology, generational theory, and practical application makes this an inspiring read. Rediscover the passionate conviction that the church is uniquely placed to make a transformational difference."

—**Lucy Moore,** Messy Church Founder and Team Leader, UK

"What Chesterton said about Christianity in general is also true of intergenerational ministry: it 'has not been tried and found wanting. It has been found difficult; and left untried.' *InterGenerate* provides workable ideas to put intergenerational vision into practice. It is like a book of travel tips from those who have gone ahead in the journey."

—**Rev. Dr. Graham Stanton,** Centre for Children's and Youth Ministry,
Ridley College, Australia

"*InterGenerate* is one-stop shopping for everything you need to know about intergenerational faith formation. This stellar group of theorists and practitioners offers solid rationales and creative methodologies for becoming a faithful, intergenerational church."

—**Ivy Beckwith,** PhD, Faith Formation Ministry Team Leader,
United Church of Christ, Cleveland, OH

"Research consistently shows that worshiping across generations helps root young people in their faith. But where are the churches in which people worship, serve, and live out their faith across generations? Unable to imagine anything else, we often default to 'church by age group.' I welcome this book as a guide for churches on the transformational journey toward being intentionally intergenerational."

—**Rev. Mary Hawes,** National Children and Youth Adviser, Church of England

"Rediscover a shape of church where old and young accompany one another in developing faith that is not only biblical but spiritually enriching for all. I hope this book will encourage churches to grow the all-age kingdom of God."

—**Martyn Payne,** author of *Messy Togetherness* and Messy Church team member,
Bible Reading Fellowship, UK

"The gift of this collection is the combined perspectives of practitioners and scholars. It is the collective wisdom from a broad range of people who care about building community across generations, and it is rooted in the guidance of God's word."

—**Gene Crume,** PhD, President, Judson University, Elgin, IL

"There are few more pressing issues for the church today than the need to rediscover what it means to actually live together in familial community. We are desperate for help in not only recognizing our relational brokenness but also discovering how to do something about it. *InterGenerate* is an invaluable resource for helping us to live together as God's people."

—**Chap Clark,** PhD, Pastor, St. Andrew's Presbyterian Church,
and author of *Adoptive Church*

Foreword by
JASON BRIAN SANTOS

InterGenerate

Transforming Churches through
Intergenerational Ministry

Edited by
**HOLLY
CATTERTON
ALLEN**

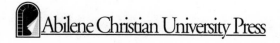
Abilene Christian University Press

INTERGENERATE
Transforming Churches through Intergenerational Ministry

ACU
PRESS

Copyright © 2018 by Holly Catterton Allen

ISBN 978-1-68426-150-5 | LCCN 2018015666

Printed in the United States of America

All Scripture quotations, unless otherwise indicated, are taken from the Holy Bible, New International Version®, NIV®. Copyright © 1973, 1978, 1984, 2011 by Biblica, Inc.™ Used by permission of Zondervan. All rights reserved worldwide.

Scripture quotations noted NRSV are taken from the New Revised Standard Version Bible, copyright © 1989, the Division of Christian Education of the National Council of the Churches of Christ in the United States of America. Used by permission. All rights reserved.

INTERGENERATE ™ is a registered trademark of Lipscomb University, used under permission of Lipscomb University. All rights reserved.

Photographs on pages 242–43 are in the public domain and have been provided by Vibrant Faith from the Visual Faith Project.

Parts of Chapter Two are drawn from a previous publication: Gareth Crispin. "A Theology of Accommodation as a Resource for Integrating Youth and Children into Intergenerational Church" from *Christian Education Journal*. Copyright © 2017 by *Christian Education Journal*. Reprinted by permission of *Christian Education Journal*.

Parts of Chapter Fourteen are drawn from a previous publication: Holly C. Allen. "Walking with Emerging Adults on the Spiritual Journey" from *A Faith for the Generations*. Copyright © 2015 by Timothy W. Herrmann, Kirsten D. TenHaken, Hannah M. Adderley, and Morgan K. Morris. Reprinted by permission of Abilene Christian University Press.

LIBRARY OF CONGRESS CATALOGING-IN-PUBLICATION DATA
Names: Allen, Holly Catterton, editor.
Title: Intergenerate : transforming churches through intergenerational ministry / edited by Holly Catterton Allen.
Description: Abilene : Abilene Christian University Press, 2018.
Identifiers: LCCN 2018015666 | ISBN 9781684261505 (pbk.)
Subjects: LCSH: Church. | Intergenerational relations—Religious aspects—Christianity.
Classification: LCC BV640 .I58 2018 | DDC 253—dc23
LC record available at https://lccn.loc.gov/ 2018015666

Cover design by ThinkPen Design | Interior text design by Sandy Armstrong, Strong Design

For information contact:
Abilene Christian University Press
ACU Box 29138, Abilene, Texas 79699

1-877-816-4455 | www.acupressbooks.com

18 19 20 21 22 23 / 7 6 5 4 3 2

I dedicate this book to my parents,
Gene and Fayrene Catterton,
with love and appreciation for their
prayers, perseverance, and faithfulness.

Contents

Acknowledgments

This book originated at the InterGenerate Conference held at Lipscomb University in Nashville, Tennessee, in June 2017. So, my gratitude goes to those who made both the conference and the book a reality.

The InterGenerate Task Force, listed below, wishes to express its profound appreciation to both GenOn Ministries[1] and Lipscomb University[2] who sponsored the conference.

GenOn Ministries bathed InterGenerate in prayer, provided initial funding for website expenses, and offered regular promotional support. In addition, at the very beginning, Liz Perraud, executive director of GenOn, created a survey, which she sent to around one hundred people we knew to be interested in intergenerational ministry, to discern the level of interest for an intergenerational conference; the strong, positive response provided the impetus to carry the conference vision forward. Several survey respondents became part of the task force, along with Shirley Carlson (GenOn board member) and Suzie Lane (GenOn program director).

Generous upfront support from Lipscomb University enabled the InterGenerate task force to begin their work. These funds were approved by Randy Lowry, president of Lipscomb University, and Danny Taylor, Lipscomb's CFO. Lipscomb's Hazelip School of Theology and the Institute for Christian Spirituality covered the costs of trademarking the word

"InterGenerate" and printing the program booklet along with other conference-related expenses.

A special thanks goes to Cory Seibel for his help in editing this text; he offered invaluable insight and suggestions for two of the chapters—besides the two chapters that he authored.

Also, we should acknowledge that two members of the task force, Melissa Cooper (a millennial) and Olivia Updegrove (a Gen Xer), created the name for the conference and for the book—*InterGenerate*; we are so glad our task force is *intergenerational*.

On a personal note, I wish to thank the women with whom I meet and pray on Tuesday evenings: Linda Blanks, Linda Bridgesmith, Mary Hemminger, Rebecca Lavender, and Kathy Musick. These women have tracked with *InterGenerate* from the beginning, catching an early glimpse of the vision, listening patiently along the way, holding up my hands when challenges surfaced, believing with me that this was God's work, and sharing the joy as this work has come to completion.

The following people formed the InterGenerate Task Force:

- Ron DeVries, Vice-Chair
  Regional Catalyzer, Faith Formation Ministries, Alberta, Canada
- John Roberto, Treasurer
  Vibrant Faith Leadership Team, Naugatuck, Connecticut
- Karen DeBoer, Secretary
  Creative Resource Developer, Faith Formation Ministries, Kitchener, Ontario, Canada
- Melissa Cooper, Website manager
  Associate, Vibrant Faith, Kissimmee, Florida
- Shirley Carlson
  GenOn Ministries board member, Port Clinton, Ohio
- Darwin Glassford
  Executive Pastor at Harderwyk Ministries in Holland, MI; and Director of Graduate Programs and Online Learning at Kuyper College, Grand Rapids, Michigan
- Suzie Lane
  Program Director, GenOn Ministries, Nashville, Tennessee

- Linda Staats
  HomeGrown Faith, Phoenix, Arizona
- Olivia Updegrove
  Minister of Family and Children's Ministries at Disciples Home
  Mission, Indianapolis, Indiana

This hard-working, committed group of people stepped into the idea of convening an intergenerational conference from scratch with passion and panache. Together, we represent Christians from a number of traditions: Catholic, Churches of Christ, Christian Reformed, Disciples of Christ, Methodist, Lutheran, and Presbyterian. It has been one of the most delightful experiences of my life to envision and create something new with these remarkable people; a wonderful *esprit de corps* emerged over the eighteen months we worked together. Both the conference and this book reflect this amazing spirit, and we learned to say along the way, "To God be the glory."

Holly Catterton Allen
Chair, InterGenerate Task Force

Notes

[1]**GenOn Ministries:** www.genonministries.org GenOn Ministries equips faith communities for Christian discipleship and builds and nurtures relationships with God through Jesus Christ through intergenerational resources, trainings, conferences, and Youth Summits.

[2]**Lipscomb University:** www.lipscomb.edu Lipscomb University is a private Christian liberal arts university in Nashville, Tennessee, offering bachelors, masters, and doctoral degrees. Its primary mission is to integrate Christian faith and practice with academic excellence. This mission is carried out not only in the classroom but also by involvement in numerous services to the church and the larger community. (www.lipscomb.edu /about/mission)

Foreword

I can't remember the first time I used the word *intergenerational* in relationship to the church; but as I reflect back on the last decade of my work as an academic and a practitioner, I do recall vivid memories of my own awakening to the value and necessity of intergenerationality in our understanding of Christian formation. The idea that we could and should intentionally form all generations through some communal spiritual practices seemed so commonsensical that it didn't seem revolutionary at first. During my fourteen years of higher education, it was never presented to me as an established school of thought nor a philosophy of education for how we form people in faith. Or perhaps I just wasn't paying attention.

If I had to guess, I would say my earliest conscious engagement with intergenerational formation came during my doctoral residency. I entered that program in my mid-thirties, having spent the previous two decades enmeshed in ministries that focused on peer-oriented, age and stage ministry—children, youth, college, and young adults. I had worked in various churches and Christian traditions around the United States and in Europe.

Having the opportunity to delve into the thoughts of other educators, theologians, and scholars throughout the world on topics related to age and stage ministries was an honor, though one that came with a growing discontentment. New "types" of ministry were constantly appearing on the horizon; which one would offer the ultimate fix for our ministries no one could guess. Even with these valiant efforts, we all knew the truth: age and stage ministries weren't broken, the church was.

My epiphany came while serving as an associate pastor at a large church. I was talking with a high school student about his experience in worship on Sunday morning. He couldn't really respond to my queries; rather he shared that in all the years he and his family had been part of this congregation, he had never really spent much time in "big church" (as he called it). The lion's share of his spiritual formation had happened outside of the broader worshiping body. In that moment, I realized that *we* (of the royal variety) had taken things too far with age and stage ministry.

Perhaps our youth are abandoning church as young adults because it was never theirs to begin with. I hate to say it, because I share in the blame, but we've failed our young people and the church at large by not truly cultivating an *intergenerational* community of faith where they knew they belonged.

As a result of my newfound realization, I began experimenting with different ways of bringing the generations together. I tried intergenerational retreats and all-age VBS. Eventually, I came to a place where I cancelled the age and stage Sunday school programing and collapsed everyone into one intergenerational class. We named it "ONE," and we had over ninety people from ages three to ninety-three.

Confession time: It wasn't always pretty. In fact, it was the hardest thing I've ever taught in my life; but it was also the most rewarding class I've ever taught. It was during those experimental times that I realized that intergenerational formation could happen, and—like those divine declarations offered during creation—*it was good.*

In the midst of my exploration into intergenerational practice, I discovered a (then) newly published book by Holly Catterton Allen and Christine Lawton Ross, *Intergenerational Christian Formation: Bringing the Whole Church Together in Ministry, Community and Worship* (2012). I was thrilled that other scholars were digging deeper into the topic. This publication appeared at a critical time, and the analysis was ground breaking. I was overjoyed—and admittedly jealous that they had written it before I could. I have no doubt that it will be one of the most influential publications on intergenerational ministry for decades to come.

Today in my own work in the national offices of the Presbyterian Church (USA), where I oversee Christian formation for the denomination, I have the opportunity to teach about intergenerational formation a lot. And every time I speak or write about the topic, my inbox swells with new requests for more information. People want to talk about it. I'm convinced that it's because the concept is fundamental to who we are called to be as communities of faith. It's not only about bringing children and youth back into "big church"; it's about all of us being formed *together* as the church. It's essential to our identity as followers of Christ.

In a day and age where societal changes are happening with an unprecedented rapidity, we know the church isn't immune. We're all asking those tough questions about what and who the church is supposed to be in our shifting culture. What Allen and Ross started in their first book, this book continues, ultimately offering an almost prophetic barometric reading on what's happening in this growing field of study and practice.

Although Allen will share more about this book's origins, it's worth noting that both its title and a significant portion of its content came out of a gathering of folks invested in intergenerational formation. It was Allen's vision that guided a team of passionate leaders to host the InterGenerate Conference in late June 2017. To date, it was the largest and most diverse gathering of academics and practitioners on the topic, and the participants left excited and ready to explore new intergenerational practices in their home settings. That's why this book will also prove to be a rich contribution to the conversation; it's about as close as you can get to participating in the conference, without leaving your armchair.

In the pages that follow, you'll encounter myriad perspectives from different parts of the world and from various denominations, from scholars with theories of intergenerationality to Christian educators sharing the joys and difficulties of leading in this ministry shift. In the end, what I hope you'll find among the amazing authors in this collection is an entry point . . . or better yet, an invitation to join in the conversation about intergenerational formation.

My encouragement to you, the reader, would be this—dig deeply into this book. It will serve your thinking and your practice well. And know that as you move through the challenges and celebrate the successes of your intergenerational experiments, you are not alone.

May God's grace and peace be with you as you serve God's kingdom.

Rev. Jason Brian Santos, PhD
Louisville, Kentucky

Addressing the Two Intergenerational Questions

Holly Catterton Allen and Chris Barnett

Community churches, emerging churches, evangelical churches, mainline churches, missional churches, charismatic churches, Catholic churches—all types of Christian communities—are lamenting the silos created by age-segregated ministries. Leaders are now asking, "How can we bring the generations back together?" This renewed interest in intergenerational ministry is also grounded in a growing body of research that supports the idea that intergenerational experiences contribute uniquely to sustainable, long-term faith formation across all ages.[1]

Defining *Multigenerational, Cross-Generational*, and *Intergenerational*

In general, we will define *intergenerational ministry* in this text as Christine Ross and I (Holly) did in our 2012 book, *Intergenerational Christian Formation: Bringing the Whole Church Together for Ministry, Community and Worship*: "Intergenerational ministry occurs when a congregation intentionally combines the generations together in mutual serving, sharing, or learning within the core activities of the church in order to live out being the body of Christ to each other and the greater community."[2]

17

Though the definition is a good basic description, it is not comprehensive, and it continues to prompt clarifying questions such as: Are the terms *intergenerational* and *multigenerational* synonymous? Are the main benefits of intergenerational ministry for children and youth? Must all the generations be present for an event to be called intergenerational? How does a generationally configured church begin the process of becoming more intentionally intergenerational?

The terms *multigenerational, cross-generational*, and *intergenerational* are often used interchangeably, though they carry different connotations. A useful resource for exploring the distinctions among multi-, cross-, and inter- is the paper from the United Church of Canada, *Defining Multicultural, Cross-cultural, and Intercultural.*[3] I (Chris) have applied the language from this document to the intergenerational space, creating the following explanations:

- in the *multi*generational environment, there is tolerance living alongside superficial and polite interaction;
- in the *cross*-generational environment, there is some sharing, listening, and learning, but little individual or collective transformation; and
- in the *inter*generational environment, there is comprehensive *mutuality, equality*, and *reciprocity* that makes individual or collective transformation more likely.

In essence, the trajectory from multi- to inter- involves a greater depth of relationship, a change in the nature of the relationship, and an increasing openness to being changed through relationship with the "other."[4]

Benefiting More Than Just Children and Youth

David Goodwin's research suggests that adult engagement with children and provision of meaningful opportunities for children to be involved in worship with adults will "assist children to grow in their faith, their love of God, and their connection to the church and its faith practices."[5] His focus is on the benefit for children; however, a crucial concept for proponents of intergenerational ministry is the idea that it offers benefits for *all* ages.

While momentum toward greater intergenerationality within churches is sometimes generated by those primarily concerned with younger generations, the initial impetus regarding the importance of intergenerationality from a secular perspective arose from the field of gerontology—that is, from an identification of the benefits for older generations of deeper engagement with younger generations.[6] As Christine and I outlined in our book, there are strong biblical, theological foundations as well as solid support from developmental, social learning, ecological systems, sociocultural, situative-sociocultural, and gerontological theory[7] for asserting that an intentionally intergenerational environment encourages and sustains lifelong discipleship for *everyone*.

Intergenerational ministry is not just about (and of benefit to) children and youth; it is about (and of benefit to) people of all generations.

Must All Six Generations Be Present?

One commonly highlighted description of intergenerational ministry is, as described by James White, "two or more different age groups of people in a religious community together learning/growing/living in faith through in-common-experiences . . . and interactive sharing."[8] Basically, this definition involves different generations intentionally engaging in shared activity together; but more particularly, it highlights the fact that it requires only two generations to be present for there to be the potential for intentional intergenerational engagement. Thus, regardless of how many years are assigned to a particular generation (typically fifteen to twenty years[9]), even in congregations without representatives from all generations, there is still the opportunity to embrace—and benefit from—an intentionally intergenerational approach to ministry.

Finding a Starting Place

Just as clarity around the terms multi-, cross-, and inter- can be useful for churches, so too can clarification around the difference between a primarily *generationally* arranged community and a primarily *intergenerationally* arranged community.

In general, a *generationally configured* community defaults to age-based cohorts that sometimes join with other generations for specific activities together. For communities primarily organized in this way, the challenge is to create opportunities for the different generations to engage in well together.

An *intergenerationally configured* community defaults to all ages gathering together, though sometimes things are done separately in age-based cohorts. For communities primarily organized in this way, the challenge is to *deepen* intergenerational connections.

An initial task for churches is to discern whether they are primarily generationally or intergenerationally configured (noting that each configuration calls for a blend of age-based and multi-age experiences); this process will help determine the foundational starting point for their journey toward greater intergenerationality. Irrespective of the starting point, though, the challenge in either case is to implement more intentional intergenerational strategies that foster Christian spiritual formation for all ages.

And the chapters of this book, *InterGenerate*, were written with this precise challenge in mind.

InterGenerate: An Overview

One unique aspect of this book is that it is, like the conference, a *blended* collaboration of practitioners and scholars. Some of the chapter authors are academicians; other authors are primarily ministers in the trenches; and some of the contributors are both. Consequently, some chapters draw heavily from scholarly sources in sociological, biblical, or theological fields, while other chapters derive mainly from direct ministry experience.

The book opens with a prologue that shares four brief stories vividly illustrating how cross-generational experiences can function and bless the church. The book is then divided into five sections. The first section addresses primarily the *why* question: Why should churches become more intentionally intergenerational? Parts two, three, four, and five address the *how* question: How can churches become more intentionally intergenerational?

Part One: Becoming More Intentionally Intergenerational

Part One opens with Jason Santos's chapter that places *InterGenerate* in the context of the current post-Christian landscape by addressing the foundational question, "Why should we move toward more intentionally intergenerational faith communities *now?*" Next, Gareth Crispin and Darwin Glassford explore, in fresh ways, the biblical and theological foundations of intergenerational ministry. Last, Lynn Barger Elliott engages generational theory, creatively capturing its significance for churches that are seeking to bring six generations together.

Part Two: Leading Intergenerational Change

Though many church leaders are initially excited about the idea of becoming more intergenerational in outlook and practice, the prospect of actually *leading* their churches in that direction is daunting. Cory Seibel tackles this fear head-on with his thorough treatment of the process of leading churches through change. Next, John Roberto offers the ten-thousand-foot view, outlining for visionaries and leaders seventeen *principles* for implementing intergenerational practices effectively.

Addressing church leadership, Jessica Stollings draws on her expertise in helping businesses navigate the unprecedented reality of four generations working together in the workforce; she proposes that intergenerational church leadership is an untapped resource to help churches address complex generational challenges and thrive in the midst of change. And Joseph Conway closes part two with his boots-on-the-ground perspective as a senior pastor leading a church on a six-year journey toward becoming more intentionally intergenerational in outlook and practice. Both Jessica and Joseph led engaging, interactive workshops at the InterGenerate Conference which they have transposed into these robust chapters on leadership.

Part Three: Current Research

My coauthor Christine and I called for more empirical research to further explore the benefits and challenges of intergenerational experience,[10] so part three addresses that research gap; it shares recent research that intersects with intergenerational ministry practices. Canadian Tori Bennett Smit shares best intergenerational practices from her doctoral research with churches that have small numbers of children. Australian Joe Azzopardi describes his study designed to assess the impact of intergenerational

Christian practices on well-being. Wilson McCoy presents the poignant findings of his qualitative study of the spiritually formative impact of reading Scripture in an intergenerational small group environment; the participants in his study ranged from age ten to eighty.

Part Four: Including Every Generation

Part four highlights the impact intergenerational Christian experiences can have on four marginalized generations in the church. Dawn Rundman makes a powerful case that ministry with infants and toddlers can be *intergenerational*, employing surprising subheadings such as Early Childhood Ministry + Hospitality Ministry = Intergenerational Ministry. Dave Sanders addresses the new reality that millennials will be the primary teachers of the next generation—which he calls Screeners (others are calling the newest generation Gen Z or iGen). My chapter (Holly) explores the exit of emerging adults from traditional churches and offers insights for joining these twentysomethings on their spiritual journeys. And finally, Diane Shallue's chapter focuses on the most marginalized generation in our churches—the seniors; she describes cross-age opportunities for meaning making, storytelling, and listening that bless all who participate, fostering mutuality, equality, and reciprocity across the generations.

Part Five: Unique Ministries and Approaches

Sixteen exciting experiential workshops were presented at the InterGenerate Conference; part five offers rich descriptions from six of those (other chapters in this book derive from workshops as well, though most are drawn from papers and keynote presentations). Tammy Tolman winningly describes what intergenerational ministry is looking like in Australia; Karen DeBoer shares in her inimitable style the significance of telling our faith stories in interage settings; Linda Staats offers her unique "Cross†Generational"[11] perspective on glocal (a combination of global and local) concerns using the term *accompaniment* as the practice of "walking beside the other," as Christ walks beside us, for the purpose of restoration and reconciliation within our communities (local) and the world (global).

Liz Perraud brings her two decades of experience with GenOn Ministries[12] to the intergenerational table; her chapter tells a touching story of cross-generational reconciliation. Nancy Going shares a wonderful, simple, and spiritually formative way to engage all ages using images and Scripture. And Olivia Updegrove explains the joys and challenges she is experiencing as she leads all-age worship using Sonja Stewart and Jerome Berryman's Young Children and Worship approach.[13]

Conclusion

Cory Seibel's concluding chapter, "The Intergenerationally Sticky Church," draws from his insightful and penetrating keynote address at the conference. Cory's cake-baking imagery vividly calls the reader to consider six key ingredients that help churches strengthen cohesion between people of diverse generations.

Our Hope

Our desire for this book is that it will equip and inspire senior pastors, children's ministers, small group leaders, youth ministers, curriculum writers, and other Christian leaders to envision and create more opportunities for intergenerational experiences marked by *mutuality, equality*, and *reciprocity*, thereby fostering the spiritual transformation of children, youth, emerging adults, young adults, middle adults, and senior adults—that is, everyone in the body of Christ.

For intergenerational ministry to be genuinely transformative, it needs to be more fully understood, more deeply embraced, more genuinely modelled, more intentionally facilitated, and more strategically embedded into the culture of faith communities. The contributors to *InterGenerate* have written with these ends in mind.

"Now to him who is able to do immeasurably more than all we ask or imagine, according to his power that is at work within us, to him be glory in the church and in Christ Jesus *throughout all generations*, for ever and ever" (Eph. 3:20–21, emphasis ours).

Notes

[1] Authors, thinkers, and researchers who are highlighting the importance of intergenerational connections to sustain faithful discipleship include David Kinnaman, *You Lost Me: Why Young Christians Are Leaving Church . . . And Rethinking Faith* (Grand Rapids: Baker Books, 2011); Dr. Kara E. Powell and Dr. Chap Clark, *Sticky Faith: Everyday Ideas to Build Lasting Faith in Your Kids* (Grand Rapids: Zondervan, 2011); Kathie Amidei, Jim Merhaut, and John Roberto, *Generations Together: Caring, Praying, Learning, Celebrating, & Serving Faithfully* (Naugatuck, CT: LifelongFaith Associates, 2014); and Christian Smith with Melinda Lundquist Denton, *Soul Searching: The Religious and Spiritual Lives of American Teenagers* (New York: Oxford University Press, 2005). Beyond the North American context, movements like Here2Stay (here2stay .org.au) in Australia and Faithfull Generation (faithfullgeneration.com) in the United Kingdom are also identifying—and responding to—similar conclusions.

[2] Holly Catterton Allen and Christine Lawton Ross, *Intergenerational Christian Formation: Bringing the Whole Church Together in Ministry, Community and Worship* (Downers Grove, IL: InterVarsity Press, 2012), 17.

[3] United Church of Canada, "Defining Multicultural, Cross-cultural, and Intercultural" (Toronto, Ontario, Canada: The United Church of Canada, 2011), http://ResearchGate.net.

[4] Chris Barnett, coauthor of this introduction, brings this valuable perspective from his work in Australia.

[5] David Goodwin, *Lost in Transition—or Not? Addressing the Problem of Children Leaving the Church as They Make the Transition from Childhood to Youth* (North Richmond, Australia: Kidsreach, 2013), 23.

[6] Allen and Ross, *Intergenerational Christian Formation*, 134.

[7] Allen and Ross, *Intergenerational Christian Formation*, chapters 5–12.

[8] James W. White, *Intergenerational Religious Education: Models, Theories and Prescription for Interage Life and Learning in the Faith Community* (Birmingham: Religious Education Press, 1988), 18.

[9] Gary L. McIntosh, *One Church, Four Generations: Understanding and Reaching All Ages in Your Church* (Grand Rapids: Baker Books, 2002), 199.

[10] Allen and Ross, *Intergenerational Christian Formation*, 174.

[11] The use of the phrase "Cross†Generational" throughout Linda's chapter is used to describe the concept that all generations gather around the cross of Jesus Christ and journey together.

[12] GenOn Ministries exists to equip churches to develop disciples through intergenerational ministry and relationships. GenOn was a sponsor of the InterGenerate Conference; see www.genonministries.org.

[13] Sonja M. Stewart and Jerome W. Berryman, *Young Children and Worship* (Louisville: Westminster John Knox Press, 1989), www.childrenandworship.org.

Four Stories

The following vibrant stories illuminate how intergenerational experiences are transforming churches as they engage teens and emerging adults, encourage young married couples, support parents struggling to spiritually nurture their children, and foster *attachment* between older and younger congregants.

When the Bulletin Becomes a Menu

Melissa Cooper

A couple of years ago, I decided to spend Lent eating a vegetarian diet. For the first time in my life, entire menus weren't available to me.

Every experience eating out became a scavenger hunt. At most restaurants, I had a maximum of one or two entrée options to choose from without requiring substitutions. I didn't like always having to ask for things to be made slightly differently *just* for me.

I work in camp and retreat ministry serving hundreds of churches, so I visit churches about as frequently as I visit restaurants. I've noticed that churches and restaurants have something in common.

A menu.

You know—that piece of paper each person is handed as they enter worship.

Church menus come in all shapes and sizes—color or black and white, some with stock images of Jesus with children, or a chalice and bread on the front, some a single sheet, some a large, complicated booklet.

The intention of the bulletin is always to engage. Most immediately, the bulletin shares what you'll be doing within the next hour. But there's also always a page or more devoted to all the other activities happening throughout the week.

Those are the pages intended to get you *really* engaged—not just for an hour, but ultimately, over your lifetime. Those pages tell you how this church is the right place for you: "Look at all these things we've got going on; and here are the ones *just* for you!"

Most church bulletins have become more complicated over time. In a world of consumeristic Christianity, where we have to compete with the yoga studio, coffee shop, or church down the street, we feel like we have to show that "there's something here *just* for you!"

In order to do that, we need page after page to show what classes are available after worship, and what groups meet throughout the week, and when there's childcare and when the youth group is going on a trip . . . and . . . and . . . and.

We have to be sure everyone finds something on our "menu" *just* for them.

And we've taught them to expect this—we've told them we will be sure there is something for everyone.

And yet . . . what if you're a vegetarian? What if you were not carefully considered when the menu was created?

When I look at these bulletins—"church menus"—I seldom find anything I can eat. I'm not one of the desired consumers who was carefully considered as the menu was crafted.

I'm thirty-two years old. I've been married for eight years. I don't have children, and I don't plan to. I very seldom find anything "*just* for me."

And even when I do, as a millennial, I've been catered to my whole life through media and community events—so I know what's going on. I know pandering when I see it.

But you know the churches I find most inviting—the ones that I feel like I could fit in the most with? It's the little country churches—small and vibrant and vital.

I don't wonder if they have something just for me; I don't have to search a long list of activities and classes to see if I've been considered. They know they can't have a menu long enough to meet everyone's needs, so they don't try. The few activities they do offer are open to *everyone*.

So I wonder . . .

How do we stop treating the bulletin like a menu?

How can we stop exhausting ourselves trying to meet the needs of each individual who walks through our doors? How can we make it clear that this church is for everyone, without having to name every group it includes?

What if we didn't have to treat our bulletins and calendars like menus? What if we instead sought ways to bring people together around common-alities other than age or stage in life?

Being intergenerational does not mean we add more items to our church calendar; it doesn't mean we add an intergenerational "program" to an already long list of groups and classes and activities. Instead, what if the majority of our existing programs were meant for everyone?

We may still have a specialty offering here and there; but if we can make the core of our church's life something that includes all and welcomes all, regardless of age or stage, then no one has to go searching for what they're allowed to attend, and no one has to ask for substitutions.

So I challenge you: As we vision and dream for the future of our churches, let's stop treating the bulletin like a menu that offers "something for everyone," along the way leaving someone out. Let's create documents that serve as invitations to participate in a vibrant, vital community. How about we make most of our "somethings" actually for *everyone*?

Parents as Partners

Amy Kippen

"What is the matter with parents these days?" "Why are parents not involved?" "Are families too busy for church?"

These were common questions at my congregation, mostly asked behind closed doors; questions that smacked of judgment; questions that produced not a solution, but increasing resentment toward parents. At the same time, more and more of our youth were "graduating" from church in their teen years.

Our faith formation approaches at the time were not accomplishing the goal of creating lifelong followers of Jesus who value Christian community.

And asking these questions produced more questions. Why are parents intensely involved in their kids' activities, but not committing to church involvement? Why does the hockey or dance coach get parents' commitment?

The answers were hard to acknowledge, and the truth was hard to face.

Parents are the primary teachers of faith whether they know and acknowledge it or not. Parents are indeed busy; however, they are constantly making choices about their time. Those coaches we resent actually expect parents to be involved; if you are going to be a dance parent, you must work the fundraiser. It comes with signing up.

Along the way, our age-specific church programs have inadvertently become just one more thing on the family's weekly schedule, no different than piano lessons or soccer practice. Yet even when parents meet our expectation that they bring their children to church, many children are not becoming lifelong followers of Jesus who value Christian community.

Acknowledging these truths meant making a significant change in the way we cultivate faith formation in our church, and we needed to find a way to get families to practice faith at home too. We needed to raise the expectation of parents both at church and at home—and ordering a new curriculum wouldn't suffice.

We needed to change the entire system.

So, just short of twenty years ago, we stopped doing Sunday school and started a weekly family program. No longer could parents drop their children off at church. Faith formation was now something families did together. There were no Sunday school classes and no teachers. We had intentionally become the church with no class.

Was this change easy? No. Were some parents upset? Yes. Were we confident that God was calling us to make this change? Yes.

So, in the midst of our fear, we stood on the knowledge that God had called *us* to be brave, visionary leaders. And if the leaders of our church didn't lead the church into a new future, who would?

We called our weekly family gathering *GIFT*—Generations in Faith Together. GIFT is a lively mix of Sunday school, VBS, family Bible camp, and worship. All ages and stages learn together, creating lasting intergenerational connections. To help alleviate parents' fears, we said again and again, "Just know that you don't need to know anything you don't already know or be anyone you're not. Just come."

And from the beginning, we communicated our mission through this motto:

Bless the child
Gift the family
Every week at church
Every night in every home

These four simple lines convey that GIFT is for the child and the family and set the expectation that faith formation happens both at church and at home. This motto serves to outline a *partnership* between parents and church, and, as in any healthy partnership, there are agreed-upon roles and responsibilities.

Every Week at Church

The *church's role* is to make GIFT engaging for people of all ages—a weekly highlight for all. We commit to modeling the love of Jesus and helping everyone know and experience God's love.

The *parents' role* is to make attendance a priority, to decide up front that "we are a family that goes to church unless we are sick or out of town." Additionally, we ask parents to be engaged with GIFT—to fully participate with positivity.

Every Night in Every Home

We challenge *parents* to practice faith through a simple, nightly, five-step faith ritual called *FAITH5*. Families get together each night for a Home

Huddle to check in, read Scripture, talk, pray, and bless one another before turning out the lights on the day. This nightly ritual sets a family on the firm foundation of shared faith enabling them to grow together spiritually.[1]

In a recent poignant conversation, a GIFT dad shared,

> I didn't want to come to GIFT with my family, and I certainly didn't want to do that FAITH5 thing every night. You know, I'm not really a churchy person. But last week, when Cali [five years old] led our FAITH5 prayer, it struck me—faith is not just something we do; this is who we are.

Moving our understanding of church from drop-off culture to partnership, and seeing parents as the main faith mentors and the church as an ally, is who we have become.

Friday Night Live

Aqueelah Ligonde

When I was in my twenties, if you had asked me how I imagined my Friday nights ten years into the future, I would have described a fabulous scene where I would be dancing and laughing with friends at fancy lounges. I would *not* have said, "At church, with a bunch of children and teens eating, playing, praying, and learning."

But as it turned out, that's exactly where I found myself in my thirties. Eating, playing, praying, learning, and laughing with a bunch of children and teens and Jesus-loving adults. Every Friday night, I found myself conversing around the table, sitting on the floor, creating with crayons, or eating cupcakes. Every Friday night was fabulously alive . . . and I wouldn't change it for the world.

First Presbyterian Church in Jamaica (known as First Jamaica) is located in the heart of Jamaica, Queens, New York. First Jamaica has existed for 350 years and has a strong history of serving and loving on the incredible community that surrounds it.

In 2010, First Jamaica began a program for families called LOGOS. LOGOS is an intergenerational ministry that has blessed congregations, communities, and families for over fifty years. Through Bible study, a shared meal, worship, and recreation, the goals of LOGOS are to live out Acts 2:42: "They devoted themselves to the apostles' teaching and to fellowship, to the breaking of bread and to prayer." The LOGOS motto represented what we wanted to live out among the families in our congregation and what we wanted to share with the community. That motto is this: "You are a child of God and I'll treat you that way." But back in 2010, the real question was, "What will it mean to show people that they are children of God, and how will we treat them that way? Where will we begin?"

We started with getting ourselves in the right frame of mind regarding what intergenerational ministry actually means. Even though we didn't use the term *intergenerational,* we knew that this ministry would be more than just putting different ages of people in the same room to eat, learn, worship, and play together. We knew that it was about building relationships and creating space for those relationships to be nurtured and to grow. It was about being at the table together with no other intention than to show this love of God that we had been called to live.

Intergenerational ministry is about living this life together. Knowing names, knowing these children of God in ways that we somehow miss on Sunday mornings during the worship hustle and bustle. It is about spending time learning things like where people are from, what they like (and don't like), and what their dreams are. It is about taking the time to get to know the people we sit next to each week, no matter how old or young they are.

It also means listening to each other.

It is amazing what you can learn about someone if you take the time to sit and really listen to them as you share a meal. There is something very intimate about taking the time to eat together. You never know what surprises might lie ahead.

One night at LOGOS, one of our adult leaders found out that Rosa was turning fifteen soon and that Rosa had been dreaming of a quinceañera. (A quinceañera is a celebration of a fifteen-year-old girl's birthday; its cultural roots are in Latin America.) Rosa's dream was beginning to fade because her mom didn't have the resources to plan such an elaborate celebration.

At the end of the night, the adult leader came up with a brilliant idea. What if we, her LOGOS family, hosted her quinceañera?

So with the help of most of the Friday night LOGOS youth, volunteers, and church staff, we were able to host her dream Sweet 15. We used all the gifts of the LOGOS family to plan and lead the religious ceremony, to decorate, and to find sponsors for the dresses and suits of the quinceañera court. LOGOS parents who were professional hair stylists, make-up artists, and photographers donated their supplies and time for the day. Another volunteer baked a three-tiered cake and decorated it with sparklers to light up the room. As a community, we were able to show Rosa that she was a child of God and that she was loved. We were living this motto out loud!

Friday nights became moments of grace, fun, and opportunities to love beyond our walls. They became a place where we could appreciate each other and experience God's love firsthand.

Friday nights became a place where middle school kids could be encouraged to say what they believed; Bible study became a place where they could express who God is to them; worship became a place that was about opening their hearts and mouths to honor God with their whole being. It was a place where a community of caring adults poured into them—a place where no one was alone, and everyone was loved.

Friday nights became alive in moments where young brown boys found a safe space in a world that often tells them they are not worthy. And a world that does not treat them as the children of God they are. A world that does not always welcome them with open arms. Here, on Friday nights, these boys could lead, be led, be loved, serve, be served, grow, and be who they are.

Friday nights became moments where strangers became family, where children became stronger, and where adults learned to laugh again—where we messed up a few times but came back every week to do it again because we believed that God was doing something far greater than what we could see in the moment.

God gave this congregation—and me—a breath of fresh air, a reason to celebrate, and a chance to be living children of God treating each other with love and respect while passing the potatoes and dancing in celebration. Twenty-year-old me might not approve of my thirty-year-old Friday nights. But right now, forty-year-old me is grateful to God for the blessing of a group of adults, children, and teens who made me a better person and reminded me that I am a child of God and absolutely treated me that way.

The Caring Church:
Intergenerational Caring as a Foundation for Church Life

Jim Merhaut

"Then the LORD God said, 'It is not good that the man should be alone . . .'"
—Genesis 2:18 (NRSV)

"The best thing to hold onto in life is each other." —Audrey Hepburn

Resting quietly beneath the flurry of church administration hides an often-overlooked foundation that is both soft and potent: the expressions of love that we call caring. Like God breathing life into dead clay, caring expressions of love across the generations are the animating principle of Christian congregations. Human beings are wired for caring connections. Dr. Susan Johnson, clinical psychologist and researcher, often comments that emotional connection among human beings is like oxygen. It is no exaggeration to say that warm, intimate, and continuous caring expressions of love are essential for human life and for Christian community.

Johnson tells a story of a Spanish bishop in 1760 who worked in an orphanage. He recorded in his journal that there were some children in the orphanage who were dying from loneliness. He could discern no other cause for their decline and death. Nearly two hundred years later, psychologist John Bowlby developed his theory of child attachment that confirms the essential importance of intergenerational caring for human thriving.[2]

Bowlby concluded, "the infant and young child should experience a warm, intimate, and continuous relationship with his mother (or permanent mother substitute) in which both find satisfaction and enjoyment."[3] Notice the careful choice of words that paint a picture of deep intergenerational connection: warm . . . intimate . . . continuous intergenerational relationship in which both generations find satisfaction and enjoyment. The benefits of human connection run in both directions up and down the generations. This is not something that church leaders can accomplish with a packaged program or resource. Building affectionate and continuous experiences of human attachment requires changing the culture of congregations from peer-centered efficiency to places where relationships of all kinds reign supreme. In the caring church, getting things done is not as important as with whom and for whom we get things done.

How many times in churches are young children and older adults excluded from activities or experiences because they might "slow things down"? When the center of our target becomes accomplishment and not relationship, we cease to be Christian. The celebrated spirituality expert Michael Downey once said, "If you are what you do, when you don't . . . then you're not."[4] This doesn't mean that doing is unimportant; it simply means that the foundation for all Christian activity is caring relationships.

Bowlby's career ended before he could test his child attachment theory on adults; however, Phil Shaver and Cindy Hazan carried on his work at the University of Denver. They tested attachment theory on adults in the 1980s and found that the emotional attachment needs that form the foundation of thriving for children do not go away as we grow up.[5] The myth of the detached, stoic, independent adult as the paradigm of adult maturity was shattered by Shaver and Hazan and has continued to disintegrate in study after study on adult thriving. Adults need caring expressions just as much as children do, and when they are experienced across the generations, they can be even more powerful for adult growth and development.

One church in Ohio set the following goal: to inspire and support friendships across the generations. In the spirit of this goal, they have transformed their Vacation Bible School into an intergenerational learning experience. Parents, grandparents, and other adults are enriched by the presence of children as they together enjoy lively and engaging activities around biblical themes. They have also developed a youth ministry initiative to empower adults to reach out in friendship to teens on Sundays. This was accomplished by giving brief presentations to all adult groups in the church with information about the power of intergenerational friendship, and then offering three simple strategies to adults for how they might connect with teens around Sunday worship:

1. Make eye contact and smile.
2. Deliberately seek out teens during the offering of peace.

3. Ask teens about school, hobbies, work, friendships, prayer, etc.

At the end of the presentation, every adult was given a small card with the three strategies and a pin that read, "We love our teens!" At the same time, children and teens were being encouraged to take on roles in the congregation that traditionally were reserved for adults. This church did not have to add new programs; it simply had to bring the generations together in programs that already existed. It's so simple. It's so powerful. Imagine what your congregation can do by connecting the generations with expressions of care.

One of the best things we can do for both young and old is structure our churches in ways that facilitate continuous caring encounters across the generations so that all ages can be enfolded in the warmth of the full body of Christ. It is when the full body is engaged with all its generational diversity that both the church and the world will experience a congregation's transforming power.

Notes

[1] See www.faith5.org for a fuller explanation of the FAITH5 process.

[2] Dr. Sue Johnson, *Hold Me Tight: Seven Conversations for a Lifetime of Love* (New York: Little, Brown and Company, 2008), 16–27.

[3] John Bowlby, *Maternal Care and Mental Health: A Report Prepared on Behalf of the World Health Organization as a Contribution to the United Nations Programme for the Welfare of Homeless Children* (Geneva: World Health Organization, 1951), 13.

[4] Michael Downey, "Magnificent Distractions: Hurdles to Living Contemplatively," paper presented at the monthly meeting of the First Friday Club of Greater Youngstown (OH), January 5, 2017.

[5] Cindy Hazan and Philip Shaver, "Romantic Love Conceptualized as an Attachment Process," *Journal of Personality and Social Psychology* 52, no. 3 (1987): 511–24.

Part One

BECOMING MORE INTENTIONALLY INTERGENERATIONAL

Chapter One

Why Now?

Jason Brian Santos

Twenty-five years ago, I took my first full-time gig as a youth worker. I was a bright-eyed nineteen-year-old who desperately wanted to help lead other young people into a relationship with Jesus Christ. I was studying youth ministry in a small Assemblies of God liberal arts college when the opportunity surfaced to take the reins of my own ministry—an offer I couldn't refuse. I remember gathering with that motley crew of teenagers in the dank church basement that was filled with tattered furniture and a colorful banner hanging from the wall with my newly designed name—Cutting Edge Youth Ministry. Little did I realize then, the name I chose for the ministry was ironically prophetic for many of the efforts we've made in children's and youth ministry over the past few decades.

Truth be told, my fledgling ministry didn't end up being on the cutting edge of anything. It did have the effect of being cutting edge, albeit, not in the innovative, dynamic sense of the phrase, but in a divisive and, in many ways, damaging way. I remember telling parents that they should steer clear of the work I was doing with their children and harshly vetting adults who wanted to be a part. I, like many youth workers over the years, had bought into the idea that youth needed to be pulled away from the larger body to do their spiritual seeking. I believed that parents and other adults would only muddy that process with their attempts at offering pat answers for what it meant to be a Christian. As far as I was concerned, young people needed a welcoming environment filled with people their own age in order to wrestle with their faith and ask hard questions without embarrassment. Who better to mentor those teenagers than a cool, almost-twenty-year-old who was convinced he knew what it meant to follow Christ?

In the years that followed, I persisted in this philosophy of ministry, forming children and youth in the faith in various basements across the nation and globe. Over that time, my thinking began to shift. As I watched high school graduates exit my youth programs and spread their wings into the wide blue yonder, I began to notice an unsettling trend—many of them weren't returning to the church. This pattern, unfortunately, wasn't an anomaly confined to my particular ministry; it was increasingly being noted throughout the nation and across denominational lines.

In ecclesial and academic circles, we made valiant attempts to offer correctives for this growing trend. We created new paradigms of youth ministry, each with the promise of fixing the failures of the past (e.g., purpose-driven, contemplative, mission-oriented, etc.). While these efforts proved helpful for a time, in retrospect, most ended up being Band-Aids that only temporarily covered up the deeper, more systemic issues befuddling our efforts to form our children and youth in the faith. Nonetheless, we plodded on, trapped in a cycle of creating new, innovative ways of reaching young people.

Then, in the late 1990s, practitioners and scholars began noting a subtle trend in the spirituality of young adults, particularly among Generation Xers, who seemed to be abandoning the faith communities of their upbringing in favor of ecclesial traditions characterized by more formal liturgy and historical Christian practices.[1] Others simply left the church all together. Though there was noted concern with this shift, it didn't cause widespread panic until the Xers' younger siblings followed suit. The millennial generation, equally discontent with the vast offerings of North American spirituality, made a much stronger statement in the most powerful way imaginable. They just left. Often characterized by the phrase "spiritual, but not religious," large numbers of millennials simply stopped affiliating with institutional religion, giving rise to a new category of American spirituality known as the "Nones."[2]

This hemorrhaging of young people from the life of the church has profound effects. The most obvious is that the perceived future of the church is threatened. Common sense tells us that if this trend continues, ultimately, there won't be any bodies left to fill our pews. Like all institutions, active membership is a significant indicator of vitality and longevity. Without a new generation to carry on our religious traditions, the societal impact of the institutional church may disappear. Consequently, for the first time in history, youth and young adult spirituality became a significant area of research, most fully realized through the National Study of Youth and Religion—the largest, most comprehensive longitudinal study of religion and young people.[3] Along the way, scholars began to argue for a new stage of life they call "emerging adulthood"[4]; these scholars argue that we are seeing, in essence, a shift in how we understand "adulthood." Traditionally defined markers—like the completion of education, marriage, a house, and children—are checked off later in life, if at all. Theoretically (and historically), once these markers are met, these adults return to the church. Though we've witnessed this return anecdotally among some Generation Xers, there is little evidence to demonstrate that time and maturity will eventually work in our favor.

A Generational Divide

I'd like to suggest, however, that there is more at play in this cultural shift than a growing generational distrust with religious institutions or the extension of a generation's transition into adulthood. Rather, I'd argue that what we're seeing are the effects of an increasingly individualistic, peer-oriented society that celebrates personal experience and self-fulfillment over a communal ethos and ethic. Naturally, this shift has a significant impact on the way the church relates to the culture. As we navigate this turn, I believe it is critical that we examine our ecclesial contexts through the lens of generational theory,[5] a topic that will be addressed more fully in Chapter Four, Lynn Barger Elliott's chapter.

For the purposes of this introduction, however, consider these brief descriptions. The silent generation, born between 1925 and 1942, were the survivors who came of age in an era shaped by the Great Depression and the Second World War. Helping to rebuild the country on the heels of the GI generation, they worked to strengthen societal institutions through civil participation. Largely characterized by a *cultural morality*, they conflated Christianity with good citizenship.

The baby boomers, born between 1943 and 1960, came of age during massive changes in our culture—the civil rights movement, women's liberation, and the sexual revolution—partly prompted by the boom in psychological research which championed the values of personhood. Ultimately, this existential awakening yielded a generation that embraced therapeutic individualism unabashedly. Unlike the generations that succeeded them, boomers attempted to reform the church rather than abandon it altogether, giving rise to non-denominationalism and consumer-driven Christianity. Arguably, peer-oriented spiritual formation found its beginnings during this era.

Generation X, born between 1961 and 1981, was the smallest generation of the past century. Returning to a parentless home after school earned Xers the moniker "latchkey kids." Highly distrusting of institutions, particularly religious ones, they are often characterized as having a deistic view of God, echoing the abandonment of their childhood. Growing up in a culture of "church hopping and shopping," they wrestled with the virtues of a market-driven, "build-it-and-they-will-come" spirituality.

Finally, the millennials, born between 1982 and 2004 (comprising the largest generation thus far), are the ones who have communicated their discontentment with institutional religion via their absence. As the first technological natives, they are the most individualistic with a vast capacity to shape their ever-changing identities and social relationships. Undoubtedly, they make up the most diverse generation. Millennials are often unfairly stereotyped as self-absorbed, despite their being known for their collaboration and social activism. They are also among the most studied generation—especially in the area of spirituality.

In 2005, the National Study of Youth and Religion offered evidence that not only are we doing a poor job of handing down faith to our children, but that the faith we're handing down is lacking. Teenagers were found to be largely inarticulate about their faith, lacking a religious or theological vocabulary from which to draw. While the young people interviewed didn't have negative views about spirituality in general, their perception of Christianity painted a grim portrait. The researchers asserted that we've handed down a faith the authors labeled Moral Therapeutic Deism (MTD). In short, MTD is the belief that religion is there to teach us what is right and wrong (morality), that it functions to help us feel good about life and ourselves (therapeutic), and that while God is real, this divine being is not really concerned with our everyday lives (deistic).

Generationally speaking, MTD is a far cry from the civic Christianity of the silent generation that understood the church as a *pastoral* institution that offered spiritual comfort and moral formation. After the Second World War, religious communities experienced a surge in attendance and the pastoral model lost its efficacy, giving rise to a multi-staff, *programmatic* emphasis. Associate pastors and ministry directors were hired to accommodate the influx. Moreover, this trajectory, undergirded by the explosion of developmental psychology, inspired boomer leaders to develop "age and stage" ministries as a means to address the needs of specific age groups.[6]

During this period, it made perfect sense to pull our children and youth away from the corporate worshiping body in order to focus on the particular needs of each stage of faith development. Consequently, youth ministry burgeoned into a whole new category of ministry with endless opportunities for study, innovation, and, ultimately, professionalization. While children's ministry didn't quite mushroom to the level that youth ministry did in terms of research and publications, it too experienced tremendous expansion and became a powerful marketing tool to draw the larger family unit into the folds of the church. In the end, these peer-oriented efforts moved the spiritual formation of our youth and children from the multi-generational body to the fringes of our communities.

Van Gogh Mickey

What was the result of this shift? A Van Gogh Mickey Mouse. Imagine with me for a moment the face of Mickey Mouse, but with only one ear. In this image, Mickey's face represents the larger body of the church (big church); the remaining ear represents where our children and youth experienced their formation. Essentially, we removed them from the corporate life of the church to be formed primarily in the peer-oriented, largely fun-and-games, snack-filled programming of Mickey's ear.[7] Bear in mind, there are many virtues associated with this type of church programming

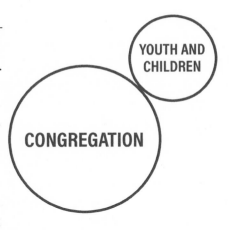

that have proven effective for forming people. In fact, I would suggest that the church at large could learn something about faith formation by taking a thoughtful look at the creative ways peer-oriented ministries have engaged our children and youth. Nevertheless, we must also critically reflect on the ways we've failed in our zeal to make spiritual formation attractive, because somewhere along the line we started calling our young people toward fun rather than Christ. In the end, what we won them *with* is what we won them *to*.[8] Perhaps we shouldn't be surprised when youth abandon the corporate body of the church after graduation—it wasn't theirs from the start.

I'm certain, as I write this, that there are countless children and youth workers that are bristling at my assertions, holding their ground that we've raised our young people faithfully. After all, this argument casts a shadow of doubt on much of our ministry efforts (including mine) over the past few decades. Whether these objections are reasonably warranted or not, the fact is that young people are walking away from what the church is offering. They don't have a problem with Jesus per se; they have a problem with the Christianity the church is attempting to sell.

This peer-oriented shift in the church, coupled with the rampant individualism that flourished during the boomer era, left our young people, in the words of Robert Putnam, "bowling alone."[9] A culture that was once defined by an ethic of communal practice is now filled with individuals wandering the streets enchanted by little screens with hopes of finding connection and community. Religiously speaking, the "sacred canopy"[10] that existed not so long ago in our collective past has been repurposed into smaller umbrellas. In fact, spirituality has become so personal, we've forgotten the biblical notion of a covenant people who were intended to be intergenerational and communal. Put differently, this generation of young people no longer trusts the consumeristic culture of boomer Christianity, nor do they relate to the institutional Christianity of the silent generation. As a result, the millennials have—literally—left the building.

Anchoring and Identity Formation

Lacking a deeper connection to their faith communities, Xers and millennials have set out on a path of self-discovery. Phrases like, "I need to find myself" and "I'm trying to figure out who I am" have become commonplace for these generations. Because much of their spiritual formation has been peer-oriented, they intuitively turned to their own age group to understand who they are and how they ought to live in an increasingly diversifying society. This isn't a difficult task considering the rapidity at which technology has expanded, while at the same time culture and the church have become more focused on the needs of the individual. Finding people "just like you" no longer poses the same challenge it did for prior generations. With a few taps, a young person can be connected with people just like them.[11]

I would argue, however, that at the core of their attempts to find themselves, there sits a deep void in terms of self-identity. While human identity has long been a topic of academic research and writing, in recent years, it has garnered more attention in popular culture and in Christian education and formation.[12] The issue of self-identity deals with how individuals view themselves. For centuries, these identities were formed in collective societies that focused on communal formation and the social construction of identity. The aim of social practice was the enculturation of the individual into the larger structure of a social milieu. An individual would (typically) conform to the customs, behavioral patterns, and norms related to their culture of upbringing, consequently creating an "anchored identity." In our increasingly diverse culture where social practice and individual ideologies are widespread, forming an anchored identity has become far more challenging.

Sociologist Peter L. Berger sheds light on this challenge through his understanding of socialization, which he divides into two stages: primary and secondary.[13] According to Berger, primary socialization takes place from birth to early childhood (six to eight years of age) and is characterized by the emotional connection a child has to those in her immediate surroundings—parents, extended family, church community, and the like. These emotional connections provide contextual relationships through which norms and maxims are formed and ingrained. In other words, an anchor identity is established in the vortex of the individual's perception of self in conjunction with her relationship to the world. Secondary socialization begins in later childhood (beyond six to eight years of age) and tends to challenge aspects of the primary socialization. When other worldviews, patterns of practice, and social customs are encountered, the anchor identity is challenged and a process of adaptation, assimilation, or rejection occurs in the individual's understanding of self.

When an individual has a poorly established anchor identity, the process of secondary socialization is confounded, making it more difficult to navigate. The result often boils down to what child psychologist David Elkind calls a "patchwork identity."[14] He asserts that the process of integrating other views into one's own is negatively affected when one lacks the foundation of an established identity. And Berger says this established identity—what he calls anchored identity—is most successfully formed in the context of a highly connected, emotionally supportive environment that reinforces communal behavior. In that light, we must consider how our efforts to form young people spiritually, in peer-oriented environments, have failed to anchor a Christian identity.

When spiritual formation primarily takes place alongside one's own peers, a broader understanding of the church is distorted. Individuals begin to see themselves at the center of the faith community rather than part of the larger whole. Church becomes one more thing to consume in our culture. When children and youth are raised in a truly intergenerational environment defined by a pattern of intentional Christian practices, they learn to understand themselves in relationship to the larger body of faith. Moreover, they begin to see that their faith development isn't isolated to a particular age or stage, but rather that it is a longer journey with all the generations traveling *together.*

According to situated learning theorists, individuals develop a deep sense of belonging and identity through something called "legitimate peripheral participation."[15] Proponents of this theory suggest that identity is most successfully formed by "doing" the things that are the most important and central to a community. In this way, individuals move from the periphery of a community to the center through participating in what the larger community does. For example, every time a teenager celebrates communion, he or she is able to look around at the congregation and see that this is a practice that defines the whole body. Over time, their participation in this act contributes to a communal identity that in turn forms them individually.

If a young person's spiritual practices are largely confined to Mickey's ear, he may search for an environment that resembles that experience later in life because those norms were established during childhood and adolescence, for example, a unigenerational, casual gathering that sings current praise songs that change every few months. Conversely, when children and youth are exposed to the central and sacred practices of an intergenerational community and it comes time for them to locate themselves in a Christian community, they are more likely to look for one that mirrors what they experienced in their upbringing.

These assertions are supported not only by situated learning theories, but also by communal memory theory, which identifies ritualized and embodied practices as the central means for how communities carry on tradition. Sociologist Paul Connerton, in his book *How Societies Remember,* explains how human identity is formed in the present by drawing upon a social memory.[16] According to Connerton, these memories are shaped through commemorative ceremonies enacted and reenacted through bodily action and performative behaviors. In this light, social memory is not only a link to the past, it has a powerful formative influence in our current contexts. As individuals draw upon experiences from their past, both personally and socially, a process of legitimization occurs in the present, giving rise to a type of shared memory linking both the history of the individual to the present and the individuals in the present context to each other.

This communal memory functions like a lock within our *habitus*—the ingrained dispositions that orient our lives and actions without us even realizing it.[17] Though they develop throughout our life span, the base memories are stored during childhood and reinforced through regular and repetitive participation. It is our job to make sure those foundational memories include multiple generations. For Connerton, "the older members of a group should not neglect to transmit these representations to the younger members of the group."[18] In the context of religious communities, intergenerationality becomes even more important, as the wider historicity of Christian practice is transmitted through each successive generation. In short, this is how the rituals of faith are handed down and a communal Christian identity is formed.

There is truth behind Proverbs 22:6: "Train up children in the way they should go, and when they are old, they won't depart from it."[19] At the end of the day, if we want our young people to be connected to the church, we must first address what's killing it. Peer-oriented ministry cannot be, and never should have been, the primary way they are formed in the faith. There is no magic bullet or pre-packaged solution to correcting the malaise we're witnessing among our younger generations toward the church, but there are things we can do to help reverse this trend. And, I believe those things begin *intergenerationally.*

Notes

[1] See Tom Beaudoin, *Virtual Faith: The Irreverent Spiritual Quest of Generation X* (Hoboken: NJ: Jossey-Bass, 2000), and Colleen Carroll Campbell, *The New Faithful: Why Young Adults Are Embracing Christian Orthodoxy* (Chicago: Loyola Press, 2002).

[2] See David Kinnaman, *You Lost Me: Why Young Christians Are Leaving Church . . . And Rethinking Faith* (Grand Rapids: Baker Books, 2011), and James Emery White, *The Rise of the Nones: Understanding and Reaching the Religiously Unaffiliated* (Grand Rapids: Baker Books, 2014).

[3] See the National Study of Youth and Religion in Christian Smith with Melinda Lundquist Denton, *Soul Searching: The Religious and Spiritual Lives of American Teenagers* (New York: Oxford University Press, 2009), and Kenda Creasy Dean, *Almost Christian: What the Faith of Our Teenagers Is Telling the American Church* (New York: Oxford University Press, 2010).

[4] See Jeffrey Jensen Arnett, *Emerging Adulthood: The Winding Road from the Late Teens through the Twenties,* 2nd ed. (New York: Oxford University Press, 2015), and Robert Wuthnow, *After the Baby Boomers: How Twenty- and Thirty-Somethings Are Shaping the Future of American Religion* (Princeton, NJ: Princeton University Press, 2007).

[5] William Strauss and Neil Howe, *Generations: The History of America's Future, 1584 to 2069* (New York: William Morrow, 1991).

[6] See Erik H. Erikson, *Identity: Youth and Crisis* (Austen Riggs Monograph) (New York: W. W. Norton, 1994), and James W. Fowler, *Stages of Faith: The Psychology of Human Development and the Quest for Meaning* (New York: HarperCollins, 1981).

[7] Stuart Cummings-Bond, "The One-Eared Mickey Mouse," *YouthWorker Journal* 6 (Fall 1989): 76.

[8] See James K. A. Smith, *You Are What You Love: The Spiritual Power of Habit* (Grand Rapids: Brazos Press, 2016).

[9] Robert D. Putnam, *Bowling Alone: The Collapse and Revival of American Community* (New York: Simon & Schuster, 2000).

[10] Peter L. Berger (*The Sacred Canopy* [Garden City, NY: Doubleday, 1967]) developed the idea that religion in the past was like a large, encompassing, sacred canopy under which whole religious societies felt covered and protected from outside chaotic forces; Berger further argued that in the highly pluralistic twentieth century world, these sacred canopies collapsed.

[11] Andrew Zirschky, *Beyond the Screen: Youth Ministry for the Connected but Alone Generation* (Nashville: Abingdon Press, 2015).

[12] Christian Smith, *What Is a Person? Rethinking Humanity, Social Life, and the Moral Good from the Person Up* (Chicago: University of Chicago Press, 2010).

[13] Peter L. Berger and Thomas Luckmann, *The Social Construction of Reality: A Treatise in the Sociology of Knowledge* (Garden City, NY: Doubleday, 1966).

[14] David Elkind, *All Grown Up & No Place to Go: Teenagers in Crisis,* rev. ed. (New York: Perseus Books, 1998).

[15] Jean Lave and Etienne Wenger, *Situated Learning: Legitimate Peripheral Participation* (New York: Cambridge University Press, 1991).

[16] Paul Connerton, *How Societies Remember* (New York: Cambridge University Press, 1989).

[17] Pierre Bourdieu, *The Logic of Practice,* trans. Richard Nice (Stanford, CA: Stanford University Press, 1992). See also Smith, *You Are What You Love,* 2016.

[18] Connerton, *How Societies Remember,* 38.

[19] Translation mine.

Chapter Two

Intergenerational Communities and a Theology of Accommodation

Gareth Crispin

Every now and again on *The Antiques Roadshow,* someone brings along a piece of furniture or art they've owned for years that they thought was worthless. After it is dusted off and brought out into the light to be observed, it turns out to be of value after all. That is somewhat akin to what can happen when rummaging around in the attic of historical theology, a place people do not normally visit to find inspiration in contemporary Christian mission and ministry. Here can be found theology that has been known for years, but whose practical theological value has perhaps gone unnoticed.

This chapter explores how the historical theology of accommodation is one such discovery. It's not an overarching theological framework for intergenerational ministry, but it does provide theological resources to aid in the implementation of intergenerational practices. In this sense, it is simply one possible piece of the jigsaw puzzle that might be used to help construct this picture of church life that we now call intergenerational.

This particular piece of the puzzle suggests that in forming intergenerational communities, it will be important for all within the community to adopt a posture of accommodating others. However, it also suggests that as a person's knowledge of God and authority within the church increases, so does their responsibility to accommodate.

What Is Accommodation?

The word *accommodation* simply means to make room for someone or something; but hidden within this concept is the assumption that someone is doing the accommodating. This common sense understanding of the word lies at the heart of the meaning of accommodation as a theological category, where God is the one who does the accommodating by making room for humanity. In theological language, God "comes down" rather than "moves over," but *accommodation* still captures the sense of movement.

Theologically speaking, accommodation is necessary because of God's transcendence; that is, God is infinite and holy, and humanity is finite and unholy. This being the case, God cannot be known by humanity without some movement on God's part to communicate, act, and appear in such a way that humanity might know God. Humanity needs God to come down—hence the title of this chapter. Accommodation requires some kind of coming down, some form of stooping.

Accommodation in Historical Theology

There are layers of richness within the theology of accommodation; layers that have been laid down over centuries. In the patristic period, the church was familiar with accommodation. Origen, for example, pictured accommodation as akin to when we speak to small children; we adapt ourselves "to the weakness of our charge." God seems to deal with us, says Origen, in the same way, "making the capacity of the hearers, and the benefit which they were to receive, the standard of the appropriateness of its announcements [regarding him]."[1] God adapts, says Origen, accommodating what he says in such a way that humanity can understand.

Calvin also spoke of the need for accommodation in terms of God's transcendence and echoed the idea of asymmetry found in the adult-child relationship, asserting, "As nurses commonly do with infants, God is wont in a measure to 'lisp' in speaking to us." Calvin suggested, "Such forms of speaking do not so much express clearly what God is like as accommodate the knowledge of him to our slight capacity. To do this he must descend far beneath his loftiness."[2]

Calvin took things in an interesting and crucial direction that Origen only hinted at. Yes, God's accommodation is communicative, said Calvin, but it is also behavioral; God *acts* in an accommodating way. This can be seen in God's provision of sacraments for humanity. Calvin says communion, for example, involves "physical signs, which thrust before our eyes, represent to us, according to our feeble capacity, things invisible."[3] In addition, Ford Lewis Battles argues that, for Calvin, the everyday ministry of the church is also part of God's accommodation to humanity: "The very choice of a human ministry to proclaim the saving message and to nurture us in spiritual growth is in itself an act of accommodation by God to our capacity."[4] John Balserak takes this further by showing how, for Calvin, the pastoring of the people by human leaders is another example of God's accommodation "so that they do not need to run around . . . in search of revelations, and at the same time that they might be taught familiarly according to their capacity."[5]

Accommodation in Biblical Theology

Of course, historical theology is not devoid of biblical theology, but a more direct look at biblical theology reveals a number of crucial steps we need to take on our journey toward the practical, theological application of accommodation to intergenerational mission and ministry. The Bible itself is an accommodation; it comes to us from God but via human authors, in human language. However, within the story of the Bible, we also see an accommodation of humanity in God's actions and the beginnings of a basis for accommodation as a principle governing practice in the church.

God accommodates in creation; Romans 1:20 tell us that the visible creation shows us qualities of God that we would not otherwise know. After the fall, God's presence is so dangerous to humanity that God constrains his presence by housing it in the tabernacle and temple (a literal accommodation) allowing safe relationship between God and people. God's accommodation to humanity is also evident in the Old Testament theophanies. The injunction against seeing the face of God (Exod. 33:20) and the promise that in the new creation God's people will "see his face" (Rev. 22:4) suggest that the theophanies of the Old Testament are an accommodation needed because of humanity's fallen state.

Ultimately, however, it is in the incarnation where God most fully accommodates himself to humanity for "no one has ever seen God. It is God the only Son, who is close to the Father's heart, who has made him known" (John 1:18 NRSV).

In the recent past, much has been made of the significance of incarnational theology for the mission, life, and practices of the church. However, the incarnation itself has perhaps been overlooked as a paradigmatic example of accommodation that challenges us to reflect on our own ecclesial life and practices in light of Christ's example.

In Philippians chapter 2, Paul presents the incarnation as a model of accommodation for the whole church. In the incarnation, Jesus, though he was in the form of God, "did not regard equality with God as something to be exploited, but emptied himself, taking the form of a slave, being born in human likeness. And being found in human form, he humbled himself and became obedient to the point of death—even death on a cross" (Phil. 2:6–8 NRSV).

The context of Philippians 2 strongly suggests some measure of disunity and selfishness within the church in Philippi (2:3–4, 14). Within this context, the Philippian church is called upon to have "the same mind" as Jesus (2:5 NRSV),[6] the humble Christ who altered his very form for the sake of humanity, specifically taking on the form of those he sought to identify with and serve.

The church is to be like Christ in its relationships, to humbly change for the sake of the other, to identify with those who are different. Humans cannot take different form in the way in which Christ did, but individuals within the church can adopt a posture of willingness to change for the sake of identification with and service of the other.[7]

And this principle applies to all. In the same way that Paul implores all the Ephesians to "be subject to one another" (Eph. 5:21 NRSV), so he desires all to have that "same mind" as Jesus, willing to change for the sake of identifying with and serving the rest. Everyone within the church should accommodate one another; at root, therefore, accommodation in church life is destined to be, in some way and at some time, a mutual process.

Paul also suggests, however, that within this fundamental mutuality, accommodation will vary depending on the circumstances. In much the same way that he spells out what being subject to one another looks like for people in different situations (Eph. 4 and 5), so also we can deduce that accommodation is applied differently in different situations. While Philippians 2 is a formative text for the general principle of accommodation, passages such as 1 Corinthians 8:1–11:1 help illustrate how accommodation varies depending on individuals' circumstances.

The church in Corinth was experiencing problems with how those who possessed knowledge of God used that knowledge. Some people knew that food sacrificed to idols was fine to eat as "no idol in the world really exists" (8:4 NRSV), but they are described by Paul as not knowing this in the correct way (8:2), suggesting that they were not acting rightly in relation to others within the community of faith. Some found it difficult to understand that they were free to eat food sacrificed to idols (8:7), so Paul pleads with those with the knowledge and freedom to eat meat sacrificed to idols to not do so on account of others with a weak conscience (8:13). Those with knowledge were free in the abstract to act how they liked; but in the context of the relationships within the community of faith, they needed to alter their behavior to accommodate those who did not possess this knowledge.

In this context, Paul uses knowledge of God to mean facts about God, but not divorced from relationship with him. The people who "knew" things about God didn't simply know facts about God; they knew something about God as person. They had knowledge about God in a factual sense, but this was intrinsically linked to their knowledge of God in a relational sense.[8]

Paul then switches from knowledge to authority in chapter 9, where he establishes that he has the rights of an apostle, but has not "made use" of these rights (9:12 NRSV). He will endure laying aside his rights; indeed, he will "endure anything rather than put an obstacle in the way of the gospel of Christ" (9:12 NRSV). In not enforcing his rights, he is making an accommodation to those in the churches he has planted; Paul is accommodating from a position of authority.

Paul extends this progression to suggest that he will use his freedom to lay aside his rights to win as many as possible (9:19). He is not a slave, but he will become one; he is not under the law, but will become like one who is; he is not a pagan, but will become as one who is; he is not weak, but he will become so (9:19–22). He does these things so that by all possible means, he might save some (9:22).

Gordon Fee comments on these categories of people to which "Paul has been willing to accommodate himself 'in order to win.'"[9] Applying this to contemporary practice, Fee adds that those in authority might

> ask in terms of their own ministries how their "use" of their rights might at the same time become a "misuse"—of such a kind that the gospel itself is not so clearly heard in our day. It would not seem to require a lot of imagination to think of several such misuses, even in the most innocent of circumstances.[10]

Crucially, Paul finishes this section of 1 Corinthians by tying this principle of accommodation back to Jesus: if you do these things, he says, you follow Christ's example (11:1). This is, as Peter Richardson puts it, a summary of the argument since the beginning of chapter 8 and "summarizes especially clearly his principle of accommodation."[11] Importantly, "what is unusual about Paul's view is not so much that he is accommodatory, but that he states his practice unequivocally and expresses it as an important matter of principle."[12]

Knowledge and authority are of course not binary. Knowledge of God is attained gradually over time. There is no point at which a Christian knows everything about God, and also no time when they know nothing. Equally, while there are some important senses in which people do or do not have authority within the church (for example, those appointed as church leaders), authority also exists as a range. People in churches have both formal authoritative positions as leaders and informal authority gained from a variety of means, including long-term participation in church life, general standing in the community, or wealth.

This understanding leads to a model that, building upon the foundation of mutual responsibility to accommodate, suggests that people within the church have an increasing responsibility to accommodate as their knowledge of God and their authority in the church increase. Put starkly, a four-year-old does not have the same responsibility to accommodate as an adult minister.

It should be noted at this point that Paul is not arguing for theological accommodation. He is not suggesting a change in doctrine merely to fit the times or advocating for putting aside right belief in order to make the Christian faith more palatable. Nor is he encouraging mere pragmatism by suggesting the church try out practices to just find out "what works."[13] What he is setting out is a principled posture for those within the church to adopt by continually reviewing their communal life and practices.

Accommodation in Practical Theology

As this old doctrine of accommodation is dusted off and examined afresh, very striking contemporary resonances appear with the aims and objectives of intergenerational mission and ministry. Alongside the biblical, developmental, and sociological arguments for the "why" of intergenerationality (see other chapters in this volume), there is here a theological foundation for the "how" of implementing intergenerational practices. God accommodates, God comes down in Christ, and we are implored to be like Christ (Phil. 2:5 and 1 Cor. 11:1). So when considering how to implement intergenerational practices, accommodating—making room for the other—will be vitally important.

In any one community of faith, a range of tastes, abilities, preferred styles, personalities, and desires will be found. In implementing intergenerational practices, decisions will inevitably be made as to what the community of all ages does when it gathers and interacts, and why. Naturally, this will present instances where someone will not warm to or relate well to particular elements of intergenerational life and practice. As many are discovering, implementing cross-age church practices is not a problem-free process. But if those within the church approach the coming together of the church family with the posture of accommodating others, this transition can be smoothed.

As briefly explored above, embracing accommodation as a *mutual* activity is only one aspect of the process; as a person's authority in the church and knowledge of God increase, so too does the responsibility to accommodate—and how leaders accommodate will deeply impact the life and practices of the church.

Church leaders within local churches will have a particular set of values and cultural preferences that will inevitably (to a lesser or greater extent) shape what the church looks and feels like. In promoting an intergenerational church, a theology of accommodation can help church leaders think carefully about the extent to which church practices reflect their own personal or generational preferences—and what church practices might look like if more attention were paid to accommodating a broader range of preferences. With this broader range in mind, church leaders could review the type and style of liturgy, language, music, media, participation, space, illustrations, and examples used within church gatherings and wider church life.[14]

But this only takes us so far. Church members have a range of likes and dislikes and preferences and come from a variety of generations and subcultures. So how can church leaders decide whom to accommodate if accommodating one necessarily implies not accommodating another?

This is where knowledge comes in. According to 1 Corinthians 8:1–11:1, it is incumbent on the Christian with more knowledge to accommodate the Christian with less. Thus a theology of accommodation can provide theological reasoning and motivation for Christians with relatively more knowledge to set aside their own tastes and desires and seek ways to develop church structures and practices that aid those with less knowledge to participate within the community of faith.

Naturally, Christian knowledge is not about age per se, but there will be, to some degree, a natural positive correlation between the two; as people get older, their knowledge of God should increase. The correlation may not be one-to-one, but it should be positive. Therefore, in general, a theology of accommodation will often suggest an accommodation of the young by the old (though mutual accommodation will be taught, modeled, and practiced as well).

In Paul's example of food sacrificed to idols, this meant the more knowledgeable refraining from eating meat, although eating meat was something they liked and wanted to do—there was a cost to this accommodation. Similarly, when a more knowledgeable Christian accommodates another Christian in some area of church life or practice, they give up something they like, possibly something they more readily identify with and relate to. They do so because they are willing to suffer the loss of the familiar and meaningful precisely because they understand the faith already; they have more knowledge, including the awareness that others might not have such knowledge.

Practical applications of accommodation can be taken from any aspect of contemporary church life. Communion, for example, is one area where accommodation can be practiced, with church leaders and more knowledgeable Christians accommodating most. Established liturgical forms of communion are likely to be familiar to church leaders and more knowledgeable Christians; they are likely to relate to and identify with a specific form of communion, if only due to significant repetition over time. However, those less familiar with such forms of communion (including the young) may not understand or appreciate them in the way others do. Church leaders and more knowledgeable Christians may not be aware of this because, as Pete Ward comments, "viewed from within, it is very hard to make a distinction between the gospel and the church's own particular cultural expression of the faith."[15]

At the extremes, children and young people might not participate in communion at all due to their lack of familiarity with the form of communion used. As Jonny Baker argues with respect to communion, because language and culture are always changing, "by keeping things the same, their meaning actually changes over time and becomes irrelevant."[16]

Explaining church practices and training the young in the ways of a faith community are essential parts of church life. However, this does not mean those practices should remain unchanged over time. Applying a theology of accommodation to the practice of communion might imply changing the form to fit the capacity of the young. This would be worked out differently in each context. It may impact the words used, the music played (if any), the physical setting, and, given the image-based culture within which youth and children live, might include a move toward the use of more images. Additionally, whether explaining to youth and children the current forms of communion or seeking to change such forms to suit their capacity, accommodation will imply *including young people in the discussion* about which forms might work best in this setting.

Stephen Cottrell provides helpful material in considering how to "reclothe" communion[17] for people new to faith, but also for children and young people.[18] He suggests ways in which language might be altered and how participation can be fostered to aid understanding. However, ideas for change are only one part of a change process. Also needed are theological resources and frameworks to aid the implementation of ideas. A theology of accommodation is one such resource and framework.

Affection for particular ways of doing things can run deep, and the cost of giving up established forms of worship and ways of church life may well be costly for some. However, fostering a culture of *mutual accommodation* while also adopting a posture of accommodation *that increases with knowledge and authority* will greatly enhance the likelihood of a smoother transition to a more intergenerational church life.

Notes

[1] Origen, "Origen: Contra Celsum," in *Ante-Nicene Christian Library: Translations of the Writings of the Fathers Down to A.D. 325,* eds. Alexander Roberts and James Donaldson (Edinburgh: T&T Clark, 1872), 236; (Brackets in the original).

[2] Calvin, *Institutes*, vol. 13, bk. 1, no. 1, *Institutes of the Christian Religion*, ed. John T. McNeill, trans. Ford Lewis Battles (Philadelphia: Westminster, 1960), 121.

[3] Calvin, *Institutes*, 1371.

[4] Ford Lewis Battles, "God Was Accommodating Himself to Human Capacity," *Interpretation* 31, no. 1 (1977): 33.

[5] John Balserak, "The God of Love and Weakness: Calvin's Understanding of God's Accommodating Relationship with His People," *Westminster Theological Journal* 62, no. 2 (2000): 191.

[6] This line of thought follows the "ethical approach" to Philippians 2:5, rather than the "kerygmatic approach," outlined in Tod J. Billings, *Union with Christ: Reframing Theology and Ministry for the Church* (Grand Rapids: Baker Academic, 2011), 136–43.

[7] Even if one is uncomfortable with incarnational analogies due to the uniqueness of the incarnation, it is still possible to see Christ's humility as a precedent for the Christian life (Billings, *Union with Christ*, 138).

[8]In this context, Paul uses knowledge of God to mean facts about God, though not divorced from relationship with him; for Paul, "factual" knowledge about God is intrinsically linked to "relational" knowledge of God.

[9]Gordon D. Fee, *The First Epistle to the Corinthians,* The New International Commentary on the New Testament (Grand Rapids: Eerdmans, 1987), 423.

[10]Fee, *The First Epistle to the Corinthians,* 422.

[11]Peter Richardson, "Early Christian Sources of an Accommodation Ethic: From Jesus to Paul," *Tyndale Bulletin* 29 (1978): 125.

[12]Richardson, "Early Christian Sources," 141.

[13]Paul's approach can be seen in action when he circumcises Timothy for the sake of the Jews in Lystra (Acts 16:3), but is vociferous in his condemnation of circumcision when it is made a condition of salvation by the "circumcision group" (Gal. 5:1–2).

[14]There are some similarities to Chap Clark's "adoptive youth ministry" approach here, especially with respect to the relationship between those in churches with power and those without, though the foundation of accommodation is completely different. See Chap Clark, ed., *Adoptive Youth Ministry: Integrating Emerging Generations into the Family of Faith* (Grand Rapids: Baker Academic, 2011), 2.

[15]Pete Ward, ed., *Mass Culture: The Interface of Eucharist and Mission,* 2nd ed. (Abingdon, UK: Bible Reading Fellowship, 2008), 20.

[16]Jonny Baker, "Rhythm of the Masses," in *Mass Culture: The Interface of Eucharist and Mission,* ed. Pete Ward, 2nd ed. (Abingdon, UK: Bible Reading Fellowship, 2008), 43.

[17]Stephen Cottrell, "Parable and Encounter: Celebrating the Eucharist Today," in *Mass Culture: The Interface of Eucharist and Mission,* ed. Pete Ward, 2nd ed. (Abingdon, UK: Bible Reading Fellowship, 2008), 67.

[18]Cottrell, "Parable and Encounter," 69–72.

Chapter Three

Learning to Love Together

Darwin K. Glassford

The terms "intergenerational" and "intergenerational ministry" are buzz-words within ministry circles. These terms are often employed to validate program or ministry ideas; rarely are these terms clearly defined.

The intent of this chapter is to provide a broad outline for a biblical theology of intergenerational ministry: first, we will describe the nature of the task before us; next, we will offer a brief survey of understandings of intergenerational ministry; and last, we will provide an outline of a biblical theology of intergenerational ministry.

The Nature of the Task

Practical theology is a theological discipline of intimate dialogue between a scriptural understanding of faith and concrete experience. It enhances the community's understanding of the text, and enables more faithful Christ-following.[1] Practical theology invites theological reflection of experiences. This systematic theological reflection, based on David Kolb's experiential learning theory, often flows from a disequilibrating event that propels one to reflect on the adequacy of his/her beliefs for interpreting the experience.[2]

I was holding my ten-month-old granddaughter in my arms as we passed the communion elements around the circle. As I was passing the bread to the person next to me, she reached out to take a piece of bread. Of course, I stopped her. Then it struck me: she was a baptized member of the community, and I had denied her the community meal. While reflecting on this experience, it became apparent to me that my belief system did not permit a meaningful interpretation of this experience. Thus, I was propelled to begin a study of infant communion, the Passover, Jesus's institution of the Lord's Supper, and Paul's first letter to the church at Corinth. With study, my understanding of the Lord's Supper and children at the Lord's Table shifted in significant ways, which influenced my present practice.

Practical theology and theological reflection are generally done within a theological tradition. This tradition shapes the questions asked and responses considered. A person's understanding of baptism and its role in the Christian life will inform questions about children at the Lord's Table. The preceding story points to a theological tradition that practices infant baptism[3]; within this tradition, the church's worship and discipleship ministries (including educational ministries) are seen as theological disciplines.

Differences in understandings of intergenerational ministry are more than simple disagreements; they reflect deeply held, and often unquestioned, theological commitments. The task before us is a challenging theological task that must seriously engage the Scriptures[4] along with our own experiences.

Intergenerational Ministry: Select Definitions

The phrase intergenerational ministry is freely employed and rarely defined. The term lends itself to a self-evident descriptive definition: intergenerational ministry involves two or more generations interacting in a shared space. This description captures the intergenerational aspect, but does not adequately address the ministry component. In this section, we will examine select representative definitions of intergenerational ministry and related terms in order to illustrate a biblical theology of intergenerational ministry and address the ministry application component.

The definitive work on intergenerational ministry is Holly Catterton Allen and Christine Lawton Ross's *Intergenerational Christian Formation*. Allen and Ross thankfully define/explain *intergenerational* in the introduction:

> To convey our understanding of intergenerationality we will unpack three phrases: *intergenerational outlook, inter-generational ministry and intergenerational experiences.* An intergenerational outlook acknowledges that the gifts every generation brings to the spiritual formation of other generations strengthens the whole church. A faith community that practices intergenerational ministry will use these gifts, creating frequent opportunities for various generations to communicate in meaningful ways, to interact on a regular basis, and to worship and serve together regularly. And intergenerational experiences are experiences in which multiple representatives of two or more generations are present, and those present are engaged in *mutual* activities.[5]

The Allen and Ross description is holistic and rightly focuses on the community aspects, the use of gifts for the whole community, and their contribution to spiritual formation.

Allen and Ross's understanding was shaped in part by an earlier work entitled *The Church for All Ages*, which is focused on intergenerational worship. In a section titled "Clarifying the Term," intergenerational worship is defined as "worship in which people of every age are understood to be equally important."[6]

David Fraze, in *Owning Faith*,[7] provides a helpful understanding of intergenerational ministry as well as *inclusive* and *multigenerational* approaches to ministry. His definitions capture subtle differences between approaches (or philosophies of ministry) and programming. He notes that multigenerational programming aims to put different generations in the same place, but "does little to put the various groups into meaningful contact or dialogue"[8] and is not synonymous with intergenerational ministry. He further notes that "inclusiveness" approaches to ministry seek to eliminate "age-specific ministry programs all together."[9]

Writing specifically on the field of youth ministry, Fraze writes, "An intergenerational youth ministry approach views the roles of parents and the surrounding adult community as the primary influence on a student's spiritual formation. As a result, intergenerational youth programming is designed to create opportunities for spiritual growth across generational lines."[10] Like Allen and Ross, Fraze views the role of intergenerational ministry as fostering spiritual formation, and recognizes that everyone should grow spiritually.

These previous definitions identify three significant common characteristics in definitions of intergenerational ministry:

- *Intergenerational ministry is intentional*; it seeks to foster interaction between distinct age groups and generations in a variety of contexts. It explicitly calls into question a cultural tendency to isolate age groups and generations from each other.
- *Intergenerational ministry is strategic*; it creates opportunities for generations to interact for a specific purpose—Christian spiritual formation.
- *Intergenerational ministry is intertwined*; that is, it informs a ministry's other programs. Intergenerational ministry does not require discrete age-specific programming, but understands that age-specific programming complements a church or ministry's commitment to intergenerational ministry.

The following definition incorporates these characteristics: *intergenerational ministry intentionally facilitates and creates contexts where people of different ages and generations constructively interact and equip each other for ministry in a manner that fosters spiritual formation.*

What does it mean to "foster spiritual formation"? What does it mean to be "spiritually formed"? In order to address these questions, it is necessary to explore the central role of intergenerational ministry in the biblical narrative by developing a biblical theology of intergenerational ministry. A biblical theology of intergenerational ministry provides the essential grounding for practicing ministry intergenerationally.

Toward a Biblical Theology of Intergenerational Ministry

Biblical theology, according to Geerhardus Vos, "deals with the process of the self-revelation of God deposited in the Bible."[11] Constructing a biblical theology of intergenerational ministry involves identifying how the intergenerational theme is developed within the biblical narrative. The intent of this section is to provide an outline of a biblical theology foundational for a commitment to intergenerational ministry and guidance in discerning the intent of spiritual formation.

A biblical theology of intergenerational ministry must begin in the Garden within the creation narrative (Gen. 1–2). The Garden reveals a picture of the created order as God intended. Within the Garden exists a most perplexing element—the tree of the knowledge of good and evil—of which the man and woman were instructed not to eat (Gen. 2:15–17). As my daughter at the tender age of eight asked, "Why did God put the tree in the Garden in the first place?"

The tree of the knowledge of good and evil and the tree of life were both located within God's garden. The man and woman were created and placed within the garden to worship God and obey him by tending the garden (Gen. 1:28–31). As the man and woman fulfilled their responsibilities, they were to grow in loving the things that God loves, in the way that God loves. Though Adam and Eve succumbed to Satan's temptation to take a self-destructive shortcut to the knowledge of good and evil, their failure did not change God's ultimate desire for them to love the very things that God loves.

Intergenerational ministry, like all ministries, is informed by the creation narrative. The man and woman in the Garden were to live lives of faith by learning to love the things that God loves, in the way that God loves. As beings created in the image of God, like the man and woman in Genesis, we are called to live just as Adam and Eve were called to live. Spiritual formation involves learning to live lives of faith, which includes learning to love the things that God loves, in the way that God loves.

The Fall (Gen. 3) disrupted the created order. The man and woman hid from God, blaming each other and denying responsibility for their decisions. God acted by disrupting their relationship with the creation so that they would be reminded of their dependence on him, and sent them out of the Garden.[12]

However, the Pentateuch from Genesis 3 forward is the story of God actively creating a people who walk by faith, a faith lived out in community, and who are committed to loving and obeying God. Throughout the story, God calls the people to a life of faith, and God institutes feasts, festivals, and sacrifices that instruct the people in the life of faith. Responsibility for passing on the life of faith is vividly described in Deuteronomy 6:1–9.

Deuteronomy is the final book in the Pentateuch and is addressed to the people of God—Israel. Chapter 6 is a foundational passage in constructing a biblical theology of intergenerational ministry. Verse 5, commonly referred to as the *Shema,* is the summons to "love the LORD your God with all your heart and with all your soul and with all your strength," which echoes the earlier call to learn to love the things God loves in the way that God loves. Learning to love God requires instruction, and these verses identify two concurrent commitments. One of the commitments involves being vigilant in teaching the faith and sharing the stories of faith with children and young people. The other commitment is between the community and parents; they are to hold each other mutually responsible for the passing on of the faith to the next generation.

Thus far, a biblical theology of intergenerational ministry summons us to develop a life of faith that involves learning to love the things God loves, in the way that God loves, by passing on the faith to the next generation by the community and parents who hold each other mutually accountable.

After Israel entered the promised land, Judges 2:10 expresses this stunning observation: "After that whole generation had been gathered to their ancestors, another generation grew up who knew neither the LORD nor what he had done for Israel." This passage reveals that both the community (Israel) and parents failed to fulfill their responsibilities to their children, young people, and each other.

The failure of this community and the parents to hold each other accountable for passing on the faith undermines the very faith Israel is called to preserve. Israel's faith was to be expressed through loving obedience to the law. In failing to instruct the next generation on a proper understanding of the faith, their narrative became vulnerable to syncretism and distortion. This distortion subtly developed as legalism that claimed obedience to the law as evidence of faith. Israel continued to wrestle with this distortion and the relationship between faith and the law throughout the remainder of the Old Testament. It is important to note that within the Old Testament story, there are two Israels—ethnic Israel and spiritual Israel (which is composed of those who live by faith).[13]

Transitioning to the New Testament, the summons to a life of faith is also central to the proclamation of the gospel (Eph. 2:8–9). The life of faith is open to all, especially to children whom Jesus highly regards because of their ability to trust him (Matt. 19:14). His words to those who would injure their faith are strong and echo the commitments of Deuteronomy 6:1–9.

The emphasis from Deuteronomy 6 is picked up by Paul in Titus 2 as he writes about the role of sound teaching across the generations. The role of sound teaching is consistent with Jesus's admonition to form disciples (Matt. 28:18–20). A disciple is in the process of becoming more Christlike, with a response of gratitude for what Christ has accomplished. Throughout the New Testament, the followers of Christ are called to live lives of gratitude increasingly characterized by the fruit of the Spirit (Gal. 5:22–23). Discipleship involves learning to love the things God loves, in the way that God loves, because of the atoning work of Christ and through the power of the Holy Spirit.

The New Testament affirms the three themes identified in our discussion of the Old Testament. The Christian life is a life of faith. Children and young people should be disciples who are taught central truths of the faith. Both parents and the community are mutually accountable to each other and mutually responsible for this teaching.

The following processes and aspects of discipleship or Christian spiritual formation draw on and are informed by the brief biblical theology offered above. A maturing disciple of Christ will exhibit the following:

- A growing love and understanding of Scripture through regular reading and reflection; this aspect represents the centrality of Scripture in Christian theology (2 Tim. 3:16–17; 2 Pet. 1:21).
- A growing understanding and skill in explaining how a person's life is informed by the Ten Commandments, the Lord's Prayer,

the Sacraments, and the Apostles' Creed (or other belief statement)—these are summaries of the Christian faith.

- A growing understanding of the gospel and what it means to live
missionally as an adopted son or daughter of God; this process
reflects what it means to live out one's identity in Christ (Rom. 8).
- A lifestyle that increasingly manifests the fruit of the Spirit, stewardship of resources, caring for the poor and the marginalized,
and generous support of the church; this process seeks to describe
how the gospel transforms a person and the person's resulting
outlook on life.
- A desire and ability to share one's story and the Story of the gospel
with others, reflecting that we are to bear witness to the good
news of the gospel (1 Pet. 3:15–16).
- An ongoing investment in the life of a local church through regular attendance, participation in worship, and involvement in the
church's ministries (Acts 2:42).

Intergenerational ministry in the Scriptures is committed to cultivating
a life of faith through teaching God's story in a context where each generation is using their gifts (1 Cor. 12) and learning from the others so that
everyone is growing in loving the things that God loves, in the way that
God loves.

Conclusion

Intergenerational ministry has a rich theological foundation and history
within Jewish and Christian traditions. The robust understanding offered
in the biblical text invites each local church and ministry to recognize
its place in forming children, young people, and the whole community.
Intergenerational ministry is rooted in a commitment to mutual account-
ability within the community. Within Western culture's fascination with
age appropriateness and segregating by age and stage, intergenerational
ministry is refreshingly counter-cultural.

And yet, becoming more intentionally intergenerational in outlook
and practice is not an end in itself. It is a means that God uses to form
Christians and the Christian community through encouraging and building

each other into Christlikeness (1 Thess. 5:11; Phil 2:5–11). Intergenerational ministry is a tool for forming disciples that are learning together to love the things God loves, in the way that God loves.

Notes

[1] Nancy T. Ammerman, Jackson W. Carroll, Carl S. Dudley, and William McKinney, eds., *Studying Congregations: A New Handbook* (Nashville: Abingdon Press, 1998).

[2] David A. Kolb, *Experiential Learning: Experience as the Source of Learning and Development* (Upper Saddle River, NJ: Prentice-Hall, 1983).

[3] This particular tradition is the Continental Reformed tradition, which is a unique blend of Reformed theology and German Lutheran Pietism as articulated in the Ecumenical Creeds (Apostles' Creed, Nicene Creed, and the Athanasian Creed) and Reformed Confessions (Heidelberg Catechism, Belgic Confession, and Canons of Dort).

[4] Findings in the social- and neuro-sciences also inform the rationale for intergenerational ministry, and are addressed in other chapters of the book (see, for example, Chapter One by Jason Santos and Chapter Four by Lynn Barger Elliott).

[5] Holly Catterton Allen and Christine Lawton Ross, *Intergenerational Christian Formation: Bringing the Whole Church Together in Ministry, Community and Worship* (Downers Grove, IL: InterVarsity Press, 2012), 20–21.

[6] Howard Vanderwell, ed., *The Church of All Ages: Generations Worshiping Together* (Herndon, VA: Alban Institute, 2008), 11.

[7] David Fraze, "Friends, Mentors, Heroes: Connecting with Other Generations," in *Owning Faith: Reimagining the Role of Church and Family in the Faith Journey of Teenagers,* eds. Ron Bruner and Dudley Chancey (Abilene, TX: Leafwood Publishers, 2017), 219–40.

[8] Fraze, "Friends, Mentors, Heroes," 222.

[9] Fraze, "Friends, Mentors, Heroes," 222.

[10] Fraze, "Friends, Mentors, Heroes," 222.

[11] Geerhardus Vos, *Biblical Theology: Old and New Testaments* (Edinburgh, UK: Banner of Truth Trust, 2007), p. xx.

[12] Brian J. Walsh and J. Richard Middleton, *The Transforming Vision: Shaping a Christian World View* (Downers Grove, IL: InterVarsity Press, 1984); Albert M. Wolters, *Creation Regained: Biblical Basics for a Reformational Worldview,* 2nd ed. (Grand Rapids: Eerdmans, 2005).

[13] Douglas J. Moo, *The Epistle to the Romans,* The New International Commentary on the New Testament (Grand Rapids: Eerdmans, 2015); Jack Cottrell, *Romans,* vol. 1, The College Press NIV Commentary (Joplin, MO: College Press, 1996).

Chapter Four

Generational Theory and Faith Communities

Lynn Barger Elliott

In Grand Rapids, Michigan, there is a popular restaurant called Rose's overlooking a marina on Reeds Lake. Rose's is as packed on a beautiful day in June as on a snowy night in January. It's like our Cheers bar with a generational twist: you can't walk in and be known by name, but you can always find someone you know. People of all ages come to Rose's.

- Kids come to chase geese off the lawn.
- Teens come for the caramel-coated popcorn.
- Twentysomethings come for the buns on the wait staff.
- Thirtysomethings come for the happy hour half-off glasses of wine.
- Fortysomethings come for the extensive wine list.
- Fiftysomethings come for the view.
- Sixtysomethings come for the late dinner.
- Seventysomethings come for the early dinner.
- Eightysomethings come for the buns on the table.
- Ninetysomethings come because they haven't been there before.[1]

There is something for everyone at Rose's.

This is often the way churches define "intergenerational"—that is, *something for everyone*. However, hosting multiple generations under one roof is not the same as being intentionally intergenerational and finding unity and purpose as the body of Christ. To effectively work toward being intergenerational, a congregation must first consider the five or six generations that are present, as well as the various understandings of *community* that these generations might have.

Shifts in Community Life

Barry Wellman, sociologist and author, identifies three shifts in community life over the last century.[2]

- Door-to-Door
- Place-to-Place
- Person-to-Person

Until the Industrial Revolution, "door-to-door" relationships were the manner in which people related to each other. Community was where your feet could take you. Face-to-face interactions were with people within a limited geographical proximity. Community was experienced in traditional neighborhood—picture a town center with a few shops, the First Methodist Church, a Roman Catholic Church, a fire department, and a library.

To participate in this kind of community, one needed to simply live there. This manner of community required a specific space and time. Spoken and unspoken rules were known: attend church; support the Fourth of July parade; go to high school football games. In a door-to-door community, one sought to reinforce and extend an *identity* through the relationships experienced in daily life.

It wasn't until the 1970s that the shift to "place-to-place" community life significantly impacted American culture. This form of community happened where your car could take you.

It could be experienced at a mall, instead of the town square; or at a megachurch thirty minutes away, instead of the local church; or on a travel sports team, instead of a local high school team. It was not determined by one's home, or populated with those who lived in a similar neighbor-hood. This "convened" community was comprised of others who had also uprooted themselves for a desired experience.

The demands of this kind of community are simple: show up! When a person does not show up, he or she no longer carries the identity of a convened community. The nature of relationships is now secondary to the desired *experience.*

The next community shift is to a "person-to-person" mode, deter-mined by neither time nor space. "I-alone" is the sole agent and portal of all social connection. Phone numbers no longer reach places; they reach persons. Addresses no longer refer to fixed places; they go directly to an individual. Groups no longer represent people who are bound together by time or space; they are created networks.

Participating in a person-to-person community is simple—yet compli-cated. Person-to-person community travels with the "I," so it can happen anytime and anywhere. No two communities are alike. The demands of this community are placed on the "I," who must create, engage, grow, and curate the network.[3]

Though this community exists without a specific place and time, this limitation does not lessen its impact. The network of relationships provides a powerful—though often fleeting—sense of *belonging.* The individual is effectively able to experience community without actually having community.

Recently, I was sitting in the Atlanta airport waiting for a connecting flight when I saw on Facebook that a friend of mine from seminary had lost his battle with cancer. The post prompted several comments from long-lost friends full of memories. My friend had become a professor, and soon his students started sharing more recent memories. For about thirty minutes, in an airport waiting area, I experienced community without being in a community! Through a shared feeling of loss, I experienced a connection with a network of friends and strangers, most of whom I will never see again in my life. And it was *real.* In a person-to-person culture, individuals seek to *belong* so they can feel a sense of social support. This sense may not come from being in the same room or on the same street or even on the same continent.

One of the reasons community is so hard to develop in a congregation is that different generations are familiar and comfortable with a particular way of being a community. An individual can experience community in all of these forms. However, the dominant mode of community at the time of childhood shapes one's understanding and expectations, as well as the commitment to what one is willing to offer to create community.

Particular generations align with these different forms of community. As a congregation considers steps to create an intergenerational approach to ministry, it must keep in mind that these three very different concepts of community are operative and dynamic. As described below, each of the six generations not only brings its own historical and cultural uniqueness to the community but it also comes with its own expectations of the community.

Door-to-Door	Place-to-Place	Person-to-Person
Greatest/Silent	Boomers/Gen X	Millennial/Gen Z

Six Generations

Defining a generation is more art than science.[4] Though it is impossible to stereotype 60–80 million people at a time, it is true that prevalent patterns arise which can be traced to historical events and innovations. The world into which one comes of age shapes hopes and expectations. The exact year a generation begins and ends varies from study to study, but it is generally agreed that generations span approximately twenty to twenty-five years.[5]

It is important to note that much of the research on generations has been conducted in the United States and is based on its historical events.[6] It is also limited in that it has been conducted with a white, college-educated population and does not represent a wide range of ethnic or socioeconomic groups. However, with widespread globalization, millennials and Generation Z can now be discussed in common terms across the world.

Most multigenerational congregations consist of six generations: the "greatest generation," the silent generation, baby boomers, Generation X, millennials, and Generation Z.

Greatest Generation: Born 1901–1924

Tom Brokaw coined this term for the generation that grew up during the Great Depression and came of age at a time when they could serve in WWII. After attending several funerals of his father's peers and hearing their life stories, Brokaw observed, "It is, I believe, the greatest generation any society has ever produced."[7] These men and women fought not for fame or recognition, but because it was "the right thing to do."

The culture that shaped this generation was united in the singular purpose of defeating evil in the world, which was embodied at that time as Nazism. Victory over this evil launched national celebrations that ushered in optimistic attitudes toward the future. Institutional trust—particularly in a government that navigated a victorious war, took care of its veterans, and rebuilt an economy—was at an all-time high. Interestingly, eight U.S. presidents hail from this generation (John F. Kennedy, Lyndon B. Johnson, Richard Nixon, Gerald R. Ford, Ronald Reagan, Jimmy Carter, and George H. W. Bush).[8]

Community for this generation was the place where they lived. It was an extension of the values they held and reinforced their hopes of a better future. It was the source of strength, inspiration, and affirmation, and a place worthy of time and investment. This strong sense of community translated into a positive view toward the institutional church; one worshiped where one lived. The church provided an extended experience of values; one could be confident that the Sunday school lessons reinforced the words spoken at home. The church was a place people turned to for guidance.

Most in this generation joined a local church because "it was the right thing to do." Membership carried with it the assumption that one would lead wherever needed and be involved in groups that provided additional social connections with others in the town or surrounding neighborhood.

Silent Generation: Born 1925–1942

The moniker for the next generation came from a description in a 1951 *TIME* magazine cover story:

Youth today is waiting for the hand of fate to fall on its shoulders, meanwhile working fairly hard and saying almost nothing. The most startling fact about the younger generation is its silence.[9]

The struggles the men and women of this generation faced being born during or shortly after the Great Depression taught them to strive for stability. They were patriotic and loyal, and expected these traits from others. They were willing to stay with the same company their whole lives (partly due to the fact that the company existed their entire careers). They understood hierarchy and sought their place in the system. No members of this generation have served as a president of the United States.

Community for this generation also took place where they lived and was an extension of their values and identity. Because this generation put high value on loyalty and hard work, community involvement and volunteering were the responsible things to do. Finding comfort in the status quo meant there was little effort made for change. This outlook translated again into a positive view toward the church, though perhaps less dynamically. One remained loyal to the community church and assumed leadership and volunteer roles as duty to the community.

Baby Boomers: Born 1943–1960

The boomers were born during the economic- and baby boom following World War II. Though much of their childhood was saturated with a positive outlook toward the future and an assurance of prosperity, this worldview shifted as they came of age and witnessed the walls of cultural institutions cracking. The Civil Rights movement challenged the status quo, and its televised violence brought disturbing visions into the home. The vision of an invincible U.S. president splintered as a nation witnessed an assassination on the streets of a city in Texas, and then saw another president impeached for obstructing justice. Furthermore, their country required their commitment through a draft into a war it could not clearly define or win.

They paid their dues so they could retire and enjoy life. They ushered in a culture less committed to the values and norms of collective society and moved the focus toward individual preferences. Bill Clinton was the first boomer to serve as president, followed by George W. Bush, Barack Obama, and Donald Trump.

The concept of community shifted significantly for boomers. It was no longer something they settled for because it was at their doorstep. This generation began to consider what experiences they desired, and then made the effort to go find them. A sense of community, now secondary to organic relationships, was achieved when united with others who shared the desire for the same experience.

This shift had an enormous impact on the church. No longer did one feel the obligation to attend a church in the immediately surrounding community, but instead "shopped" for the place that would offer the desired experience. Against the backdrop of waning institutional trust was the fading assumption that one needed to play a leadership role in the organization. Local churches declined while staff-heavy regional churches grew in size and stature.

Gen X: Born 1961–1981

Generation X, originally called the "baby busters" due to declining fertility rates, came of age in a less than optimistic trajectory. They were the first "latchkey kids," who let themselves into their homes after school because both parents worked. This generation experienced the peak of divorce rates in America,[10] which necessitated the development of skills to navigate homelife on two fronts. Their daily lives shaped them to think independently.

As teenagers, they experienced the AIDS epidemic, MTV, and the fall of the Berlin Wall. They saw their parents devote their lives to work, only to be laid off when companies needed to consider the bottom line. No longer could one blindly trust the government, economy, or the institutions that had once created neighborhoods.

This generation decided to work smarter and to seek a balance between life and work. As they considered commute times, family commitments, and the career needs of a spouse, compromises were made at the expense of promotions and career successions. They introduced the concepts of job sharing, working at home, and business casual. Though they are still young, no member of this generation has yet served as a president of the

United States. It is noteworthy that Justin Trudeau, the prime minister of Canada, and Emmanuel Macron, the president of France, were both born within this generation, and shaped by parallel histories.

When it comes to community, Generation X brings a unique blend of seeking the desired experience while considering the time it will take away from family life. Community life is no longer something that assumes involvement over a lifetime. Membership is approached with caution as the distrust around institutions and the desires to protect family time have increased. For the church, this means participation in congregational life depends on the flexibility of the institution and what it has to offer the family. Not only does a church need to meet the criteria for the desired experience, it also needs to demonstrate value for family involvement. Leadership and volunteer roles within the church are evaluated in terms of whether it is in conflict with efforts to protect family time.

Millennials: Born 1982–2004

Millennial is the most common term used to refer to those who came of age in the new millennium. This generation is the largest to date in U.S. history and is more diverse than previous generations, with 42 percent being part of a minority race or ethnic group.[11] Unlike their (mostly boomer) parents who lived by the mantra, "Don't trust anyone over thirty," millennials get along well with their parents. Colleges, graduate schools, and businesses have noticed parents increasingly accompanying their adult children to interviews and helping them make life decisions.

"Millennials . . . were raised during the boom times and relative peace of the 1990s, only to see their sunny world dashed by the Sept. 11 attacks and two economic crashes, in 2000 and 2008. Theirs is a story of innocence lost."[12] Though they have been considered indulgent and individualistic, they have also been lauded for their communal spirit, tolerance, creativity, and adaptability, all necessary for times of rebuilding.[13] They like being part of a team and are more comfortable with collaboration than leadership.

Millennials experienced the explosion of the Internet and all remember the day they got their first cell phone. Technology has created a landscape with seemingly limitless opportunities, which has created commitment problems due to the fear of missing out (FOMO). The new world economy has provided pathways for millennials to rise to professional levels that do not take into account age or life experience.

Concepts of community have shifted radically with technology. Proximity in time or space is no longer necessary. Video games can be played any hour of the day with strangers from all over the world. Close relationships can form and be sustained without face-to-face contact. Immediate access to superiors challenges the hierarchies honored by previous generations. Advice, support, and information are only a tap away—as are slander, exclusion, and misinformation.

The brick-and-mortar church that holds a meeting at a specific time each week struggles to compete with the millennial's constant access to community. Institutional trust has plummeted as scandals have been exposed and issues like poverty and inequality go unaddressed. Though the majority of millennials continue to espouse a faith, many are opting to pursue it outside of a church community. This "spiritual, but not religious" group is joining the ranks of atheists and agnostics to form what sociologists are calling the rapidly growing "none" category (when asked about their religious affiliation, many in this group respond with the answer "none").[14]

Millennials who opt to stay within the church seek immediate purpose and authenticity. They care about creating a better world and want to be involved today, not groomed for future leadership. They assume they have useful skills and insights and want to put them to use right away. Sadly, many churches still choose leaders based on age and experience and miss the opportunity of millennial leadership.

Generation Z: Born 2005–2025

Generation Z is difficult to characterize primarily because some are not yet born and none have come of age. However, patterns can already be observed. They are all "digital natives," meaning they do not remember life without technology, a smart phone, or social media. They are remarkably multiethnic and biracial. Between 2000 and 2010, the country's Hispanic population grew at four times the rate of the total population. The number of Americans self-identifying as biracial rose 134 percent.[15]

As Generation X's offspring, they have absorbed the "sober sensibility" of their parents.[16] They are conscientious, hardworking, and somewhat anxious about the future. They are more likely to go to ACT prep camp than art camp. Unlike the millennials whose childhoods were disrupted, this generation has had open eyes from the beginning. They were born into the war on terror and the Great Recession. As one Gen Zer said, "I think I can speak for my generation when I say that our optimism has long ago been replaced with pragmatism."[17]

"Texting is the preferred way to connect with others, followed by messaging apps."[18] Having seen the online carelessness of the millennials, they are much more thoughtful about presenting a curated persona on social media.[19] Recalling the earnest and cautious silent generation, sociologist Neil Howe observes, "Put it all together—the privacy, the caution, the focus on sensible careers—and Generation Z starts to look . . . like their grandparents (or, in some cases great-grandparents)."[20]

Community for this generation brings a sense of belonging and meaning in a networked, yet fragmented, world. The desire to find authentic relationships overlaps with a sense that time must be used wisely. Meeting kindred souls should happen on a mission trip or a nonprofit board.

Church is an organization to which one can belong, but it does not automatically produce a sense of belonging. Generation Z is accustomed to navigating multiple networks at once, so this generation needs the church to offer a sense of belonging, *coupled with* a meaningful use of time and connection. They want to develop community alongside others from whom they can gain wisdom, experience, or opportunity.

Into the Future

With so many conflicting models for seeking and contributing to community, the question remains, "How does the church unite and function as the body of Christ?" The answers might be at the marina on Reeds Lake: Rose's knows each generation is seeking a unique experience, and Rose's assumes it has what generations are seeking.

As the church considers what it means to be intergenerational, I propose we think like Rose's:

- *Know that each generation is coming with different expectations for community.* It is imperative that generations understand their differences and appreciate what each has to offer. This is a strength, not a cause for divisiveness. Understanding brings vitality and opportunity to our common purpose to witness the love of Christ.

• *Assume that we have the essence that all generations are seeking.* Each generation has desires for identity, experience, and belonging. As God's people, united in forgiveness and called to serve, the church is uniquely qualified to offer all three.

Differences will continue to increase as technology accelerates the pace of change. As the church seeks to be authentic in the twenty-first century, rediscovering its call to be intergenerational will be its faithful pathway forward.

Notes

[1]Ideas for this list came from "Joke of the Week Where Should We Eat?" accessed February 26, 2017, www.clevelandseniors.com/forever/jow127.htm.

[2]This description can be found in Barry Wellman, ed., *Networks in the Global Village: Life in Contemporary Communities* (Abingdon-on-Thames, UK: Routledge, 1999). I rely on the summary presented by Andrew Zirschky, *Beyond the Screen: Youth Ministry for the Connected but Alone Generation* (Nashville: Abingdon Press, 2015), chapter 4.

[3]Zirschky goes into great detail on the demands of person-to-person community in chapter 5.

[4]This text will be using the Strauss and Howe generational birth ranges. See William Strauss and Neil Howe, *Generations: The History of America's Future, 1584 to 2069* (New York: William Morrow, 1991); William Strauss and Neil Howe, *The Fourth Turning: An American Prophecy—What the Cycles of History Tell Us about America's Next Rendezvous with Destiny* (New York: Broadway Books, 1997).

[5]Samantha Raphelson, "From GIs to Gen Z (Or Is It iGen?): How Generations Get Nicknames," NPR, October 6, 2014, www.npr.org/2014/10/06/349316543/don-t-label -me-origins-of-generational-names-and-why-we-use-them/.

[6]For example, many from the greatest generation fought in or knew someone who fought in World War II. The silent generation experienced childhood as the nation rebuilt after a war. Boomers were born after World War II and came of age in the '60s when protests of the Vietnam War filled our streets and Watergate weakened the institutional trust found in previous generations. Though there may be parallels in other national histories, these events are specifically based in the cultural psyche of the United States.

[7]Tom Brokaw, *The Greatest Generation* (New York: Random House, 1998), xxxviii.

[8]"American Generation Fast Facts," CNN Library, August 27, 2017, www.cnn.com/2013 /11/06/us/baby-boomer-generation-fast-facts/index.html.

[9]"People: The Younger Generation," *TIME*, November 5, 1951, http://content.time.com /time/subscriber/article/0,33009,856950,00.html.

[10]Ana Swanson, "144 Years of Marriage and Divorce in the United States, in One Chart," *Washington Post,* June 23, 2015, www.washingtonpost.com/news/wonk/wp/2015 /06/23/144-years-of-marriage-and-divorce-in-the-united-states-in-one-chart/?utm _term=.960d4ffb7d9a.

[11]"American Generation Fast Facts."

[12]Alex Williams, "Move Over, Millennials, Here Comes Generation Z," *The New York Times,* September 18, 2015, www.nytimes.com/2015/09/20/fashion/move-over-millennials -here-comes-generation-z.html?_r=0.

[13]Williams, "Move Over, Millennials."

[14]"'Nones' on the Rise," *Pew Research Center,* October 9, 2012, www.pewforum.org /2012/10/09/nones-on-the-rise/.

[15]"'Nones' on the Rise."

[16]"'Nones' on the Rise." According to a survey of risky behavior by the Centers for Disease Control and Prevention, the percentage of high school students who have had at least one drink of alcohol in their lives declined to about 66 percent in 2013, from about 82 percent in 1991. The number who reported never or rarely wearing a seatbelt in a car driven by someone else declined to about 8 percent, compared with about 26 percent in 1991.

[17]"'Nones' on the Rise."

[18]"Generation Z: New Insights into the Mobile-First Mindset of Teens," Think with Google, March 2017, storage.googleapis.com/think/docs/GenZ_Insights_All_teens.pdf.

[19]"Gen Z: A Look Inside Its Mobile-First Mindset," Think with Google, April 4, 2017, www.thinkwithgoogle.com/interactive-report/gen-z-a-look-inside-its-mobile-first -mindset/#dive-deeper.

[20]Williams, "Move Over, Millennials."

Part Two

LEADING INTERGENERATIONAL CHANGE

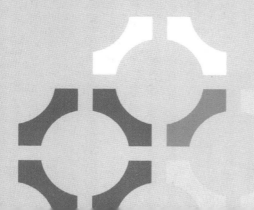

Chapter Five

From *Multi*generational to *Inter*generational

Cory Seibel

> By faith Abraham, when called to go to a place he would later receive as his inheritance, obeyed and went, even though he did not know where he was going. (Heb. 11:8)

All leaders who desire to help their *multigenerational* churches grow as intentionally *intergenerational* communities of faith are destined to encounter two practical challenges. First, in many churches, attempts to implement intergenerational ministry represent a departure from the age-segmented frameworks that have predominated in recent decades. The desire to move toward an intentionally intergenerational approach to ministry thus forces us to grapple with how to bring about change in relation to existing structures. Second, thinking about change also raises the question of how to shepherd congregations through the process of change.

As we set out to initiate change, we are likely to feel much like how Abraham is described in Hebrews 11. We might sense that God had called us to embark on a journey into something new. We might even be confident God will lead us. However, we also might be keenly aware that we do not really know where we are going. This can be unsettling.

In this chapter, I will argue that the process of change for multigenerational churches that desire to become purposefully intergenerational is like being called to a place we do not yet know. Understanding this can set the tone for the changes we undertake, enable us to adopt realistic expectations, and help us avoid a number of pitfalls we might otherwise encounter.

Thinking Unrealistically about Change

The suggestion that the process of becoming an intentionally intergenerational church is akin to Abraham's journey might strike us as an unappealing prospect. Perhaps we might prefer the journey of Moses. Who would not rather be called to embark on a path that, from the first step, has an identifiable Promised Land as its destination?

Much of modern literature on organizational change would have us believe that change processes are about moving as efficiently as possible to reach the Promised Land. Once we have formulated a clear, compelling, and comprehensive vision, "change is merely a matter of spanning the distance between present reality and envisioned future, between present behaviours and desired behaviours."[1] However, this "straight-line" conception of change rarely rings true to experience; for example the people of Israel managed to extend their 240-mile journey to forty years and two generations.[2]

As we endeavor to guide our churches, we would certainly hope to avoid the pitfalls to which Israel succumbed. However, it is fair to anticipate that there will be some unexpected twists and turns along the way. In reality, the assumption that change occurs through a straight-line progression into an envisioned future does not correspond with reality; we can describe this assumption as a "straight-line fallacy."[3] When church leaders allow this fallacy to guide them, troubles and frustrations frequently follow.

Thinking Adaptively about Change

The primary reason Abraham's journey provides a fitting metaphor for the process of change can be explained through the work of Harvard scholars Ronald Heifetz and Marty Linsky. They make a distinction between *technical* and *adaptive* challenges.[4] A technical challenge occurs when a situation arises for which existing systems and structures provide adequate solutions. The changes required by technical challenges can be accomplished sufficiently within the current order of things.

An adaptive challenge, on the other hand, arises in a situation where the existing systems and structures cannot offer sufficient answers. Adaptive challenges thus require us to engage in experimentation and a process of learning. They necessitate changes in behavior, values, and attitudes. In essence, they challenge us to embark on a journey to a land we do not currently know.

In many multigenerational congregations today, the process of helping church members adopt an intentionally intergenerational approach to ministry poses an adaptive challenge. In his book *Culture Making*, Andy Crouch provides a framework for understanding the adaptive change phenomenon. Crouch defines culture as "what we make of the world."[5] Culture, he says, is visible in the various "artifacts" or "goods" that humans create.[6]

Every cultural artifact is shaped by the underlying values, attitudes, and beliefs that we bring to our creative endeavors. According to Crouch, these values, attitudes, and beliefs cause us to approach the creative process with certain assumptions about "the way the world is" and "the way the world should be."[7] As a result, the artifacts we create also tend to define our "horizons of possibility and impossibility" in ways that reflect these assumptions.[8] In other words, our cultural products make some things possible, while making other things impossible, or at least extremely difficult.

Crouch's insights provide us a way to think about the ministry structures churches employ. We must acknowledge that these structures are cultural artifacts; they are the products of human creativity. As such, they have been shaped by underlying assumptions about "the way things are" and "the way things should be."

For example, much has been written about how the embrace of certain assumptions concerning human development and educational theory led to the formation of highly age-segmented approaches to ministry. In addition, the Church Growth Movement's philosophical commitment to "homogeneity" has reinforced the belief that ministries must be designed to target identifiable demographic groups in order to be effective. For many North American adherents to the assumptions of the Church Growth Movement, this "Homogeneous Unit Principle" has meant developing distinct ministry strategies and structures to appeal to each generational cohort, or even deciding to focus the church's whole ministry upon a specific generational cohort (e.g., families with young children).[9]

It is important to consider the profound ways in which these structures have defined the horizons of possibility and impossibility for churches. Born out of sincere efforts to be faithful, these structures have enabled churches to accomplish many good things. Yet, because they were not designed to facilitate intergenerational interaction, they have made it difficult for people of different generations to build community together. In fact, many of these structures are grounded in values and assumptions that actually discourage bringing the generations together. As a result, the horizons of possibility and impossibility in many congregations hinder them from envisioning a more intergenerational approach.

This being said, leaders who endeavor to guide their multigenerational churches toward becoming purposefully intergenerational must recognize that they face an adaptive challenge. Holly Allen and Christine Ross caution that helping churches become flourishing intergenerational communities requires more than a new method; it calls for a new mindset.[10] Our values, assumptions, and priorities must undergo transformation. This is an adaptive challenge—one that necessitates culture change within the church. As Drew Zahn notes, this aim of "building a permanent culture of intergenerational cooperation" is not easy.[11] Thus, leaders who desire to guide their congregations toward becoming intentionally intergenerational must see this deeper cultural work as a critical task.[12]

The adaptive journey of becoming an intentionally intergenerational church will challenge us to learn new behaviors and adopt new attitudes and allegiances. This is true for us as leaders and for all who join us on this journey of change, a journey that extends beyond the horizons of possibility and impossibility to which we are accustomed. This is a journey to a place that many of us have never truly been before. The process we employ must take this into account.

A Framework for Adaptive Change

When attempting to bring about change, it can be helpful to adopt a change model to guide the process, particularly one that has been developed through solid social-scientific research. This can help leaders anticipate necessary stages in the journey of change and order their steps accordingly. This can be especially valuable as we attempt to step into the unknown of adaptive change and to invite others to come along on this journey.

With this in mind, I will devote the remainder of this chapter to exploring how one change model could be used to guide the adaptive process of becoming more intergenerational in outlook and practice. I will employ a framework inspired by Everett Rogers's *Diffusion of Innovation* research and adapted by several church consultants.[13] This is certainly not the only approach to change one might take, but I have selected it because it has proven helpful to many churches engaged in adaptive change.[14]

Rogers devoted much of his life to studying how change takes place within cultures. He found that the integration of new ideas happens according to a discernable pattern consisting of five key movements. His insights demonstrate that change takes time and is accomplished through small, intentional steps. The approach Rogers's research inspires does not promise the rapid transformation of an entire organization. Rather, it emphasizes the steady, intentional cultivation of cultural change.

To demonstrate how this framework might help guide churches on the journey toward becoming purposefully intergenerational, I will briefly explore each of its five movements. I also will incorporate practical advice from others who have written about helping churches become more intergenerational and will suggest how their insights connect with the five stages of this process.

Stage One: Awareness

Michael Frost and Alan Hirsch assert, "People must be convinced that there is a problem before they are interested in a solution."[15] Thus, the crucial first step in the change process is to foster awareness of the intergenerational issues that the church faces. As leaders talk with their congregations, they are likely to discover that many people are already grappling with questions and feelings about these issues.[16] Leaders sometimes attempt to address these feelings by moving directly to strategies, plans, and programs. However, what is most needed is for leaders to create "a listening space" to aid parishioners in becoming aware of what is happening within them and among them.[17]

Several authors who have written about intergenerational ministry emphasize the importance of engaging key leaders in the earliest stages of the change process. However, in order to foster broader engagement, it is important to invite others to participate as well. To move in this direction, leaders might choose to form an intergenerational team. Jim Merhaut and John Roberto suggest something along these lines in recommending that churches consider developing an Intergenerational Integration Team.[18] At this stage, this team's role is not to design or plan, but rather to participate in conversations focused upon listening to one another and developing a growing awareness of the core intergenerational issues they face.

Leaders must exercise care in assembling an intergenerational team. When developing these teams, leaders often choose individuals who seem most representative of their respective generations.[19] However, such people often have the hardest time transcending their own generational preferences. Recognizing this, Gil Rendle recommends selecting "edgy" participants; these people "live close to the edge of their own value preferences and overlap with individuals who live close to the edge of the competing value system."[20] As a result, they are able to understand and express their own value system without being narrowly tied to it.

Stage Two: Understanding

In this stage, participants are provided time to develop deeper understanding of the issues they face. Most people cannot simply jump into a new idea; cultivating understanding, therefore, is an essential leadership task. Brenda Snailum identifies "lack of understanding of the basis and need for intergenerationality" as one of the key barriers to creating an intergenerational culture within churches.[21]

During this stage, it is crucial for leaders to nurture a culture of intergenerational learning. As Rendle expresses, "The shift from doing something about our differences to learning about our differences requires a different space . . . where reflection and learning are possible."[22] Several authors address this point by stressing that leaders who desire to help their churches become intergenerational communities must serve as "educators."[23] Christine Ross, for example, encourages leaders to commit to patient, continuous teaching.[24]

In addition, nurturing a culture of intergenerational learning necessitates providing participants with opportunities to exchange ideas and concerns,[25] to listen to one another so that they can hear the underlying questions and issues that are being voiced. Leaders must help to bridge the "understanding gap,"[26] creating ways for congregants to communicate with one another effectively in order to understand their differences better.[27] Good leadership at this stage might actually involve engaging the tensions between the generations in order to fully capitalize upon the learning opportunities they present.[28]

As time is provided for discussion, understanding will deepen and new insights will emerge. Participants will begin to recognize the ways in which their horizons of possibility and impossibility have been limited by previous assumptions about "the way things are" and "the way things should be." They also will begin to get a fresh glimpse of what God is doing in their midst.

Stage Three: Evaluation

In the third stage of the journey, "the congregation examines current actions, attitudes, and values in light of the new understanding they are gaining. People can now consider whether specific activities, programs, and commitments are congruent with their newly emerging awareness and understanding."[29] Well-crafted evaluative questions become an essential tool during this stage.[30]

This is still not the time for action, but rather a time for discernment and decision-making. Leaders are likely to be tempted to develop action steps. However, as Alan Roxburgh and Fred Romanuk caution, "if a congregation does not take enough time for awareness, understanding, and evaluation, then most solutions will yield only a short-term burst of hope and energy, but then the congregation will return to its previous state."[31] Thus, this time dedicated to evaluation is crucial in helping achieve lasting change.

Stage Four: Experimentation

Allen and Ross observe that becoming an intentionally intergenerational church "entails actually bringing the generations together for cross-age activities, events, and experiences."[32] Thus, the fourth movement in this process constitutes a key stage in the journey of change. It invites participants to begin to put new insights into action by initiating new practices and participating together in intergenerational ministries "that cross barriers of style and preference."[33] This is a time for experimentation to be nurtured. As people experiment with what they have been learning, true cultural change can become embedded in the life of a congregation.[34]

In the face of adaptive challenges, the tendency of leaders to impose ambitious, far-reaching plans can cause anxiety and conflict. In reality, successful efforts at change often come from the margins of an institution rather than from a direct attempt to alter the center of its life. Thus, rather than taking on "the whole system at once,"[35] this fourth stage calls for "experiments around the edges" that avoid overwhelming church members.[36] These experiments are meant to engage the entire system without changing the whole system.[37]

This may involve experimentation with "one or two pieces" of the church's life.[38] This approach is consistent with Zahn's advice that, instead of a "complete overhaul," churches should aim to begin with a number of "small, experimental forays into intergenerational ministry."[39] Churches might also consider Snailum's recommendation of "beginning where they are" by identifying ministries that already have some cross-generational components as places to start.[40]

The experiments undertaken during this stage are not chiefly intended to become permanent fixtures in the church's life.[41] Rather, they are about discovering how God's Spirit is leading the congregation. They are meant to provide opportunity for new habits and values to become embedded in the life of the congregation. They enable the church to experience "early victories," while also encouraging long-term cultural change.[42]

Allen and Ross emphasize the importance of participants engaging in evaluation together to learn from their early efforts of implementing intentionally intergenerational activities.[43] They should also be encouraged to share their stories of success in hopes that others will become inspired to participate. The invitation "to join the journey" should be consistently extended to the whole congregation.[44]

This approach can be challenging for leaders experienced in more technical approaches to leadership. Thus, as Merhaut and Roberto suggest, it is important for leaders to adopt a collaborative and empowering style, to lead by example, and to work with teams to design and implement projects.[45] Ross also offers several suggestions that are helpful at this stage. She notes that leaders play an important role in encouraging church staff members and other leaders to work together to implement intergenerational approaches to ministry. She also emphasizes the need for leaders to remind others continuously about the shared vision that is emerging.[46]

Stage Five: Commitment

In the final stage, as participants continue to implement intentionally intergenerational approaches to ministry, they will begin to recognize that they are operating in ways that transcend their prior horizons of possibility and impossibility. New habits become engrained in the life of the congregation. Confidence grows as more people become involved. In turn, "the innovation becomes a part of the deep values of the culture, and the congregation begins to carry on its usual business according to the innovation."[47] Merhaut and Roberto speak of this transformation in describing how practices that were "planned at the beginning of intergenerational programming" now become "the spontaneous and natural way that church members treat each other intergenerationally."[48]

These final strides toward a full embrace of intentional intergenerational ministry will unavoidably impact previously existing structures of the church. However, because of the widespread adoption of innovation that has already been achieved, changes proceed much more rapidly as the need for these changes becomes clear to a majority of congregants.[49] Structural changes can now be accomplished—not because they have been championed by a particular leader, "but because the people themselves have taken on a new way of being church together."[50]

Conclusion

The journey of adaptive change for many multigenerational churches desiring to become intergenerational in outlook and practice is indeed a journey to an unknown land. The framework explored here can help us navigate the pathway from here to there. It enables us to adopt new values, attitudes, and assumptions and to learn to live in ways that transcend our previous horizons of possibility and impossibility. This process requires an investment of time, patience, and perseverance. However, if we are willing to embark on this journey, we may eventually be surprised and delighted to discover where we have arrived together.

Notes

[1] Cory L. Seibel, "Intergenerational Reconciliation and Justice as Essential Dimensions of Missional Renewal in the Post-Modern Transition" (PhD thesis, University of Pretoria, 2009), 465, repository.up.ac.za/handle/2263/28779.

[2] Merrill F. Unger, "The Exodus," In *The New Unger's Bible Dictionary*, ed. R. K. Harrison, rev. and updated ed. (Chicago: Moody Press, 1988), 384–85.

[3] Alan J. Roxburgh and Fred Romanuk, *The Missional Leader: Equipping Your Church to Reach a Changing World* (San Francisco: Jossey-Bass, 2006), 82; Patrick Keifert, *We Are Here Now: A New Missional Era* (Eagle, ID: Allelon Publishing, 2006), 48–49.

[4] Ronald A. Heifetz and Marty Linsky, *Leadership on the Line: Staying Alive through the Dangers of Leading* (Boston: Harvard Business School Publishing, 2002).

[5] Andy Crouch, *Culture Making: Recovering Our Creative Calling* (Downers Grove, IL: InterVarsity Press, 2008), 23.

[6] Crouch, *Culture Making*, 28.

[7] Crouch, *Culture Making*, 29.

[8] Crouch, *Culture Making*, 28–29.

[9] I provide a more detailed analysis and critique of the Homogeneous Unit Principle in my PhD thesis. To explore this topic further, please refer to chapters 3, 4, 5, and 7 of Seibel, "Intergenerational Reconciliation and Justice."

[10] Holly Catterton Allen and Christine Lawton Ross, *Intergenerational Christian Formation: Bringing the Whole Church Together in Ministry, Community and Worship* (Downers Grove, IL: InterVarsity Press, 2012), 178–79.

[11] Drew Zahn, "Connecting the Generations," *Christianity Today*, April 1, 2002, accessed July 15, 2017, www.ctlibrary.com/le/2002/spring/3.37.html.

[12] Jim Merhaut and John Roberto, "Leadership for an Intergenerational Church," in *Generations Together: Caring, Praying, Learning, Celebrating, & Serving Faithfully*, eds. Kathie Amidei, Jim Merhaut, and John Roberto (Naugatuck, CT: LifelongFaith Associates, 2014), 159.

[13] Everett M. Rogers, *Diffusion of Innovations*, 5th ed. (New York: Free Press, 2003); Roxburgh and Romanuk, *The Missional Leader*; Keifert, *We Are Here Now*.

[14]By the time Patrick Keifert published *We Are Here Now* in 2006, his organization, Church Innovations, had employed this framework through more than two decades of consultancy work among one thousand congregations, seventy-five national and mid-governing bodies, and two dozen denominations in seven countries and all across the United States.

[15]Michael Frost and Alan Hirsch, *The Shape of Things to Come: Innovation and Mission for the 21st-Century Church* (Peabody, MA: Hendrickson Publishers, 2003), 191–92.

[16]Another key facet of this framework is the "diffusion of innovation curve." This concept reflects the understanding that some people are eager to participate in innovations, while others will only embrace an innovation with time. This process is based in the assumption that there are "innovators" and "early adopters" in every congregation who will want to be involved from the earliest stages. See Keifert, *We Are Here Now,* 55–57, and Roxburgh and Romanuk, *The Missional Leader,* 103–4.

[17]Roxburgh and Romanuk, *The Missional Leader,* 87.

[18]Merhaut and Roberto, "Leadership for an Intergenerational Church," 160.

[19]Bob Whitesel and Kent R. Hunter, *House Divided: Bridging the Generation Gaps in Your Church* (Nashville: Abingdon Press, 2000), 131.

[20]Gil Rendle, *The Multigenerational Congregation: Meeting the Leadership Challenge* (Bethesda, MD: Alban Institute, 2002), 130.

[21]Brenda Snailum, "Implementing Intergenerational Youth Ministry within Existing Evangelical Church Congregations: What Have We Learned?" *Christian Education Journal,* 3rd ser., 9, no. 1 (Spring 2012): 135–47.

[22]Rendle, *The Multigenerational Congregation,* 119.

[23]Merhaut and Roberto, "Leadership for an Intergenerational Church," 166.

[24]Christine Ross, "Four Congregations That Practice Intergenerationality," *Christian Education Journal,* 3rd ser., 9, no. 1 (Spring 2012), 143.

[25]Allen and Ross outline several exercises that could be helpful, including studying scriptural examples of intergenerational life, discussing the factors that led to the church adopting age-segregated approaches to ministry, and exploring some of the theoretical support for learning and growing together (*Intergenerational Christian Formation,* 181).

[26]Carolyn A. Martin, PhD, and Bruce Tulgan, *Managing the Generation Mix: From Collision to Collaboration* (Amherst, MA: HRD Press, 2002), 40; Jean M. Twenge, PhD, *Generation Me: Why Today's Young Americans Are More Confident, Assertive, Entitled—And More Miserable Than Ever Before* (New York: Free Press, 2006), 8.

[27]Angie Williams and Jon F. Nussbaum, *Intergenerational Communication across the Life Span* (Mahwah, NJ: Lawrence Erlbaum Associates, 2001), 216–17.

[28]Rendle, *The Multigenerational Congregation,* 5, 8.

[29]Roxburgh and Romanuk, *The Missional Leader,* 95.

[30]Merhaut and Roberto provide an "Intergenerational Audit Worksheet" that could be a great resource in this evaluative process ("A Congregational Toolkit for Becoming Intentionally Intergenerational," in *Generations Together,* 102). Allen and Ross also outline a number of discussion points that can be helpful to churches in this evaluative process (*Intergenerational Christian Formation,* 182).

[31]Roxburgh and Romanuk, *The Missional Leader,* 96.

[32]Allen and Ross, *Intergenerational Christian Formation,* 188.

[33] M. Rex Miller, *The Millennium Matrix: Reclaiming the Past, Reframing the Future of the Church* (San Francisco: Jossey-Bass, 2004), 82.

[34] Roxburgh and Romanuk, *The Missional Leader*, 82.

[35] Keifert, *We Are Here Now*, 90.

[36] Roxburgh and Romanuk, *The Missional Leader*, 99.

[37] Keifert, *We Are Here Now*, 92.

[38] Roxburgh and Romanuk, *The Missional Leader*, 84.

[39] Zahn, "Connecting the Generations."

[40] Snailum, "Implementing Intergenerational Youth Ministry," 170.

[41] Roxburgh and Romanuk, *The Missional Leader*, 61.

[42] Keifert, *We Are Here Now*, 85.

[43] Allen and Ross, *Intergenerational Christian Formation*, 187.

[44] Allen and Ross, *Intergenerational Christian Formation*, 185.

[45] Merhaut and Roberto, "Leadership for an Intergenerational Church," 161, 163, 167.

[46] Ross, "Four Congregations That Practice Intergenerationality," 145.

[47] Keifert, *We Are Here Now*, 53.

[48] Merhaut and Roberto, "Leadership for an Intergenerational Church," 103.

[49] Keifert, *We Are Here Now*, 53–54.

[50] Roxburgh and Romanuk, *The Missional Leader*, 102.

Chapter Six

Intergenerational Principles and Three Stories

John Roberto

Christian congregations are rediscovering the importance of intergenerational faith formation and are making cross-age relationship building a defining characteristic of their community lives. Research is now providing evidence of the enduring importance of intergenerational experiences for the formation of faith in the younger generations, as well as in adults and the whole family.

Over the last two decades, congregations from a variety of Christian traditions have been developing new models of intergenerational faith formation and learning. Intergenerational learning provides a way to educate the whole community, bringing all ages and generations together to learn with and from each other, build community, share faith, pray, celebrate, and practice the Christian faith. The key is that everyone is learning together—young and old, single and married, families with children and empty-nest families, and children, parents, and grandparents—in a shared experience of the Christian faith.

Three Intergenerational Stories

Since the early 2000s, St. Elizabeth of Hungary Church in Acton, Massachusetts, has been offering monthly intergenerational learning as the core faith formation experience for all ages. Their curriculum is liturgically centered, connecting faith formation with the realities of daily experience and the Eucharistic celebration. For St. Elizabeth, the Sunday Eucharist is the heart of all efforts to know, love, and serve Jesus Christ. This is where their community accompanies everyone on their journey of life and faith. They hold intergenerational learning sessions each month between Labor Day and the Easter season with four sessions per month to accommodate the large number of participants and their different schedules. Every session begins with a meal. What follows varies from month-to-month, but usually includes an opening activity in common and age-appropriate breakouts (grades K–4 with at least one parent, middle school, high school, and adult). Each session runs no longer than two and a half hours. Each month's theme is drawn from one of the Sunday lectionary readings in that month. Some years they adopt a theme—2017–18 was Discipleship—while other years have a monthly theme drawn directly from the lectionary readings. In addition to monthly programs, St. Elizabeth sponsors a twenty-four-hour intergenerational experience of prayer, learning, service, and worship called "24 Hours with the Lord" and has sponsored an intergenerational mission trip.[1]

While St. Elizabeth is a large suburban parish, Our Lady of Fatima is a small-town church in New York State. Since the early 2000s, they have been holding monthly intergenerational faith formation gatherings called GIFT, a parish model of intergenerational, life-long, event-centered faith formation. All ages gather once a month for a learning session around a yearly theme. In 2017–18, they focused on Mary, the mother of Jesus, and learned through her about the life of Jesus. Gatherings are on Saturday, and begin with a potluck supper immediately following the 4:00 P.M. Mass.[2]

St. Anthony on the Lake parish in Peewaukee, Wisconsin, has been offering intergenerational faith formation for over twenty-five years. They started with twenty families and have grown to over 350 families, which includes adult-only households. Offered on Sunday mornings or Monday evenings (whatever is most convenient for people), twice a month from mid-September through March, the program begins with an intergenerational activity and breaks into age-group learning where both parents/grandparents, children, and youth explore faith themes covering the Bible, the Creed, sacraments, morality, and prayer and spirituality. The Sunday program begins at 10 A.M. with fellowship and concludes at noon; the Monday program begins with a light supper at 5:30 P.M. and ends at 7:30 P.M.[3]

Research Descriptions

The findings in this chapter are based on two research projects (2006 and 2013) on intergenerational faith formation along with a survey of intergenerational principles with the participants in the 2014 Symposium on Intergenerational Faith Formation.

The 2006 research was conducted with over one thousand Catholic parishes involved in the Generations of Faith Project,[4] a Lilly Endowment funded project sponsored by the Center for Ministry Development.[5] At the conclusion of the Generations of Faith Project in 2006, qualitative (focus groups) and quantitative (survey) research was conducted to determine the effects of intergenerational faith formation on participants, church leaders, and the whole faith community. The qualitative research study involved parish staff in seventy-nine parishes; the quantitative online survey was completed by 434 of the approximately one thousand Catholic parishes that participated in the project.

In 2013, my colleague Jim Merhaut and I identified over two hundred parishes that were involved in intergenerational faith formation from the original 2001–06 group of churches as well as new parishes that began after 2006. Fifty parishes completed a survey on the status of intergenerational faith formation in their churches. They were large, medium, and small-sized churches in suburban, rural, and urban settings. Some were combined with, or in the process of combining with, another church. We asked faith formation leaders in churches to tell us what they had learned over the past decade. They told us about content, methods, sustainability, and the impact that the intergenerational model has had on them and the congregations they serve.

A summative review of these two research studies (along with relevant literature) surfaced a substantial list of intergenerational faith formation principles. In 2014, I sponsored a cross-denominational[6] symposium on intergenerational faith formation; prior to the symposium, a survey outlining and describing these principles was sent to the one hundred registered participants of the symposium. The purpose of the survey was to test the importance and application of these principles for intergenerational faith formation.

Drawing on these three research studies, this chapter proposes seventeen principles for the effective design, implementation, and facilitation of intergenerational learning. These principles can serve as guides for developing, enhancing and expanding, and evaluating intergenerational learning in a congregation.

Principles of Intergenerational Faith Formation

This section presents seventeen principles, drawn from the research described earlier, to guide the design, implementation, facilitation, and leadership of intergenerational learning in a congregation. The principles are organized into four categories:

- Promoting Christian Identity
- Building Relationships and Community
- Fostering Learning and Growth
- Empowering and Collaborating Leadership

These principles can be seen in the stories of St. Elizabeth, Our Lady of Fatima, and St. Anthony on the Lake; and they can serve as guides for developing, enhancing and expanding, and evaluating intergenerational learning in a congregation.

Promoting Christian Identity

Principle 1. Through intergenerational faith formation, Christian commitment is formed and strengthened as people develop relationships and actively participate in intergenerational faith communities that teach, model, and live out the community's beliefs.

Principle 2. Through intergenerational faith formation, people learn the ways of the faith community and how to live as a Christian today as they participate authentically and relationally with more experienced members of the community.

Principle 3. Through intergenerational faith formation, people identify with their faith community and participate more fully with all ages and generations in the life and ministries of the faith community.

We know from the research findings that participation in intergenerational learning leads to greater involvement in church life, including Sunday worship, sacraments, service projects, and the ministries of the church; also, participation in these all-age learning activities leads to a deeper understanding of the core events and practices of the Christian faith.

One of the ways churches promote Christian identity and church participation is by focusing the learning on the central events of the Christian faith. For example:

- *The feasts and seasons of the church year* provide a natural rhythm and calendar to the curriculum: Advent and Christmas, Lent and Holy Week, Easter Season, Pentecost, and more.
- *The Revised Common Lectionary*[7] provides a rich curriculum for the whole community with its three-year cycle of Scripture readings. The *Narrative Lectionary* provides a four-year cycle following the sweep of the biblical story, from Creation through the early Christian church.
- *Ritual, milestone, and sacramental celebrations* provide events rich in theological meaning that celebrate the faith journey throughout life: baptism, confirmation, first Bible, first communion, graduation, marriage, funeral, and more.
- *Acts of service and justice*—locally and globally—provide a focus on mission to the world and put in action biblical and church teachings on service, justice, and care for the earth.

When intergenerational faith formation is focused on the central events of the Christian faith, churches have the opportunity to *prepare* people with the appropriate knowledge and practices for participation, to *immerse* them in the events and experiences of church life, and to guide their *reflection* upon the meaning of the event and how to live/practice that learning in daily life. For example:

- People learn about worship and how to worship in intergenerational settings; experience Sunday worship with the faith community and practice worshiping; and live the Sunday worship experience at home and in their daily lives (with activities and resources delivered online).
- People learn about the Bible and how to read it, interpret it, and apply it to their lives; experience the Bible at Sunday worship and at home; and develop their own practice of Bible study and reading (with activities and resources delivered online).
- People learn about Jesus and the Christian tradition and what it means for life today; experience the teachings of Jesus and the Christian tradition through participation in the events of church life; and continue to learn and live the Christian faith in daily life today (with activities and resources delivered online).
- People learn about prayer and spirituality and how to develop their spiritual lives through prayer and spiritual disciplines; experience the prayer life of the faith community; and develop their own practice of prayer and the spiritual disciplines (with activities and resources delivered online).
- People learn about the justice issues of our day and the biblical and church teachings on justice, service, and care for creation in intergenerational settings; experience acts of justice and service with the faith community—locally and globally; and engage in the practices of serving those in need, caring for creation, and working for justice—as individuals, with their peers, with their families, and with their church and other groups and organizations (with activities and resources delivered online).

Building Relationships and Community

Principle 4. Intergenerational faith formation strengthens and creates new relationships among people of all ages, enhances their sense of belonging in the faith community, and increases participation in church life.

Principle 5. Intergenerational faith formation promotes a community where generational differences can be transcended rather than reinforced, and where generational understanding and positive intergenerational relationships can be experienced.

Principle 6. Intergenerational faith formation affirms each person's value in the total community (regardless of age), and promotes understanding of shared values and respect for individuals in all stages and ages of life.

Principle 7. Intergenerational faith formation fosters a climate that includes valuing, nurturing, and employing the gifts of every person from young to old.

Principle 8. Intergenerational faith formation creates a welcoming and safe environment—of warmth, trust, emotional safety, acceptance, and care—conducive to promoting faith sharing, group participation, mutual support, and care for one another in the congregation and in the community.

We know from the research findings that one of the most significant features of intergenerational faith formation is the way it builds community among people, and fosters relationships across ages and generations. Central to building relationships and community is creating an atmosphere of hospitality and welcoming at intergenerational learning sessions where everyone feels a sense of belonging, acceptance, and respect. *This welcoming spirit is as important as the content being taught.*

The intergenerational learning model creates the environment and experiences where people of all ages learn from each other and grow in faith together. Adults gain meaningful insights from their interactions with children and youth; and children and youth experience meaningful support from nonparental adults. Intergenerational learning creates an environment in which participants feel safe to learn, ask questions, and grow in faith on a deeper level.

Fostering Learning and Growth

Principle 9. Intergenerational faith formation addresses the social and developmental needs of age groups, and speaks to the relevant concerns and challenges people face today.

Principle 10. Intergenerational faith formation addresses the variety of faith styles and religious experiences of people in the congregation by engaging people of all ages in a variety of activities that are developmentally appropriate, experiential, multisensory, interactive, and participatory.

Principle 11. Intergenerational faith formation settings are authentic learning environments made up of individuals at various stages in their faith journeys who teach and learn from each other.

Principle 12. Intergenerational faith formation encourages faith growth and practice in all generations, and provides "up close and personal" faith experiences as children, teens, young adults, midlife adults, and older adults engage in sharing faith, teaching, learning, serving, celebrating, and praying for one another.

Principle 13. Intergenerational faith formation has a positive effect on both the older and younger generations by creating intentional opportunities for young and old to meet together, to share stories, to create something together, or merely to talk with each other.

Principle 14. Intergenerational faith formation supports families by surrounding them with a community of faith, by engaging the whole family in caring, celebrating, learning, praying, and serving together, and by providing parents with opportunities to learn from Christians who are practicing their faith and raising faithful children.

Principle 15. Intergenerational faith formation equips people to live their faith in daily life and engages them in service to others, locally and globally.

We know from the research that intergenerational learning works most effectively when it engages people in a variety of learning activities that are experiential, multisensory, and interactive, and involve faith sharing. People of all ages and generations learn best when the learning program engages them experientially through their heads, hearts, and lifestyles. In order to accomplish this, churches should design intergenerational learning with these ideas in mind:

- Respect the variety of learning styles among the participants with a diversity of learning experiences, recognizing that some people learn best through direct, hands-on, concrete experiences, some through reflective activities, others through exploration and analysis, and others through active experimentation with the new knowledge and practices.

- Recognize the multiple intelligences (linguistic, spatial, musical, logical, bodily-kinesthetic, intrapersonal, interpersonal, and naturalist) among the participants, and design learning methods and activities that address the variety of intelligences in the group.
- Incorporate a variety of methods that are appropriate for all ages learning, and encourage people to participate in a variety of learning activities, even if the activities are new for them.
- Utilize as many of the five senses as possible throughout the learning experience through multisensory methods that engage the whole person—art, drama, music, dance, storytelling, media, prayer, and rituals.
- Teach and model the skills for listening and sharing across generations, creating an environment conducive to storytelling and faith sharing.
- Engage people in collaborative and group-centered formats for study, inquiry, activities, and sharing.
- Incorporate real-life learning application by helping people experience new ways to practice their faith during the session, and find ways to transfer learning from the session to their daily lives.

We know from the research that intergenerational learning strengthens parental and family faith by encouraging the whole family to participate—children, teens, parents, and grandparents. It equips parents (and grandparents) to be faith formers of their children by developing their competence and confidence through such faith-forming experiences as sharing stories, celebrating rituals, praying together, reading the Bible, and more. Intergenerational learning provides activities that model the practices that churches want parents and families to live at home. The research findings also revealed that families *enjoy* opportunities to pray, learn, and be together (even if parents may resist participating initially).

Empowering and Collaborating Leadership

Principle 16. Intergenerational faith formation is led by congregational leaders who embrace a collaborative, team-based, and empowering style of leadership, and have a shared vision of an intergenerational church.

Principle 17. Intergenerational faith formation ministry and programming is facilitated by teams who work collaboratively in designing and conducting programming, and are well prepared and supported in their ministry.

The research showed that the churches that implemented intergenerational faith formation *effectively* demonstrated several important leadership characteristics. First and foremost is consistent leadership; that is, from the pastor to the coordinator to the volunteer leaders, they all share a common vision for intergenerational faith formation that they share with the whole church community.

In addition, the practice of intergenerational learning requires a diversity of leaders who practice a *collaborative* and *empowering* style of leadership. This style of leadership is exercised by not just the pastor and coordinator of intergenerational faith formation, but also by the entire leadership team. Intergenerational learning requires committed volunteer leaders who are engaged in a variety of roles in lifelong faith formation: planning, teaching, organizing, and supporting. Teamwork and collaboration are essential for the effective planning and implementation of intergenerational learning.

Conclusion

These seventeen principles can help every church in making intergenerational learning an essential foundation for lifelong faith formation. These principles are excellent guides for developing, enhancing and expanding, and evaluating intergenerational learning in your congregation.

For the complete Generations of Faith research study, articles, case studies, and interviews with leaders on intergenerational learning, email John Roberto at jroberto@lifelongfaith.com.

Notes

[1] To learn more about their work, go to www.seoh.org/faith-formation/gift. (Download the annual plan with themes.)

[2] To learn more about their program, go to www.rcda.org/churches /OurLadyOfFatima/faith_formation.html. (Download the annual plan with themes.)

[3] To learn more about their program, go to www.stanthony.cc/family-program.

[4]I served as the project coordinator for the Generations of Faith Project. The Generations of Faith intergenerational model is based on the work of James White in his book *Intergenerational Religious Education* (Birmingham: Religious Education Press, 1988). White identified four patterns of relationships that shape the four components of an intergenerational religious education learning experience: 1) in-common experiences, 2) parallel learning, 3) contributive occasions, and 4) interactive sharing.

The model created by the Generations of Faith Project expanded upon White's components to include gathering together, opening prayer, all-ages learning experiences, in-depth learning experiences, sharing reflections and application, and closing prayer.

[5]The Center for Ministry Development is a Catholic nonprofit organization serving diocese and parishes in youth and young adult ministry, family, and intergenerational faith formation.

[6]Survey participants represented eight Christian denominations: American Baptist, Christian Reformed, Episcopal, Lutheran ELCA, Presbyterian (USA), Roman Catholic, United Church of Christ, and the Unitarian Universalist Association.

[7]Lectionaries from the Episcopal, Presbyterian, Lutheran, and other Christian traditions offer similar guidelines.

Chapter Seven

Unlocking the Power of Intergenerational Leadership

Jessica Stollings

As an experiential learning activity, one of my corporate clients divided its leaders up by generation, challenging each group to go through an "Escape Room," a physical adventure game where participants are locked in a space from which they must escape within a certain timeframe using the hidden clues that are in the space. The results of this activity were fascinating.

The boomer group struggled with the lack of clearly defined rules, roles, or step-by-step processes. They were constantly tidying after interacting with the room. A centralized leader emerged, and everyone followed him—right down the wrong path. They were stuck.

The Generation X group was anxious. "What is this activity about?" they asked. "Is it tied in with our bonus?" In the room, they were skeptical of one another, and each tried to solve the problem independently. One group member actually said to another, "How do I know you're not a spy for the other team?" They were stuck.

The millennial group was right at home in the chaos of the room; if anything, the uncertainty inspired teamwork. Their challenge became excessive flexibility, which prevented them from creating a structured plan. They never found a direction or game plan to get out of the room, and they were stuck.

I can't help but wonder what would have happened if my client had put an intergenerational team in the room together. Would they have escaped? How could we, as the church, lead the charge in finding out?

From Stuck to Success

The Escape Room experiment caused me to ponder parallels and questions for churches and ministries. Even with the best of intentions and a shared passion for living and sharing faith, many of our congregations still operate in age and stage silos—similar to the single-generation groupings in the experiment.

How do we break down the walls and give all generations a place to belong together? How do we escape surface-level differences—things like worship style, music selection, staff schedules, and work locations—that seem to hinder relationships among people?

In the church—one of few places where up to six living generations converge on a regular basis—could intergenerational leadership, teams, and community be an untapped differentiator to solve complex challenges, forge deeper connections, and thrive in the midst of change?

The time to explore these questions is now, as we are in the middle of one of the greatest demographic and culture shifts in history. Along with globalism, technology disruption, and the fast-moving complexity of modern society, we're living in what generational theorists consider to be a "fourth turning"[1]—a time in which America's institutional life is torn down and rebuilt from the ground up. It's certainly not the first time this has happened; but thanks to the rapid pace of change, the current generational shift is arguably the most dynamic and ripe with opportunity for impact.

I believe the church is uniquely positioned to apply intergenerational principles in a way that impacts faith trajectories for decades to come. How do we do it? Consider the following clues on how to successfully unlock bringing generations together to solve our collective challenges—in ministry and beyond.

Unlock Understanding

To lead wisely and successfully through complexity, we must develop a competency called "multi-vocal leadership," as Brian Uzzi explains in *Harvard Business Review.*[2] This means becoming the kind of leader who can identify with every member of the ministry team and congregation and bring their perspectives together for the benefit of all.

The first step is recognizing that there are real reasons why each generation has reached its perspective, and these reasons are worth understanding. To increase your congregation's, your staff's, or your own generational IQ, try these ideas:

- Host a speaker, training session, or education series about generations in society and in the Bible.
- Invite members of your staff or congregation to share their stories, experiences, and lessons learned. For example, host a cross-generational panel on life, relationships, and faith. This can help each generation see where others are coming from.

Exercises like these can help everyone see how one generation is not *better* or *worse* than another. One generation's way of doing things should not be glorified while another's is ignored. Every generation has unique strengths, and the generations complement one another.

Unlock Appreciation

Once you understand some of the attitudes, values, and perspectives of each generation, adapt to meet them where they are. This can be hard, especially when their style clashes with yours, but it's important to honor and celebrate each generation's uniqueness.

When confronted with a generational difference that rubs you the wrong way, take a deep breath and consider these steps to pivot frustration into appreciation and advantage:

- Pause and think before responding. Consider whether a generational misunderstanding could be at the root of the issue.
- Explore how your generational experiences shape your views—including how the era you grew up in influenced your ideas about church norms and expectations. Is your generational "filter" hindering you from seeing younger or older congregation members in an accurate or positive light?
- Step back to consider how different generational experiences shape others' views. Why is your younger or older colleague's approach frustrating you? Is it wrong, or is it just different and reflective of the era in which they grew up? Are you taking time to listen and ask questions?
- Adapt by using generational insights to improve interactions and outcomes, seeking ways to work together for a win-win solution that leverages all points of view.

Sometimes the bridge-building process is easy. Often, commonalities emerge that organically provide strong foundations of connection. If similarities do not emerge, consider facilitating ways to find them. For example, put intergenerational groups together and ask them to find one thing—outside of church—that they all have in common.

Other times, combining differences is a bit more challenging and requires a mindset shift from "this *or* that" thinking to "this *and* that" thinking.

Author Malcomb Gladwell, speaking at the Society for Human Resources Management's 2012 conference in Atlanta, noted that older generations typically understand how workplaces and social organizations function in terms of *hierarchy*; Gladwell stated in contrast that millennials have moved from *hierarchies* to *networks* in their understanding of how the world operates.[3]

"The current generation has stumbled on an incredibly powerful model for changing the world and dealing with the workplace. All of us can learn from them when it comes to the network." However, Gladwell added: "Networks may be able to start revolutions, but they can't finish them. One form is not better than the other. They're two different forms with very different sets of strengths and weaknesses.[4]

"What we need," Gladwell concluded, "is a system where we bring out the best of networks and combine them with the best of hierarchies."[5]

There are key moments when bridging differences is a real challenge; two mindsets are locked and unwilling to change. For example, I once worked with a church that had lost a majority of its young adults and families over a conflict about the starting time of Sunday services. In these situations, it's important to consider what author Stephen R. Covey explains in his book *The 3rd Alternative*.[6] Covey indicates that in any conflict, the first alternative is "my" way, and the second alternative is "your" way, and the usual outcomes are continued divisiveness or compromise. Compromise stops the fight, but without breaking through to new results; a third alternative is that kind of breakthrough. It comes by asking if we can do better, defining what success looks like, imagining what third alternatives exist, and then arriving at synergy—a place of transformation.[7]

Unlock Collaboration

Certain demographics, such as youth, often get isolated from the rest of the church body. This can make it hard for them to merge back in when they are older. Groups for people of a similar age and stage are often appropriate, but they should be balanced with opportunities to learn and grow with other generations.

Consider these ideas to help build intergenerational connections within your church:

- Mix up your church ministries, for example pairing a youth group and a seniors group for activities or service projects.
- Provide services, Sunday school classes, and small groups that engage people of multiple ages in worship and discussion.
- Include people of a variety of ages on your boards, leadership teams, and committees. Expect a learning curve for younger members, and treat mistakes along the way as opportunities for coaching and mentoring.

- Organize intergenerational committees to solve your complex problems.

The goal of creating opportunities like this is—literally and figuratively—to get all generations in the same room. Only when they're comfortable looking at each other across the table can the door to intergenerational problem solving and benefits for all be unlocked.

Unlock Communication

All too often, messages get "lost in generational translation," meaning members of different generations, even though well-intentioned, fail to communicate effectively because they are unaware of the other generation's paradigm. Understanding these perspectives—and how to message to them effectively—is critical to reaching people effectively. To communicate in ways that all generations can hear, consider these tips:

- Use a variety of channels for your message, such as newsletters, email, and social media. If you're not sure what members of your congregation need or want, ask them!
- Use stories as much as possible. This time-tested communication form unites us all as humans, regardless of age.
- Ask questions, allowing each person to relate the issue to his or her personal experience.
- Use multigenerational imagery in your communication materials. These images can say a lot about your church or organization and who is welcome there.
- Create classic, timeless brands; focus on a message that appeals to all people, regardless of generation.

When communicating about a specific issue, try using the Intent, Behavior, Results model (or IBR) to help you share your message clearly:

- **Intent:** *Why are you having the conversation or meeting?*
- **Behavior:** *What action steps will you need to take?*
- **Results:** *How will you know when you're successful?*[8]

Unlock Wisdom Sharing

Are you doing all you can to equip and empower the next generation? Are you teaching them what you've learned and sharing your faith forward? Think about whose life you could be investing in.

At the same time, consider that mentoring is a two-way street; reverse mentoring is learning from people who are younger than you are. For example, I have seen youth directors strengthen their faith because of deep questions posed by the adolescents in their ministry. Here are some ways I have seen churches leverage wisdom sharing within their congregation and community:

- Have your youth interview and capture the stories of older church members. This is a great way to help preserve the legacy of those who've gone before and a solid learning tool for young people.
- Create forums for wisdom exchange. For example, you might host an event geared toward the needs of young adults—such as budgeting, cooking, or car repair basics—where experienced leaders can teach them how to do these things.
- Help young people identify their talents, passions, and calling. You might provide personality tools, spiritual gift surveys, or leadership assessments—and mentors who could nurture their gifts.
- Celebrate milestones, promote responsibility, and practice cross-generational appreciation through rite-of-passage events.

Investing in the next generation is both helpful to young people and beneficial to their mentors. According to the authors of *Growing Young*, the starting point for deep connections is extending empathy and helping young people wrestle with three questions:

1. **Identity:** Who am I?
2. **Belonging:** Where do I fit?
3. **Purpose:** What difference do I make?[9]

If you are interested in mutually beneficial mentoring but don't know how to structure it, consider this framework developed by Ken Blanchard and Clair Diaz-Ortiz:

- **Mission:** Create a clear purpose statement for the mentoring relationship. Why are you together as mentor and mentee, and what do you hope to get out of it?
- **Engagement:** Establish how and when you'll engage with each other and figure out what those meetings will look like.
- **Networking:** Discuss how you might expand each other's horizons in faith, vocation, and life.
- **Trust:** Take time to build a culture of trust in your mentoring relationship.
- **Opportunities:** Ask what new opportunities you might create for each other.
- **Review and Renewal:** Periodically check in with each other to see how your relationship aligns with the mission you set out and make sure it's still a good fit as you both grow and change over time.[10]

Release a Faith That Endures

Right now, we sit at a crossroads of challenge, change, and opportunity for the church to thrive. Faith communities are in a unique position to apply generational insights, and the choices we make now will echo in our culture for decades.

One of the great commonalities true to all generations is that in a tumultuous period of intense social change, we all need each other. We need the stability and wisdom of those who have gone before us to teach us what they have learned and to affirm that a hope-filled future awaits. We also need the energy and passion of the next generation—and the insights they have gained—to sustain that faith.

Ultimately, we need to invite all generations into the room so that we may intentionally ensure, as instructed in Exodus 3:15, that the Lord is remembered from generation to generation.

Notes

[1] See, for example, William Strauss and Neil Howe, *The Fourth Turning: An American Prophecy—What the Cycles of History Tell Us about America's Next Rendezvous with Destiny* (New York: Broadway Books, 1997).

[2] Brian Uzzi, "Great Leaders Can Think Like Each Member of Their Team," *Harvard Business Review* online, July 8, 2015, hbr.org/2015/07/great-leaders-can-think-like-each-member-of-their-team/.

[3] John Scorza, "Millennials Usher in New Social Paradigm," *Society for Human Resource Management,* June 25, 2012, www.shrm.org/hr-today/news/hr-news/pages/millennialsusherinnewsocialparadigm.aspx.

[4] Scorza, "Millennials Usher in New Social Paradigm."

[5] Scorza, "Millennials Usher in New Social Paradigm."

[6] Stephen R. Covey, *The 3rd Alternative: Solving Life's Most Difficult Problems* (New York: Free Press, 2011).

[7] Covey, *The 3rd Alternative*, 8–15.

[8] Dusty Staub, CEO of Staub Leadership International, taught an "Intent, Behavior, Results" workshop in Charleston, West Virginia, in March 2014. I was in the audience and asked his permission in 2016 to use the tool for my speaking, training, and writing. He has allowed me to use the tool.

[9] Kara Powell, Jake Mulder, and Brad Griffin, *Growing Young: 6 Essential Strategies to Help Young People Discover and Love Your Church* (Grand Rapids: Baker Books, 2016), 95.

[10] Ken Blanchard and Claire Diaz-Ortiz, interview by Donald Miller, "How to Create a Mutually Beneficial Mentoring Relationship," *Building a StoryBrand with Donald Miller,* June 26, 2017, podtail.com/podcast/building-a-story-brand-with-donald-miller-cla/50-ken-blanchard-and-claire-diaz-ortiz-how-to/.

Chapter Eight

In It for the Long Haul

Joseph P. Conway

In recent years, as we have witnessed a rising enthusiasm for intergenerational ministry and congregational life, a surprising clarity is emerging: we must reassess our age-segregated practices and bring the generations back together. As leaders, we must retrace the steps that brought this clarity in the hopes that we can communicate the journey to others.

In the late 1990s, I was in college majoring in youth ministry, absorbing the best insights and theories of the time—mostly age-separated programming. From 2000 to 2006, I poured my heart and energy into ministering to adolescents based on all I had been taught: I decorated a designated room for the teens with posters and couches; I taught them to rely on Jesus and each other; and I tapped parental resources when I needed a driver or homemade cookies. The Jesus of my ministry never bored them, and we experienced close relationships. After I moved away, I earnestly followed the continuing journey of those beloved adolescents, the ones who had been part of my youth groups. Over the years, these teens graduated, went to college, moved from home, and started their young adult lives.

Sadly, the outcomes of this particular youth ministry microcosm mirrored the outcomes that can be seen nationally. Approximately one-fifth to one-fourth maintained some type of church connection in their twenties. Another one-fifth to one-fourth walked away from their faith entirely. The other half entered into a murky, churchless religious sentiment while maintaining a loose Christian identity.[1]

A Different Way

From 2007 to 2011, I experienced my second youth ministry tenure with a congregation. Already sensing that low retention was connected in some way to age separation, I looked for a different way. Around this time, the findings of the landmark National Study of Youth and Religion[2] was greatly shaping the conversation. Works by Christian Smith, Melinda Lundquist Denton,[3] Kenda Creasy Dean,[4] Kara Powell,[5] Chap Clark,[6] and Thomas Bergler[7] demonstrated the shortcomings of traditional youth ministry. Separating kids into generational silos and focusing on short-term outcomes of attendance and safe adolescent behavior somehow minimized the depth and sacrificial aspects of the historic faith.

During those years, I attended a teen ministry conference where three speakers in a row focused their presentations on the infamous picture of a "one-eared Mickey Mouse"; the one ear represents the separate-and-apart-from-others appendage of the typical youth ministry model. Most everyone agreed with the shortcomings, but few could conceive how to re-vision and retool amid typical expectations built upon the almost universally accepted youth ministry apparatus that already existed.

Perhaps the most meaningful influence on my journey was a short article describing a Baylor University study on faith retention; the study found the highest faith retention rate to be among teens participating in ongoing community service and reflection *alongside adults.*[8]

Shaped by these resources and personal experiences, I decided to incorporate ongoing *intergenerational* community service as a principal focus of my second youth ministry tenure. Moreover, I minimized the importance of having a close personal connection with every single teen, instead surrounding them with *other* adults. The outcomes have been better for these adolescents; that is, a higher percentage of the teens in that youth group have retained their faith thus far.[9]

By the time I accepted my current ministry position in 2011, I had come to a firm conviction: we must reassess our age-segregated practices and bring the generations back together. However, while the goal seems clear, the path there appears foggy. Local church practitioners face an urgent need to translate enthusiasm into tangible action that differentiates between a critical reorientation and mere temporary trends. How can we develop and sustain an intergenerational vision for the long haul?

I serve as the sole minister for a small urban congregation just south of downtown Nashville, Tennessee. This previously childless, aging congregation has experienced revitalization over the past two decades. As young families began coming into this church that had little to no recent history of children and teen ministry, a fascinating laboratory for intergenerational experimentation began to emerge, teaching us key lessons along the way.

Challenges

First, I must be clear about the challenges. While most smile and nod their heads at the idea of bringing the generations together, the implementation often proves to be a fearful undertaking. Consider the recent context. While many Gen Xers and millennials have left church life, the remaining ones have mostly fond memories of generation-specific ministries. Academics can postulate how those strategies did not work for many; however, they *worked* for the very ones who are being encouraged to change. When we ask parents to move toward an intergenerational approach, we are requesting that they move away from the age-specific practices that apparently bore good fruit in their lives. For example, many adults in church grew up on experiences geared toward their specific generation with few adults around—certainly not parents. They grew up on high-energy games, pop-culture-infused devotionals, and music geared for their generation. When we try to convince them to surround their kids with games, devotionals, and music that make space for all the generations, their children may not respond enthusiastically. At this point, we can talk about research and long-term outcomes over immediate ones, but that will be a hard conversation.

On top of fear, intergenerational ministry creates uncomfortable scenarios. Small children get the wiggles just as the minister turns to the climactic point of the sermon. A person from one generation offers an unhelpful stereotype from the media, just as a person from that referenced generation was about to open up. Beyond the romance and idealism of intergenerational ministry, let me be blunt about its reality. It can be really loud. It's often chaotic. It proves messy. It may offer richness and depth— and elicit patience—but it may not be exciting and "cool."

Moreover, beyond fear and discomfort, becoming more intergenerational in outlook and practice may not merge well with our existing structures, especially in larger congregations. Building layouts, budgets, and staff titles regularly take shape around age-specific programming and strategies. Churches hire age-specific ministers and then evaluate them on the activities and programs they created for one generation. As a youth minister in the past, my evaluation process actually worked against intergenerational ministry in many ways. These current structures prove powerful and may confound our intentions.

The Good News

Despite the barriers, hindrances, and challenges to becoming more intentionally intergenerational, churches are making progress. The following strategies and postures have worked well for my congregation and others.

As we develop a long-term intergenerational vision, we must define the terms well. Religious and theological jargon can be off-putting. Find a term (e.g., intergenerational, cross-generational, whole church, cross-age), and stick with it. Then, help congregants locate and name their cross-age experiences. For example,

- Remember that night after Bible study when Mr. Bill (age 90) and Henry (age 6) counted coins for thirty minutes.
- Remember that amazing conversation about creation care that broke out between teens and adults that night at small group.

- Remember how the adults on the spring retreat taught piano and Spanish classes; then remember how the teens in turn found the space to teach mind-mapping and ballet.

What We Mean by Intergenerational

Every adult, teen, and child has a positive memory of an intergenerational experience. We must help them locate and name it. On top of that, we must name the problem. Thankfully, many have come to see isolated generational silos as problematic. Recent years have shown us the discord and frustration caused by generations no longer listening and communicating with each other. So, when given the opportunity, I point out the ways our congregation gains strength from the contributions and input from all generations. Also, without falling into demonization, I calmly yet honestly refer to overly stringent generational programming as *age separation* or *age segregation*. Certainly, the latter term can take on an inflammatory tone, depending on the context. For example, I visited a congregation that had printed this announcement in its bulletin: "During the worship, classes for kids are offered in the children's wing. Children are encouraged to attend. If your child disrupts others, they will be asked to leave." Now, to be clear, I think I understand what they meant. I get it. Adults like a quiet atmosphere for worship. With the expectations of many adults today, it can be hard to attract new members into a noisy, untidy worship service full of kids. I have seen families visit once, take in the ethos, and depart—never to be seen again. I get it. But in my public teaching, when discussing why our children are among us, I simply ask the congregation, "Would we tolerate sending away any other group of people?"

After naming and explaining, we must implement with small steps. Abruptly canceling children's worship, Sunday school, or the teen summer trip rarely achieves positive results. In our worship time (no history of children's church), we added congregational readings, object lessons, and occasional children's bulletins to connect kids with a mostly adult-themed worship. In addition, in my sermons, I often directly speak to different generations. In discipleship, we intentionally pair newly baptized teens with an adult mentor who commit together to read a book on the Sermon on the

Mount and meet for discussion three times. Besides this, one member com-piled a journal of devotionals written by adult members to give these teens.

In service and outreach, we emphasize community ministries that involve all generations. Instead of construction projects or late-night tasks, our congregation serves through hospitality, food preparation, supply collections, delivering food and supplies, visits, and prayer walks. Each summer, we plan a mission week of intentionally intergenerational service experiences such as a homeless immersion, a nature hike, a Matthew 25 prayer drive through the city, or a documentary night with panel discussion. These small steps have left the congregation expecting an intergenerational environment and wanting more.

Sustaining an Intergenerational Vision

To sustain the intergenerational vision over the long haul, we must antici-pate challenges and respond with flexibility. Several times a year, an adult kindly shares that they don't feel space to share their struggles in the midst of so many children. Adults and children who visit or attend only occa-sionally are unaccustomed to age-inclusive worship and may struggle to engage our worship service. In intergenerational experiences, we give up the laser precision of age appropriateness. At times, our kids overhear stuff they're not quite ready to process.

We seek to respond with flexibility by over-communicating and making exceptions. We intentionally create some adult-only spaces in our congregational life. We work at communicating the details of experiences beforehand. We keep some of the favorite traditions of age-specific min-istry such as Sunday school, the teen amusement park trip, Ladies Book Club, and the men's campout, but we do so in an overall intergenerational atmosphere. Put simply, instead of the default being generational separa-tion, we make the default age inclusion. Our age specific programming represents an exception, albeit a needed one.

We remind ourselves that other congregations offer traditional models for those who want them. We calmly listen to people's expectations and desires. We make exceptions when we can. But if people continue to push for a return to generational silos, we simply say, "That's not us." The leadership listens and shows flexibility in the midst of commitment, yet remains dedicated to our intergenerational stance.

The most important tool has been this: the leadership publicly and consistently embraces the vision. Our oldest, wisest members do not complain about noise; they patiently encourage younger generations that being together proves best.

Recently, we experienced a refugee simulation, led by the teens. Some young kids cried because of the intensity. Some teens let the power of being in charge go to their heads. Some older members struggled climbing stairs and cramming into crowded basement classrooms. Honestly, I wondered if we had reached the end of the intergenerational honeymoon—yet again. However, as we processed the experience upstairs afterward, an eighty-seven-year-old woman beamed: "This was great. We need to do more of this. I learned so much. Beats any VBS I've ever seen." And as we prayed, a six-year-old spoke up and said, "Don't forget to pray for the refugees."

Notes

[1] In 2013, I went over my old youth rosters and made these calculations to the best of my knowledge.

[2] "National Study of Youth and Religion," *University of Notre Dame*, youthandreligion .nd.edu.

[3] Christian Smith with Melinda Lundquist Denton, *Soul Searching: The Religious and Spiritual Lives of American Teenagers* (New York: Oxford University Press, 2005).

[4] Kenda Creasy Dean, *Almost Christian: What the Faith of Our Teenagers Is Telling the American Church* (New York: Oxford University Press, 2010).

[5] Dr. Kara E. Powell and Dr. Chap Clark, *Sticky Faith: Everyday Ideas to Build Lasting Faith in Your Kids* (Grand Rapids: Zondervan, 2011).

[6] Chap Clark, *Hurt 2.0: Inside the World of Today's Teenagers*, Youth, Family, and Culture Series (Grand Rapids: Baker Academic, 2011).

[7] Thomas E. Bergler, *The Juvenilization of American Christianity* (Grand Rapids: Eerdmans, 2012).

[8] Michael Sherr, Diana Garland, Dennis Myers, and Terry Wolfer, "Community Service Develops Teens' Faith," *Baylor Magazine*, Spring 2007, www.baylor.edu/alumni /magazine/0503/news.php?action=storyandstory=45581.

[9] The results may not be attributable solely to a more intergenerational approach; the churches were similar in many ways but were different in geographical location.

Part Three

CURRENT RESEARCH

Chapter Nine

Five Best Intergenerational Practices for Small Churches

Tori Bennett Smit

"I am sorry to bother you. You see, we only have six children in our church and our Sunday School just isn't working. Could you please recommend a curriculum that would work for just a handful of children?" This is the most consistent question I am asked as an education consultant.[1] "Our Sunday school used to be overflowing," they tell me. "We had them hanging from the rafters." But their children have long grown up, boomers and their children left the church decades ago, and very few families have come into the church to take their place. Their situation is further complicated by a lack of teachers, a discouraged Christian education committee, and a greatly diminished budget. Add to this their belief that an existing Sunday school stands as the central marker of good children's faith formation as well as a sign of congregational health and vitality, and helping congregations to think differently about children's faith formation becomes truly complicated.

The number of children within the Presbyterian Church in Canada (PCC) has been steadily and significantly declining from its peak in

1962, with an overall decline of 87 percent of our children in just over five decades.[2] In 2014, 49 percent of the 268 congregations in my synod declared ten or fewer children on their statistical reports.[3] This is true regardless of congregational size, theology, ethnicity, age, or location.

It has been my conviction that if the focus of the congregation's concern could be shifted away from the assumed necessity of a traditional Sunday school, they could begin to consider the more significant question: For congregations with few children, what are the best practices for ministry that will address the goal of transformational and lifelong faith formation? And in answering this question, they could also discover that their circumstance of having very few children might also offer new opportunities for a more suitable and biblically based model of faith formation.

Best Practices for Ministry with Ten or Fewer Children

I began by considering best practices for ministry with children, regardless of the number of children in a church community. I discerned these practices through reading, interviews, site visits, and participation in Christian education events and forums. I believe that each practice considered should be grounded in Scripture, should be welcoming of children, and should engage an approach that helps children learn the stories of faith while experiencing God in and through meaningful relationships formed in their community of faith. I then refined my list down to six key practices that I felt would be particularly suitable for congregations with very few children.

Provide Meaningful Participation in Intergenerational Worship

Children of most PCC churches are present only for a small portion of the worship service before being dismissed for Sunday school. This is a result of an emphasis on children's cognitive learning promoted during the 1950s, '60s, and '70s, leading churches to believe that Sunday school was the best place for children to learn the basics of Scripture and fundamentals of faith. Young people could then join the adults in worship when they became old enough to grasp the deeper content of worship.[4] By emphasizing cognition, the church inadvertently set aside children's spiritual experience of faith.

We now recognize that children are innately spiritual beings and experience the transcendent in their lives from their earliest days apart from any formal religious instruction.[5] With children's capacity to experience the transcendent, they need to be in a place where they can participate in the mystery and wonder of God through the rituals, storytelling, singing, and relationships found in community worship.

The church needs its children to be in worship for our body of faith to be complete. Worship is the most central practice we participate in as a church. If our children are to fully participate in the life of the church, they must participate meaningfully with all ages in worship.[6] We experience God through each other; embracing the joy and openness of younger members while benefiting from the life-long experience of those who have been worshiping over decades. Meaningful intergenerational worship must be prepared with all ages in mind. For this to happen, worship needs to become more experiential and participatory, appealing to all of the senses.[7] We need to be able to touch, see, smell, hear, and taste that the Lord is good.

For churches with few children, moving toward intergenerational worship can be viewed as an immediate solution to the problem of few children, but that is not the reason for making the shift; including children in worship welcomes them in, teaches them how to worship, and offers the opportunity for them to experience the transcendent when they are most open to the mystery of God.

Consider New Models for Sunday School

As churches invite all ages to be present in worship, the question of age-appropriate cognitive education soon arises. The field is wide open with options for accomplishing this, with each church exploring and experimenting with what works best for them. Here are some effective models:

- Prepare young children for participation in worship through contemplative and reflective models such as *Young Children and Worship*[8] or *Godly Play*.[9]
- Email educational materials to families and invite parents and children to learn together.

- Provide multisensory materials and specific instructions for responding to the Word for young children to use during worship.
- Offer midweek intergenerational programs such as *LOGOS*[10] as the primary cognitive education time for children.
- Offer seasonal age-appropriate and intergenerational educational events throughout the church year.
- Offer grandparent-led gatherings for adult children and grand-children who have an uncomfortable relationship with the church.[11]
- Create intergenerational small groups that engage all ages in study, conversation, prayer, and fellowship.[12]

When congregations move cognitive learning opportunities to midweek, they are able to increase the number of cross-generational interactions their children experience as well as open the door to unchurched children joining in.

Support and Resource Parents for the Unique Role They Play in the Spiritual Formation of Their Children

In Deuteronomy, we read that Yahweh gives primary responsibility to parents for passing their faith from one generation to the next (Deut. 6:4–9). The moment a newborn is held by her parents, she begins to form an image through her parents of the "Great Other" who has created the wonderful world she lives in.[13] The home is the first and most natural setting for sharing faith stories and practicing living out our faith in and through the rhythms of family life. Church educators agree that children's faith is best formed through the minuscule events of life with those they know best and most intimately. The quality of the relationship that parents have with their children has the greatest and most profound influence on their faith.[14]

Parents are meant to be the first and primary nurturers of their children's faith, yet the majority of parents say they do nothing in an average week to pass their faith on to their children.[15]

Parents are not unwilling, but most say they don't know how. Rather than the church taking on the role of "parent" through the provision of more and more children's programming, congregations should refocus their energy on coming alongside parents to assist them in discovering the art of faith-filled parenting.

Share Our Stories of Faith with Each Other as a Part of God's Big Story

Humans are wired to be transformed by stories. Pastoral theologian David Hogue explains that the human brain, unlike that of any other species, is able to put images and memories together to create stories.[16] Our creator has made our brains work automatically to make sense out of our experiences and the world. Always looking to answer the question "why," stories have an explanatory power; and through story listening and storytelling, we are able to interpret, select, and bring our own experience to the stories we save and tell to others.[17]

Our capacity for processing stories starts at an early age. Rabbi Sandy Eisenberg Sasso states that as we share stories of faith with children, they discover where we see ourselves in the story, and they are enabled—through *our* relationship with God—to then see *themselves* in God's story because of their relationship with us.[18] Mutually shared biblical stories of faith and experiences of God become a window to a transformative growing faith. Children and adults are drawn into the stories and imagine themselves performing the acts and behaviors of the characters in them. People relate to the characters in the stories, finding themselves and others in their community in them, and they begin to mirror these stories in their lives. Stories told and retold have the cumulative effect of coming together to become God's BIG story.

Children need to hear our personal stories of faith and share their own experiences of God and God-inspired activity so they can join in the great and wondrous story of God's interaction and love for us and the world. No matter how big or small the church community, we are bound by our stories, and we must not resist sharing our experience of God with each other.

Involve Children Intergenerationally in Service Projects and Acts of Justice

Jesus spoke of a world where all were called to care and show compassion for one another. Sadly, our children are often absent when the congregation makes decisions about how they will care for their neighbor. They rarely have the opportunity to contribute to the discussion, the financial commitment, or the "hands-on" work. Without seeing or being involved, children do not learn to practice their faith in meaningful ways.

Modeling faith is a significant factor in faith becoming embodied in children. Children make meaning by doing. Merton Strommen and Richard Hardel note in their book *Passing on Faith* that "involvement in service projects proved to be a better predictor of faith maturity than participation in Sunday school, Bible study, or worship services."[19] Children are excited and filled with energy when they are invited to participate with the congregation in community service activities. Helping to serve assists children in imagining and living into the kind of world of which Jesus spoke. Their experience of neighbor provides a reality check, builds deep connections, removes barriers, and shatters misconceptions about those with whom we share the planet.

Make "Intentionally Intergenerational" the Default Position of Your Church

Being "intentionally intergenerational" is the ideological thread that runs through each of these ministry best practices for a church with few children. Holly Catterton Allen and Christine Lawton Ross clarify that "intergenerational ministry occurs when a congregation intentionally brings the generations together in mutual serving, sharing, or learning within the core activities of the church in order to live out being the body of Christ to each other and the greater community."[20] They advocate for *intentional* intergenerational ministry, believing that an

> intergenerational educational methodology is inherently more aligned with Christian theology than an age-segregated educational model, that intergenerational ministry intrinsically stems from and teaches the essence of the biblical understanding of the body of Christ, and that intergenerationality capitalizes upon the natural multigenerational quality of a congregation.[21]

Australian church educator Chris Barnett advocates for churches to flip their present age-segregated orientation toward intergenerationality. Rather than assuming that most church activities will be age-segregated, churches should instead assume that most activities of the church will be intergenerational.[22] While not *all* activities will be intergenerational, most ought to maximize the opportunity for all ages to rub shoulders with each other. Faith is formed as we interact and practice our faith with one another in worship, study, social action, and casual conversation. Children need sustained relationships with adults whom they trust and with whom they share similar beliefs and values as they consider their faith together. With this knowledge, congregations must create ample opportunities for such relationships to flourish.

Some Conclusions

Having presented these practices to four congregations, inviting them to work with one or two self-selected practices for six months, I learned several important things. Each of the congregations chose to focus primarily on children's meaningful participation in intergenerational worship. They believed this to be the best theological, ideological, and logical place to start. One church made a complete shift while others increased children's time and participation in community worship over a number of months while maintaining a reduced Sunday school.

All of the ministers found themselves primarily responsible for developing new ways of doing worship that were attentive to all ages; they all said it was hard but very important work, worthy of the time and commitment it required. They all felt frustrated by a lack of quality resources that emphasized true intergenerational worship rather than worship for children with adult spectators. Out of their frustration, we soon developed a resource list, workshops, and a worship-planning group to help ministers lean into this new focus.

Most congregations also stated that despite months of preparing the congregation and families for the shift, they still felt they should have done more. Constant and varied forms of communication were key in helping the congregations understand the theological and faith formational "why" behind the change. When education happened, adults quickly got on board and became intentional in how they related to the children and youth now present in worship, as well as how they modeled worship themselves. Over a short period of time, most congregations claimed the change as a positive and desired move. None of the churches that succeeded in making the shift said they would return to their previous model, with one participant declaring, "to pull [the children] out of worship would be going backward."

Other practices that were adopted by the participating congregations became works in progress for them, as were the practices they did not choose to highlight. For those congregations with key leadership committed to engaging children in the life and ministry of the church, I heard stories of success and a continued commitment to the practices—not because the practices dealt with their presenting concern of having few children, but because they saw and experienced joy and growth in the faith of their children and adults, and because they were convinced that Jesus had encouraged faithful communities to be intentionally intergenerational.

By stepping back from their question about curriculum, and instead considering what they could do to best help form the faith of their children, these four churches were enabled not only to do wonderful things, but also to find hope in what they saw as a hopeless situation. There was a renewed sense of joy and community and a rediscovered awareness that we belong together.

Notes

[1] I serve as the Regional Minister for Faith Formation for the Synod of Central, Northeastern Ontario and Bermuda, Presbyterian Church in Canada.

[2] Brian Clarke and Stuart Macdonald, *Working Paper: Presbyterian Church in Canada Statistics*, Version 2.0 (Toronto: The Presbyterian Church in Canada, 2013), 3–4; *The Acts and Proceedings of the One Hundred and Forty-First General Assembly of the Presbyterian Church in Canada* (Toronto: The Presbyterian Church in Canada, 2015), 752, presbyterian.ca/wp-content/uploads/ga2015minutes-sederunt1_2015-06-04.pdf.

[3] *The Acts and Proceedings of the One Hundred and Forty-First General Assembly*, 760–768. (Each church defines "children" by their own standard; but generally, churches count all children participating in their church from birth to the completion of Sunday school at around thirteen.)

[4] David M. Csinos and Ivy Beckwith, *Children's Ministry in the Way of Jesus* (Downers Grove, IL: InterVarsity Press, 2013), 29–30.

[5] Donald Ratcliff and Rebecca Nye, "Childhood Spirituality: Strengthening the Research Foundation," in *The Handbook of Spiritual Development in Childhood and Adolescence*, eds. Eugene C. Roehlkepartain, Pamela Ebstyne King, Linda Wagener, and Peter L. Benson (Thousand Oaks: Sage Publications, 2006), 474.

[6] Csinos and Beckwith, *Children's Ministry*, 116.

[7] Rodger Nishioka, "Making Disciples: The Future of Christian Education" (workshop, Knox Presbyterian Church, Waterloo, November 2, 2013).

[8]Sonja M. Stewart and Jerome W. Berryman, *Young Children and Worship* (Louisville: Westminster John Knox Press, 1989). See Chapter Twenty-One by Olivia B. Updegrove in this text for a description of Children and Worship in a fully intergenerational setting.

[9]Jerome W. Berryman, *Godly Play: An Imaginative Approach to Religious Education* (Minneapolis: Augsburg Fortress, 1991).

[10]LOGOS is a ministry of GenOn Ministries, www.genonministries.org. See Chapter Nineteen by Liz Perraud for a fuller description of LOGOS.

[11]Rev. Chris Barnett, interview with author at *Faith Forward 2014*, Nashville, May 21, 2014.

[12]See chapter 18 in Holly Catterton Allen and Christine Lawton Ross, *Intergenerational Christian Formation: Bringing the Whole Church Together in Ministry, Community and Worship* (Downers Grove, IL: InterVarsity Press Academic, 2012),

[13]Scottie May, Beth Posterski, Catherine Stonehouse, and Linda Cannell, *Children Matter: Celebrating Their Place in the Church, Family, and Community* (Grand Rapids: Eerdmans, 2005), 153.

[14]May, et al., *Children Matter*, 152.

[15]Barna Group, "Parents Accept Responsibility for Their Child's Spiritual Development but Struggle with Effectiveness," May 6, 2003, www.barna.org/component /content/article/5-barna-update/45-barna-update-sp-657/120-parents-accept -responsibility-for-their-childs-spiritual-development-but-struggle-with-effectiveness# .VnXchTbUP_c.

[16]David A. Hogue, *Remembering the Future, Imagining the Past: Story, Ritual, and the Human Brain* (Cleveland: The Pilgrim Press, 2003).

[17]Hogue, *Remember the Future*, 89, 92.

[18]Sandy Eisenberg Sasso, "Tell Me A Story" (presentation, *Faith Forward 2014*, Nashville, May 22, 2014).

[19]Merton P. Strommen, PhD, and Richard A. Hardel, DMin, *Passing on Faith: A Radical New Model for Youth and Family Ministry* (Winona, MN: Saint Mary's Press, 2000), 95.

[20]Allen and Ross, *Intergenerational Christian Formation*, 17.

[21]Allen and Ross, *Intergenerational Christian Formation*, 14.

[22]Barnett, interview, 2014.

Chapter Ten

Well-Being, Discipleship, and Intergenerational Connectedness

Joe Azzopardi

This chapter outlines what is currently known about the intersection of well-being, discipleship, and intergenerational connectedness. These findings form the hypothesis of a research project that is in progress among ten churches in Australia.

Social Connectedness and Well-Being

The World Health Organization has recognized depression as "the single largest contributor to global disability."[1] With such a pervasive and life-threatening disability that contributes to close to eight hundred thousand suicides worldwide per year,[2] it is quite relevant to note that there is strong support from research that suggests depression is influenced by levels of social connectedness.[3]

Social connectedness is defined by Chin-Siang Ang as "the degree to which a person is socially close, interrelates, or shares resources with other persons in a number of social ecologies such as families, schools, neighborhoods, cultural groups, and society."[4] Since physical health is impacted by mental health, socially connected people have a higher life expectancy.[5] This impact is evidenced through the Blue Zone research of Dan Buettner and Sam Skemp, who investigated the world's longest-living communities. Buettner and Skemp found that the members of these communities share a highly cohesive social bond with each other.[6] Positive social connectedness influences individuals to behave in a healthy manner, which increases their survival rate; and beyond this, it also creates a stress-buffer in individuals, thus promoting healthy mental well-being.[7]

It has become evident that the greater the number of social groups people are members of, the less likely they are to become depressed; and if they do become depressed, symptoms will be fewer and less intense.[8] However, it is not merely the *number* of groups one is a part of which ameliorates depression, but rather the number of "groups with which we *identify*" that have this ameliorating effect.[9] Thus, mental health and well-being are significantly increased with improving and maintaining social group relationships, whereas a lack of social connectedness would be typically detrimental to an individual's mental health and well-being.

While it is true that no one desires to be lonely, the reality is that many people are indeed lonely, and loneliness impacts far more than the thwarting of that simple desire for companionship. One study found that "data across 308,849 individuals, followed for an average of 7.5 years, indicate that individuals with adequate social relationships have a 50% greater likelihood of survival compared to those with poor or insufficient social relationships."[10]

Furthermore, current research "indicates that the quantity and/or quality of social relationships in industrialized societies are decreasing."[11] The same study found a general decrease in relationship quantity and quality, reporting, for example, that there are three times the number of Americans who report having no confidante in their life compared to two decades ago, indicating a sharp increase in loneliness in the overall population.[12]

Intergenerational Connectedness

This chapter will focus specifically on intergenerational connectedness, or *intergenerationality,* as it has been found to be a major form of connectedness that is decreasing, particularly in the industrialized west.[13] Intergenerationality is of vital importance as it enables an exchange of both tangible and intangible resources between generations. Of more interest to this study are the *intangible* resources that are notably missing when there are few intergenerational connections. Generational segregation leads to an absence of opportunities of many worthwhile interactions between generations, such as those concerning learning and understanding and, particularly, mentoring.[14]

In an effort to explain the mechanism whereby intergenerationality provides such a wealth of benefits, Holly Allen and Christine Ross proposed the situative-sociocultural perspective on learning.[15] This theory takes the sociocultural theory of Lev Vygotsky[16] and further develops it using the situative learning approach of Jean Lave and Etienne Wenger.[17] Allen and Ross explain that the rationale for intergenerationality as an effective approach flows from three premises. The first premise is that "individuals learn best in authentic, complex environments."[18] Studies have shown that one of the most effective means of learning is in collaborative environments where real problems are resolved through a social group.[19]

The second premise is the assertion that "the best learning happens when persons participate with more experienced members of the culture (Vygotsky's zone of proximal development)."[20] This can take place by means of mentorship and modeling, whether incidentally or through a directed learning activity.

The final premise taps into Lave and Wenger's communities of practice theory which explains that individuals become a part of a community of practice through participating in that community's activities; through such participation, they learn the attitudes and practices of that community.[21] When solidarity exists within a diverse community, individuals are more likely to learn, since identifying with others typically begets trust and empathy.[22] Such trust and empathy encourages intimacy, which can deliver empowerment through tangible resources such as finances, property, or equipment,[23] and intangible resources such as education, respect, and authority.[24]

Given this understanding of the benefits of intergenerationality, it is prudent to seek contemporary examples of intergenerational communities.

However, very few such communities exist within the contemporary western world.[25] Urban planning studies have found that neighborhoods are becoming more age segregated, often due to economic advantage.[26] Though there has been a global rise in schools that try to incorporate intergenerational programs in their curriculum (and they have had positive results), these schools are the minority overall and the programs could not truly be considered all-encompassing intergenerational approaches.[27]

Interestingly, there is one kind of community that has still managed to withstand, at least to a certain degree, the barrage of generational fragmentation within the industrialized world, and this is the religious community.[28] Given the variety of religious faith communities to choose from, this study will specifically focus on intergenerational connectivity within the Christian faith.

While several authors in this book have given ample reasons as to why Christian congregations should be intergenerational,[29] the question that will be addressed in this chapter is regarding what drives connectedness—intergenerational connectedness or otherwise—in Christian congregations. Previously, we discussed the situative-sociocultural learning theory as the mechanism for intergenerational connectedness, noting that individuals learn better in complex and authentic environments via mentors and models in communities of practice. Both biblical directive and recent literature indicate that such a mechanism of connectedness is enabled through the process of discipleship.[30]

Discipleship

Discipleship is a lifelong process that results in an individual becoming more aligned with what Jesus would desire him to become and allowing God to be God, thus allowing God to transform him.[31] Reviewing both the academic literature and Scripture, three factors appear to be integral regarding discipleship: growth, faithfulness, and love.

Taking a look at growth first, ongoing personal growth is an integral aspect of discipleship; though the ultimate end goal is unachievable, it is yet worthwhile as a pursuit.[32] As disciples, we are to continually grow in our spiritual walks, becoming better people than we were in the not-too-distant past. Thus, growth is an essential part of discipleship.[33]

Concerning faithfulness, when we read Matthew 28:18–20, it can be easily argued that we are mandated by Jesus Christ to disciple. This text is often read, however, with the focus on baptizing, with relatively little emphasis on teaching. It is important to note, however, that baptizing and teaching are not separate from discipleship, nor are they themselves discipleship.[34] They are indeed *part* of the process of discipleship, and being faithful disciples means that we adhere to all that the Lord is telling us to do.

The meaning and purpose of discipleship focuses on fulfilling the Great Commission, found in Matthew 28:19–20, which is not merely the multiplicity of teaching and baptizing, but it also results in saving others from disconnection from God and gives them hope and meaning through a life of service to God and others.[35] Therefore, in the Christian mindset, reconnection and restoration to God is salvation.

Being a disciple means being obedient to what God is asking one to do. A disciple follows the commandments of God, but discipleship is not merely about keeping the commandments.[36] As disciples, we need to go beyond treating the commandments as a checklist of righteousness and surpass them, as Isaiah 30:21 directs: "Whether you turn to the right or to the left, your ears will hear a voice behind you, saying, 'This is the way; walk in it.'"

Consequently, at the center of Christ's call to discipleship is the third factor, which is love. "A new commandment I give to you, that you love one another, even as I have loved you, that you also love one another. By this all men will know that you are My disciples, if you have love for one another" (John 13:34–35 NASB). Further to this, Paul describes love in detail in 1 Corinthians 13, arguing that without love, all accomplishments and virtues are empty. In a like manner, love is what qualifies both growth and faithfulness as factors of discipleship. Faithfulness to God is simultaneously prompted by, progressed by, and a product of love, and it results in growth, which leads to more faithfulness.[37] Growth without love produces pride; and faithfulness without love cannot exist, as we are commanded to love.

Having discussed discipleship as the mechanism for connectedness within Christian congregations, it is relevant to address what discipleship produces, which is well-being. While we understand that discipleship uses growth, love, and faithfulness as its methods, the purpose is found in the summary of God's commandments, which is expressed by Jesus in three of the Gospels and is a reference for two commandments given in the Old Testament (Deut. 6:5; Lev. 19:18). Matthew's account reads,

> "Love the Lord your God with all your heart and with all your soul and with all your mind." This is the first and greatest commandment. And the second is like it: "Love your neighbor as yourself." All the Law and the Prophets hang on these two commandments. (22:37–40)

Although there may seem to be two identities in which to pursue love from this text, there are in fact three: love of God, love of others, and love of self. It is proposed that love in this sense is very similar to the term *positive connectedness,* as both concern the promotion of welfare through positive relationships—that is: (a) love of God being spiritual connectedness, (b) love of others being social connectedness, and (c) love of self being psychological well-being. Love of self is to be understood as a positive and healthy view of oneself in light of being a child of God—as opposed to narcissism, which is characterized by self-absorption and self-worship, and leads to disconnection with others and God.[38]

Current Research

The purpose of the current research with ten churches in Australia is to investigate the impact of intergenerational discipleship on well-being. In this research, *well-being* is defined as the positive functioning of the psychological, social, and spiritual aspects of an individual, integrated and interdependent with each other as a holistic and unified characteristic. In this sense, well-being is a product of loving oneself, others, and God, thus incorporating individual, social, and spiritual connectedness. From the Christian perspective, an individual who exhibits healthy well-being has positive and meaningful relationships, is capable of achieving desired goals, has a positive self-concept, is continually growing as an individual, and finds meaning, purpose, and guidance through connection with the divine.

With this discussion in mind, increasing connectedness should enhance a person's well-being. Furthermore, with the understanding that one of the largest areas of disconnection in society is due to a lack of intergenerational connectedness, it can be surmised that discipleship that takes place in intergenerational congregations may lead to higher levels of well-being. Therefore, the research question that is being addressed in this current study is: Does discipleship in an intergenerational Christian congregation contribute to better well-being?

It is the hypothesis of this study (and indeed of this book) that intergenerational Christian experiences do in fact benefit people of all ages in a number of ways. Biblical, theological, theoretical, sociological, and anecdotal support exists for this premise as well as empirical support in various forms, both large and small.[39] This current Australian study at the congregational level is part of the ongoing call for empirical research that further explores this hypothesis.

Notes

[1] World Health Organization, "Depression and Other Common Mental Disorders: Global Health Estimates," World Health Organization (Geneva: World Health Organization, 2017), www.who.int/mental_health/management/depression/prevalence_global_health_estimates/en/.

[2] World Health Organization, "Depression and Other Common Mental Disorders."

[3] Tegan Cruwys, Genevieve A. Dingle, Catherine Haslam, S. Alexander Haslam, Jolanda Jetten, and Thomas A. Morton, "Social Group Memberships Protect against Future Depression, Alleviate Depression Symptoms and Prevent Depression Relapse," *Social Science and Medicine* 98 (December 2013): 179–86.

[4] Chin-Siang Ang, "Types of Social Connectedness and Loneliness: The Joint Moderating Effects of Age and Gender," *Applied Research in Quality of Life* 11, no. 4 (December 2016): 1173–87.

[5] Catherine Haslam, Tegan Cruwys, S. Alexander Haslam, Genevieve Dingle, and Melissa Xue-Ling Chang, "Groups 4 Health: Evidence That a Social-Identity Intervention That Builds and Strengthens Social Group Membership Improves Mental Health," *Journal of Affective Disorders* 194 (2016): 188–95.

[6] Dan Buettner and Sam Skemp, "Blue Zones: Lessons from the Word's Longest Lived," *American Journal of Lifestyle Medicine* 10, no. 5 (2016): 318–21.

[7] Julianne Holt-Lunstad, Timothy B. Smith, and J. Bradley Layton, "Social Relationships and Mortality Risk: A Meta-Analytic Review (Social Relationships and Mortality)," *PLoS Medicine* 7, no. 7 (2010): e1000316, doi.org/10.1371/journal.pmed.1000316.

[8] Cruwys et al., "Social Group Memberships."

[9] Tegan Cruwys, S. Alexander Haslam, Genevieve A. Dingle, Jolanda Jetten, Matthew J. Hornsey, E. M. Desdemona Chong, and Tian P. S. Oei, "Feeling Connected Again: Interventions That Increase Social Identification Reduce Depression Symptoms in

Community and Clinical Settings," *Journal of Affective Disorders* 159 (April 2014): 145. Haslam et al. found essentially the same thing in their study ("Groups 4 Health").

[10] Holt-Lunstad et al., "Social Relationships and Mortality Risk," 14.

[11] Holt-Lunstad et al., "Social Relationships and Mortality Risk," 2.

[12] Holt-Lunstad et al., "Social Relationships and Mortality Risk," 2.

[13] Albert Sabater, Elspeth Graham, and Nissa Finney, "The Spatialities of Ageing: Evidencing Increasing Spatial Polarisation between Older and Younger Adults in England and Wales," *Demographic Research* 36, no. 25 (2017): 731–44; Richelle Winkler, "Research Note: Segregated by Age: Are We Becoming More Divided?" in cooperation with the *Southern Demographic Association* (SDA) 32, no. 5 (2013): 717–27.

[14] See, for example, Darshini Ayton and Nerida Joss, "Empowering Vulnerable Parents through a Family Mentoring Program," *Australian Journal of Primary Health* 22, no. 4 (2015): 320–26; Giulia Cortellesi and Margaret Kernan, "Together Old and Young: How Informal Contact between Young Children and Older People Can Lead to Intergenerational Solidarity," *Studia Paedagogica* 21, no. 2 (2016): 101–16; Giselle Massi, Aline Romao dos Santos, Ana Paula Berberian, and Nadine de Biagi Ziesemer, "Impact of Dialogic Intergenerational Activities on the Perception of Children, Adolescents and Elderly," *Revista CEFAC: Atualizacao Cientifica em Fonoaudiologia e Educacao* 18, no. 2 (2016): 399407.

[15] Holly Catterton Allen and Christine Lawton Ross, *Intergenerational Christian Formation: Bringing the Whole Church Together in Ministry, Community and Worship* (Downers Grove, IL: InterVarsity Press, 2012).

[16] L. S. Vygotskii, R. W. Rieber, and Aaron S. Carton, *The Collected Works of L. S. Vygotsky. Cognition and Language* (New York: Plenum Press, 1987).

[17] Jean Lave and Etienne Wenger, *Situated Learning: Legitimate Peripheral Participation. Learning in Doing* (Cambridge: Cambridge University Press, 1991).

[18] Allen and Ross, *Intergenerational Christian Formation*, 104.

[19] Heidi Yeen-Ju and Neo Mai, "Leveraging Web Technologies for Collaborative Problem-Solving in an Authentic Learning Environment," *International Journal of Social Science and Humanity* 6, no. 7 (2016): 536–40.

[20] Allen and Ross, *Intergenerational Christian Formation*, 104.

[21] Lave and Wenger, *Situated Learning*.

[22] Cortellesi and Kernan, "Together Old and Young," 101–16.

[23] Marc Szydlik, "Generations: Connections across the Life Course," *Advances in Life Course Research* 17, no. 3 (September 2012): 100–11; Kimberly A. Wade-Benzoni and Leigh Plunkett Tost, "The Egoism and Altruism of Intergenerational Behavior," *Personality and Social Psychology Review* 13, no. 3 (2009): 165–93.

[24] Arla E. Day, Kevin Kelloway, and Joseph J. Hurrell, eds., *Workplace Well-Being: How to Build Psychologically Healthy Workplaces* (Malden, MA: Wiley Blackwell, 2014); Igor Pyrko, Viktor Dörfler, and Colin Eden, "Thinking Together: What Makes Communities of Practice Work?" *Human Relations* 70, no. 4 (2017): 389–409; Marissa Salanova and Susana Llorens, "Employee Empowerment and Engagement," in *Workplace Well-Being: How to Build Psychologically Healthy Workplaces*, eds., Arla Day, E. Kevin Kelloway, and Joseph J. Hurrell (Malden, MA: Wiley Blackwell, 2014), chapter 6.

[25] Sabater et al., "The Spatialities of Ageing."

[26] Simon Biggs and Ashley Carr, "Age- and Child-Friendly Cities and the Promise of Intergenerational Space," *Journal of Social Work Practice* 29, no. 1 (2015): 1–14; Sara

M. Moorman, Jeffrey E. Stokes, and Sean C. Robbins, "The Age Composition of U.S. Neighborhoods," *Journal of Population Ageing* 9, no. 4 (2016): 375–83; Sabater et al., "The Spatialities of Ageing"; Winkler, "Research Note: Segregated by Age."

[27] Gregory Bailey, Eric Werth, Donna Allen, and Leonie Sutherland, "The Prairie Valley Project: Reactions to a Transition to a Schoolwide, Multiage Elementary Classroom Design," *School Community Journal* 26, no. 1 (2016): 239–63; Jiska Cohen-Mansfield and Barbara Jensen, "Intergenerational Programs in Schools," *Journal of Applied Gerontology* 36, no. 3 (2017): 254–76; Carey DeMichelis, Michel Ferrari, Tanya Rozin, and Bianca Stern, "Teaching for Wisdom in an Intergenerational High-School-English Class," *Educational Gerontology* 41, no. 8 (2015): 551–66.

[28] Darwin Glassford and Lynn Barger-Elliot, "Toward Intergenerational Ministry in a Post-Christian Era," *Christian Education Journal* 8, no. 2 (2011): 364–78.

[29] Allen and Ross, *Intergenerational Christian Formation*; John Roberto, "Our Future Is Intergenerational," *Christian Education Journal* 9, no. 1 (2012): 105–20.

[30] Robert H. Bolst, "Spiritual Formation through the Practice of Spiritual Disciplines within the Seventh-Day Adventist Church" (DMin thesis, Fuller Seminary, 2012); Beverly Vos, "The Spiritual Disciplines and Christian Ministry," *Evangelical Review of Theology* 36, no. 2 (April 2012): 100–14.

[31] Rick Taylor, *The Anatomy of a Disciple: So Many Believers, So Few Disciples* (Fresno, CA: The Well Community Church, 2013).

[32] Sherene Hattingh, Lindsay Morton, Kayle de Waal, Kevin Petrie, Rick Ferret, and Julie-Anne Heise, "Developing a Discipleship Measurement Tool," *Journal of Adventist Mission Studies* 12, no. 2 (2016): 86–104.

[33] Robert E. Logan and Charles R. Ridley, *The Discipleship Difference: Making Disciples While Growing as Disciples* (North Charleston, SC: CreateSpace, 2015).

[34] Neil Cole, *Church 3.0: Upgrades for the Future of the Church. Leadership Network* (San Francisco, CA: Jossey-Bass, 2010); Bill Hull, *The Complete Book of Discipleship: On Being and Making Followers of Christ* (Colorado Springs: NavPress, 2006).

[35] Taylor, *The Anatomy of a Disciple.*

[36] Brant Himes, "Discipleship as Theological Praxis: Dietrich Bonhoeffer as a Resource for Educational Ministry," *Christian Education Journal* 8, no. 2 (2011): 263–77; Beverly Vos, "The Spiritual Disciplines and Christian Ministry," *Evangelical Review of Theology* 36, no. 2 (April 2012).

[37] Diane Chandler, "Whole-Person Formation: An Integrative Approach to Christian Education," *Christian Education Journal* 12, no. 2 (2015): 314–32.

[38] Hannelie Wood, "A Christian Understanding of the Significance of Love of Oneself in Loving God and Neighbour: Towards an Integrated Self-Love Reading," *Hervormde Teologiese Studies* 72, no. 3 (2016): 1–10.

[39] See national studies by Barna (David Kinnaman. *You Lost Me: Why Young Christians Are Leaving the Church . . . And Rethinking Faith.* Grand Rapids: Baker Books, 2011); Christian Smith (Christian Smith and Melinda Lundquist Denton, *Soul Searching: The Religious and Spiritual Lives of American Teenagers.* New York: Oxford University Press, 2005); and Kara Powell (Kara Powell and Chap Clark, *Sticky Faith: Everyday Ideas to Build Lasting Faith in Your Kids.* Grand Rapids: Zondervan, 2011). Smaller studies include dozens of DMin and PhD projects, including those written by Frederick R. Fay, Lynne Kammeraad, and Larry Linderman.

Chapter Eleven

All Ages Learning Together

Wilson McCoy

Stephanie was crying when I scanned the room. Becky sat in front of her listening and speaking soft words I could not make out. They sat there for almost ten minutes, but I knew I needed to give them more time. They kept talking as the other participants gathered back into a circle in the center of the room. We were about to begin discussing our passage of Scripture for the night when Becky and Stephanie joined us.

After the session, Stephanie stayed to talk. Before I could ask her what happened, she gushed with excitement. She said she felt like God spoke to her through Becky. Stephanie went on to tell me the reason for her earlier tears. She felt overwhelmed when she partnered up to discuss the passage. The part of the text that resonated with her was another reminder of the unexpected news from earlier that week—she was pregnant with her fourth child. She and her husband were scared. So as she shared about the faith of Moses in light of uncertainty, she began to talk about the baby, her fear, and then the tears came.

Becky, about twenty years older, listened with care. Then she whispered something Stephanie did not expect, "The same thing happened to me when I was your age." Becky then told some of her story, about her unexpected third child and the blessing her daughter had been to her family. She went on to assure her, comfort her, and offer any help she needed in coming months. Stephanie later told me she was in awe, not only of how God had woven their stories together, but also because this conversation was the first time she had ever met Becky.

The Project

This encounter is one of the many surprising moments from the intergenerational experience I facilitated at my church in Lebanon, Tennessee, in the fall of 2015. The College Hills Church of Christ is a large, multigenerational church.[1] For my Doctorate of Ministry project with Lipscomb University, I wanted to create an intentionally intergenerational experience with a portion of my congregation. My main purpose was to explore the formative impact of cross-generational experiences. In other words, what difference does meaningful interaction with other generations have on the process of spiritual formation?

To explore this question, I met with two separate intergenerational small groups once a week for two months. Each group consisted of five generations ranging in age from ten to eighty.[2] One group of twelve met on Sunday nights while the other group of fourteen met on Wednesdays. In order to better compare their respective intergenerational experiences, these two groups never met together in an intentional way during the project.

Moreover, in my interaction with the group participants, I made sure the *intergenerational* dimension of the project was implicit and not overt. I did not draw attention to this dynamic on my own initiative. Instead, I wanted a scenario where participants could, on their own accord, make connections and reflections on the dynamics between the generations organically. Not until the very end of the project did I draw attention to the intergenerational aspect in an intentional way.

The method of reading Scripture we experienced together was Dwelling in the Word.[3] This spiritual practice seemed ideal due to its emphasis on encountering God and Scripture through a community. I knew by using this style of reading, the different generations would be encouraged to interact with each other. This reading practice consists of six moves:

- First, a prayer is said to invite the Spirit to guide the reading of the Word.
- Second, a passage is read aloud twice to the group. They are given two questions to consider while the passage is read: What captures your imagination? What question would you like to ask a Bible expert based upon this passage?
- Third, a time of silence is observed to allow the words of the passage to have impact.
- Fourth, each person in the group is instructed to find someone they do not know very well. They are further instructed to listen to that person in free speech[4] as they tell the listener what they hear from the passage based upon the two questions.
- Fifth, after the time of sharing, the group listens to the reports from the various participants regarding what they heard from their partner.
- Finally, the group together discerns what God might be doing among them based upon what they heard.

In every group meeting, we followed the same order over the course of an hour. We started with a time of arriving, eating light snacks, and group members sharing from their personal story or previous week. We then carried out Dwelling in the Word with Exodus 34:1–10.[5] Each week, I encouraged the participants to pair with a new person to ensure they interacted with different ages. After partnering together, we then formed a circle to share and discern before concluding our time.

In order to discern the formative impact of this intergenerational experience, I attended to the project through three distinct angles.[6] First, I took field notes each week to capture my perspective on the unfolding events with special attention to what I saw happening between the generations. Second, I distributed two questionnaires and facilitated a final focus group interview with the participants to get an insider angle on the project.[7] Third, I asked an independent expert to provide an outside angle on the experience; this person read through all of the questionnaires and gave reflections on her observations. I then brought these three angles together to ensure a thicker, more valid description of the results.

Connections to Earlier Research

Many of the results of my study confirmed existing research about the formative benefits of intergenerational ministry. First, my research confirmed the potential for robust faith development.[8] Younger participants noted how their views of faithfulness and their own sense of faith were enhanced by the diverse ages. Older participants noted a deeper sense of God's activity in their lives as they observed faith within younger generations.

Second, my research confirmed the potential for more robust views of church due to intergenerational experiences.[9] Participants noted how their reading community became like an extended family. As they experienced care from various ages, they reported a greater appreciation for the body of Christ. Some even noted a greater appreciation for the larger body at College Hills because of this church experience in miniature.

Third, my research confirmed the ways in which intergenerational experiences strengthen relationships between generations.[10] Mentors were found, life stages were navigated, and care was experienced. Perceptions of and attitudes toward different age groups improved within the groups. One participant even affirmed that the experience helped her to begin to see members of another generation as not just a stereotype, but as actual people.

New Contributions

The results of my research also offered several unique contributions to the field of intergenerational Christian spiritual formation. First, Dwelling in the Word proves to be an effective intergenerational practice. This spiritual discipline inherently cultivates mutuality between the generations, which is a key distinguishing trait of intergenerational experiences. Numerous participants noted the impact of this particular reading method with people of different ages. In fact, one of the few participants who had experienced Dwelling before noted the difference the practice made for her due to the diverse ages present. This twenty-four-year-old said,

> I am surprised how much I am getting out of the class. When it was announced that we would be "Dwelling in the Word," I was disappointed. In the past, I have not liked this method of reading. One reason . . . was because with a large group, the same individuals would share and the same comments were made each week. However, with this smaller and more varied age group, I feel each week God wants both myself and the group to hear something different.

This research shows that reading together can be an effective means of intergenerationality, and Dwelling in the Word provides one avenue for such reading. This discovery is important due to the challenge of finding inclusive ways for multiple age groups to interact with Scripture on equal levels.

Second, my research reveals that the formative potential of intergenerational experiences is enhanced when there is a common purpose and bond for the group. Numerous participants noted that part of what made their experience more meaningful was a sense of purpose to the meetings (i.e., to read Scripture). One older millennial noted that he began the process wondering what he had in common with some of the older members; but in time, he felt a close-knit connection with them. Part of this connectedness was due to having a shared purpose with people of another age group. One millennial female called this factor "common ground"; a Gen Xer called this a "common search for truth." The communal formation of the group grew in part because of this shared bond and purpose.

Third, my research uncovered an interesting insight that can inform future intergenerational experiences. I call this dimension the "me too" dynamic.[11] This phrase, growing out of the work of Brené Brown, refers to the formative impact on participants when they heard a person of a different generation express questions or concerns that they also experienced. They reported feeling normalized or more confident in their faith because they knew others also shared similar struggles; they felt a sense of solidarity and empowerment. One Gen Xer, who also happened to be a new Christian, said,

One of the great things about this experience is being able to
share our thoughts and questions with others in the group. The
diversity of the group and the differing viewpoints and understanding is helping grow my faith. This experience is teaching
me that other people have the same or similar questions about
faith as I do and that it is okay to not have all of the answers.

A seasoned Christian also mentioned the power of this open sharing,
saying, "I thought it was great to see [an eighty-three-year-old male in
her group] still asking questions at his age and maturity. It is reassuring to
know that we never have all the answers." The deeper insight for practitioners involves creating spaces where different generations can hear one
another give voice to questions, doubts, and concerns. These expressions
of vulnerability have the ability to build a more robust and shared faith.

Fourth, the specific trait of listening emerged as a formative quality
among all ages participating in the project. Almost everyone talked about
the struggle of learning to listen through this process. Some noted explicitly how listening to a person of another age group had a formative impact.
One millennial confessed halfway through the reading experience, "I have
learned so much from people in here that are younger than me, so what
might I be missing out on if I chose to listen better? God was telling me to
listen better." Similar feedback came from our older generation as well. A
seventy-one-year-old said, "The different ages and genders have helped us
to develop greater respect among us. That respect here can cultivate respect
out there." A sixty-eight-year-old said,

We can learn from each other. [God is] showing us that our
thoughts are not the only ones. . . . We need to listen to the little
ones and what they have got to say. We always think that we
need to listen to our elders. . . . I think sometimes we think that
teenagers just don't know anything. So I think we need to be a
little more open.

Previous research has indicated the potential for unique character development through intergenerational research.[12] My project extends this
research by identifying the trait of listening as both a needed means and
manifestation of successful intergenerational expression.

Fifth, this research reveals the potential for thicker faith conversations when diverse generations interact in mutual ways. One participant described how her intergenerational experience challenged her "generational group think." She and others noted how easy it is to assume other ages view faith and Scripture through the same prism as that of your peers. However, by creating a give-and-take conversation between generations, those prisms were challenged and broadened. The reminder for practitioners is to seek avenues in the life of a community of faith where diverse ideas and generational perspectives can be shared.

Personal Insights

Before this project took shape, my knowledge of intergenerational ministry was nonexistent. However, over the course of this project, my interest in and appreciation of this approach grew. Watching old and young openly question and converse around Scripture was powerful. Having conversations outside of the reading group helped me to see the ways these experiences were having a broader impact on the members. The strong, positive reactions from both groups and my personal experiences each week increased my conviction of the need for such experiences within the spiritual formation models of local congregations. I cannot see a future in my ministry where I will not look for ways to bring various age groups together in formative ways. I would encourage other church leaders to consider the powerful potential of this means of transformation in the lives of their congregations.

A Concluding Reflection

A few weeks after the project ended, I made a phone call to one of the participants about a church matter unrelated to the project. While we talked, this older woman reaffirmed the experience of reading with other ages. When I asked her why the experience was meaningful, she said that this was one of the first times in her experience of church that she had felt heard in a diverse environment. In the past, she felt that her comments were not as significant or valued in mixed group settings, so she had usually remained quiet. She said that part of the power of this project was being able to share and be listened to by people different from herself.

I called the woman back later for her permission to share that story because her words lingered with me long after the phone conversation ended. I wanted to close with that story because her experience reveals the potential power of intergenerational experiences in the life of the church. We need more spaces in our churches where people feel like they can give and receive; where they can share and be heard. We need more opportunities for people to experience a diversity of voices within the community of faith. Intergenerational Christian spiritual formation is a powerful means of creating such a culture of mutuality, diversity, and reciprocity where people can experience life in the body of Christ more deeply.

As a commentary on the entire experience, "Curtis," age seventy, shared these words about his experience in his intergenerational small group:

> What kind of church would be formed if everyone got to experience what we have experienced? It would be a church that was stronger, more devoted, and a caring church. As we were discussing this, I got to thinking about Paul's statement about neither male nor female, Jew nor Greek, slave nor free, and now we would have to add young or old, because this has enhanced our experience with God to have all of us here.

Notes

[1] This classification of "multigenerational" describes a community of faith where many different ages coexist alongside each other. This category is often held in contrast with "intergenerational" communities. As noted in this book's introductory chapter, intergenerational communities of faith are those who are intentionally and strategically bringing the generations together in ways that create mutuality and reciprocity.

[2] For the purposes of this project, I used William Strauss and Neil Howe, *Generations: The History of America's Future, 1584 to 2069* (New York: William Morrow, 1991). They breakdown generational cohorts as follows: the GI generation (1901–1924), the silent generation (1925–1942), the boomer generation (1943–1960), Generation X (1961–1981), the millennial generation (1982–2004), and the generation born after 2004, who are still developing a name and characteristics. See Lynn Barger Elliott's chapter, Chapter Four, for a fuller description of these five generations.

[3] Pat Taylor Ellison and Patrick Keifert, *Dwelling in the Word: A Pocket Handbook* (St. Paul: Church Innovations, 2011). The description and language of these steps is taken from this work.

⁴This phrase is used in order to emphasize an open, responsive posture of listening. An informal way of saying it is to "listen to this person as if what they are saying is the most important thing in the world." It is developing a posture of open, nonjudgmental listening, where you really believe that God might speak through your partner.

⁵We used this same passage every week for all eight weeks of the project.

⁶This method of evaluation is known as "triangulation." For more on this method, see Tim Sensing, *Qualitative Research: A Multi-Methods Approach to Projects for Doctor of Ministry Theses* (Eugene, OR: Wipf and Stock, 2011), 72; John W. Creswell, *Research Design: Qualitative, Quantitative, and Mixed Methods Approaches*, 3rd ed. (Thousand Oaks, CA: Sage, 2009), 191–92.

⁷The first questionnaire was given out after four weeks, at the halfway point of the experience. The second was given out after the eighth week. The focus group interview occurred on the final, ninth time of meeting.

⁸Holly Catterton Allen and Christine Lawton Ross, *Intergenerational Christian Formation: Bringing the Whole Church Together in Ministry, Community and Worship* (Downers Grove, IL: InterVarsity Press, 2012): 47–63, 156–74; Allan G. Harkness, "Intergenerationality: Biblical and Theological Foundations," *Christian Education Journal* 9, no. 1 (2012): 129–32; John Roberto, "Our Future Is Intergenerational," *Christian Education Journal* 9, no. 1 (Spring 2012): 105–9.

⁹Allen and Ross, *Intergenerational Christian Formation*; Harkness, "Intergenerationality"; Roberto, "Our Future Is Intergenerational."

¹⁰Allen and Ross, *Intergenerational Christian Formation*; Harkness, "Intergenerationality"; Roberto, "Our Future Is Intergenerational."

¹¹This expression comes from the sociological research of Brené Brown who argues for the need for connection within the human experience. She contends that one of the most powerful connectors of the human experience, and one of the biggest detractors of shame, is the expression "me too." That simple phrase serves as a locus of solidarity, companionship, and connection. This fact is especially true in moments where people are vulnerable. When people in places of vulnerability are met with "me too," then a powerful reciprocal connection occurs. They know they are not alone in their given struggle. For more on this dynamic, see Brené Brown, *Daring Greatly: How the Courage to Be Vulnerable Transforms the Way We Live, Love, Parent, and Lead* (New York: Gotham, 2012), 58–111; Brené Brown, *I Thought It Was Just Me (but it isn't): Making the Journey from "What Will People Think?" to "I Am Enough"* (New York: Gotham, 2008), 31–68.

¹²Allen and Ross, *Intergenerational Christian Formation*, 47–63, 156–74; Harkness, "Intergenerationality," 129–32; Roberto, "Our Future Is Intergenerational," 105–9.

Part Four

INCLUDING EVERY GENERATION

Chapter Twelve

Babies and Toddlers, Too?

Dawn Rundman

> I've got the love of Jesus, love of Jesus,
> Up in my brain! Where?
> Up in my brain! Where?
> Up in my brain.
> I've got the love of Jesus, love of Jesus,
> Up in my brain! Where?
> Up in my brain to stay.

These lyrics are an unfamiliar (and maybe jarring) variation of the song George William Cook composed over a century ago. Tunes about Jesus and brains aren't likely to make it into the church's canon of well-loved children's tunes anytime soon. But switching the word "heart" to "brain" points to the necessary order of how humans remember and learn. To love Jesus with our hearts, we need to know Jesus with our brains.

This chapter challenges Christian education practitioners, clergy, theologians, and others invested in the study of lifelong faith formation to consider how research on *early* brain development can help frame new ways of thinking about how and when we introduce the love of Jesus to young children. The first three years of life are an extraordinary period of human development because of the brain's rapid proliferation of neural connections. The brain's ability to form new connections in response to experiences, called *neuroplasticity,* is especially pronounced during these years.[1]

Researchers in several disciplines such as developmental psychology, neuroscience, linguistics, and music cognition have studied infant and toddler development for decades to learn when, how, and why humans develop the capabilities they do in the first years of life. More recently, they've used advances in brain imaging technology to demonstrate how experience can shape neural connections in the brains of infants and toddlers. While this research has been reported in hundreds of studies on early physical, cognitive, social, and emotional development, this chapter will present a brief snapshot of a few findings from studies of *language, early literacy,* and *music* in young children. These three areas can be viewed as central in understanding the church's unique role in providing a rich neurological context for early childhood development.

These findings are followed by several ideas for how early childhood ministry can be viewed more expansively as intergenerational ministry rather than a siloed ministry applying only to a three-year span of human development. Framed this way, early childhood faith formation can become a powerful way to support not just the young children in our midst, but also their older siblings, parents, grandparents, godparents, and many others who are part of a young child's congregational community.

Behold the Brains of Babies

By the 1990s, child development researchers had spent close to a century creating ingenious techniques for assessing infants and toddlers, including detailed facial coding systems and pacifiers that measured sucking rates. But this decade marked a time for neuroimaging technologies to become more common in research labs, including those studying young children. Dense Array Electroencephalography (dense array EEG), Magnetoencephalography (MEG), and Functional Magnetic Resonance Imaging (fMRI) allowed them to learn more about the structure and functions of different brain regions so they could view the activity in the brains of infants and toddlers. With these techniques in place, empirical research on the first three years of life has established that this is a unique and

remarkable period of development, with many neural connections forming in response to experiences, not just the programmed development in
our DNA.

Language

Dr. Patricia Kuhl at the University of Washington has studied language in
infants for four decades. (Her 2010 TED talk, "The Linguistic Genius of
Babies," is worth watching.) Kuhl has asserted that babies are what she calls
"Citizens of the World" because they are born with the ability to learn any
language that is spoken to them. In her lab, they've discovered that from
birth, infants demonstrate the ability to hear the difference between speech
sounds in any language, differences that adults (or even older infants)
cannot hear. This ability to distinguish between all the sounds in all the
languages begins to diminish at about eight to nine months of age. By
the time an infant celebrates their first birthday, they have now narrowed
the range of sounds to mostly the ones in the language they hear in their
everyday lives. They no longer need to be a "Citizen of the World," only a
citizen of *their* world.[2]

Early Literacy

Linked to the study of language is the area of early literacy, which involves
exposing infants and toddlers to physical books, to text on the page, reading aloud, basics of storytelling, the use of illustrations to support the
storytelling—in short, activities that help young children develop the concept or cognitive schema of "bookness." A 2015 study used Functional
MRIs with nineteen preschoolers who had varying levels of reading exposure in their homes. They measured this exposure by asking parents to
complete a questionnaire asking about access to books, frequency of reading, and variety of books read. Children then listened to age-appropriate
storybooks through headphones while being assessed by fMRI. Those
children with more exposure to reading showed more activity in brain
regions responsible for forming mental imagery and creating meaning,
suggesting that being read to more often meant that these children could
visualize stories more vividly in their minds.[3]

Music

In her review of studies on music perception in babies, Trehub summarizes the drastic change in researchers' understanding of infants' abilities:
"Research on infant music perception over the past four decades has
changed the conception of infants from passive and ineffectual music listeners to active listeners and adept learners."[4]

Over the last four decades, researchers have discovered that infants
are indeed adept music listeners.

- Four-month-olds look longer at the source of consonant sounds
  than dissonant sounds and fret/turn away from the source of dissonant sounds.[5]
- Just as we know that babies prefer what's called motherese, or par-
  entese—the higher pitched, slower, and more animated forms of
  conversation—infants prefer to hear infant-focused singing with
  higher pitches, slower tempos, and a more intimate quality rather
  than adult versions.[6]
- Infants and toddlers move more rhythmically to music than to
  speech and adjust the speed of their movements based on the
  tempo of music.[7]

Church as a Rich Neurological Context

Experiences shape young brains, and parents and other primary caregivers exert significant influence on their child's neurological development,
because they are the ones deciding on the contexts for these experiences.
A congregation can serve as one of these contexts for development during
the first three years, especially in the areas of language, literacy, and music.

Language

When a young child is part of the worshiping community, they hear thousands of words during the hour they are in the setting. Our pastors preach.
Our lectors read from Scripture. Our worship leaders speak the liturgy.
And during many parts of a service, an infant or toddler is surrounded by a
unique acoustic event—dozens, or hundreds, or even thousands of people
around them speaking the same words together.

As a church, we can give infants and toddlers some of their first exposure to the language of faith.

Literacy

The church can also be a context that supports early literacy by introducing the Bible as a book that is important to the child because it is important to our faith. The Bible helps us answer the big questions of life that are on the developing minds of infants and toddlers: Who am I? Who takes care of me? Will my needs be met? Whom can I trust? Who loves me? When I mess up, will they still love me?

As a church, we can develop biblical literacy in babies and toddlers right from the start so they never remember a time when they didn't see and hear God's Word read aloud.

Music

Knowing what we do about the ability of young children to connect with music and begin to understand its structure, its melodies, its patterns, and its underlying emotional content, let's consider the ways that a church, especially during worship, provides experiences that can shape young brains. Music is presented in many different formats, giving young children unique acoustic experiences that they may hear nowhere else:

- One person serving as a cantor, leading the back and forth with the congregation
- A small group or choir singing an anthem
- The acoustic sounds of a pipe organ, or piano, or drum kit
- The electric sounds of guitars, bass guitars, and keyboards
- The surround sound of congregational singing

As a church, we can design musical experiences that make an impression— literally—on the minds of the youngest ones in our midst.

Early Childhood Ministry = Intergenerational Ministry

A church has the potential to be a remarkable context for supporting the development of young children. How effectively is this happening? How often is this happening? *Is* this happening?

Without more empirical data, I can share what I've heard after speaking on the area of early childhood faith formation for the last fifteen years in mainline Protestant churches: we baptize them when they're babies, and then they start Sunday school when they're three.

What may guide this practice (aside from a we've-always-done-it-this-way mentality in some contexts) is skepticism that early childhood ministry can make any kind of difference in the lives of these young children. *With the finite congregational resources we have,* we ask, *aren't they best spent elsewhere—on Sunday school, or youth ministry, or programs for adults?*

In response to "Aren't they too young for that?" a powerful description proposed by Maria Lahman may give us a fresh way of viewing the little ones in our churches. She proposes that children be considered both vulnerable *and* competent.[8] This both/and description acknowledges that children are utterly dependent on their caregivers to meet their needs in the first years of life. But these little ones are also competent, their brains much more plastic than ours in forming connections and pruning away others in response to the environment around them.

Considering, then, these vulnerable and competent children in our church communities, what if we viewed early childhood ministry as an innovative expression of intergenerational ministry? Such a view could be a way to overcome our hurdles, blind spots, and perceived barriers. What follows are several proposed points of intersection between early childhood ministry and other people, ministries, and programs in congregations. These proposed "What if?" statements can serve as springboards for congregational dialogue, planning, and innovation.

Early Childhood Ministry + Youth Ministry = Intergenerational Ministry

What if churches provided opportunities for youth to recognize their gifts for childcare by providing ways to match young children to skilled teenage caregivers, starting in the nursery, but also for parent date nights? This practice could eventually lead to families developing relationships with youth who become their go-to babysitters. Some youth may discover a vocational calling to study early childhood development and pursue careers in this area.

Early Childhood Ministry + Marriage Care Ministry = Intergenerational Ministry
What if churches prioritized couples' marriages while their children were infants and toddlers? Marriages are especially vulnerable during this time. Parents of young children are tired and don't have much private time together. Financial resources are stressed, schedules are ever shifting, and some new parents may also be caring for their parents. Married couples need help to sustain their relationships at a time when marriage care may sink to the bottom of their priority list.

Early Childhood Ministry + Parent Ministry = Intergenerational Ministry
What if churches took the opportunity to equip parents to raise their children in the faith? By offering faith formation experiences for young children beyond baptism or baby dedication, the church makes it clear to parents that formation begins early. In his essay on developmentally responsive catechesis, Joseph D. White points to this missed opportunity in many churches: "At precisely the time that [new parents] are ready and willing to completely restructure their priorities and rearrange their lives, the parish often has little to offer."[9] By providing parent-child classes starting in infancy, churches may also discover an added benefit: educating the child often leads to educating the parents as well.

Early Childhood Ministry + Senior Ministry = Intergenerational Ministry
What if churches sought to educate and support grandparents of young children? Serving these grandparents is definitely not a one-size-fits-all approach. Some grandparents are involved in day-to-day caregiving for their grandchildren. Others live many miles away from their grandchildren and miss them dearly. In addition to supporting the needs of these grandparents, churches can give them opportunities to serve as surrogate wise elders for young children whose grandparents live many miles away.

Early Childhood Ministry + Hunger Ministry = Intergenerational Ministry
What if churches helped every child be fed? Healthy brain development is at risk when children do not have enough to eat. The single most important thing a church can do to support healthy brain development during the first three years of life is to support food shelves, nutrition programs, and

other hunger-fighting ministries so that families facing food insecurity can adequately nourish their babies and toddlers.

Early Childhood Ministry + Hospitality Ministry = Intergenerational Ministry

What if churches were deliberate in how they appealed to families with young children that are seeking a church home? Radical hospitality means things like making sure the men's room has changing tables, giving young children seating that's their size in fellowship areas, and offering free childcare at church events, not just worship.

Early Childhood Ministry + Worship Planning = Intergenerational Ministry

What if every worship service had songs you could learn by heart, colorful liturgical images, and opportunities for movement and praise? When every facet of a worship service is designed for adults and no one is representing the vulnerable and competent babies and toddlers, we miss a major opportunity to design worship that connects to all God's people. The amazing thing is that such simple parts of worship often connect very deeply with adults as well.

Early Childhood Ministry = Young Children Ministering to Others

Finally, I want to affirm that early childhood ministry is bidirectional. We do not just minister *to* young children. Young children minister to *us* by their presence, their vulnerability, and their embodiment of who Jesus calls us to be, "for the kingdom of God belongs to such as these" (Luke 18:16). They are followers of Jesus; not when they're old enough, but right here and right now.

The church has a window to create lasting, lifelong neurological impressions on young children that will offer them opportunities to learn, remember, and cherish who Jesus is . . . up in their brain to stay.

Notes

[1] For a helpful review, see Adrienne L. Tierney and Charles A. Nelson, III, "Brain Development and the Role of Experience in the Early Years," *Zero Three* 30, no.2 (November 1, 2009): 9–13.

[2] Patricia K. Kuhl, Erica Stevens, Akiko Hayashi, Toshisada Deguchi, Shigeru Kiritani, and Paul Iverson, "Infants Show a Facilitation Effect for Native Language Phonetic Perception between 6 and 12 Months," *Developmental Science* 9, no. 2 (April 2006): F13–F21.

[3] John S. Hutton, Tzipi Horowitz-Kraus, Alan L. Mendelsohn, Tom DeWitt, Scott K. Holland, "Home Reading Environment and Brain Activation in Preschool Children Listening to Stories," *Pediatrics* 136, no. 3 (August 2015): 466–78.

[4] Sandra E. Trehub, "In the Beginning: A Brief History of Infant Music Perception," *Musicae Scientiae* 14, no. 2, supplement (September 2010): 71–78, http://doi.org/10.1177/10298649100140S206.

[5] Marcel R. Zentner and Jerome Kagan, "Infants' Perception of Consonance and Dissonance in Music," *Infant Behavior and Development* 21, no. 3 (December 1998): 483–92.

[6] Laurel J. Trainor, Elissa D. Clark, Anita Huntley, and Beth A. Adams, "The Acoustic Basis of Preferences for Infant-Directed Singing," *Infant Behavior and Development* 20, no. 3 (July–September 1997): 383–96, http://doi.org/10.1016/S0163-6383(97)90009-6.

[7] Marcel Zentner and Tuomas Eerola, "Rhythmic Engagement with Music in Infancy," *Proceedings of the National Academy of Sciences* 107, no. 13 (March 2010): 5768–73, doi:10.1073/pnas.1000121107.

[8] Maria Lahman, "Always Othered: Ethical Research with Children," *Journal of Early Childhood Research* 6, no. 3 (2008): 281–300. https://doi.org/10.1177/1476718X08094451.

[9] Joseph D. White, "Forming Lifelong Disciples through Developmentally-Responsive Catechesis," *Church Life Journal*, May 22, 2017, churchlife.nd.edu/2017/05/22/forming-lifelong-disciples-through-developmentally-responsive-catechesis/.

Chapter Thirteen

Millennials and Screeners

Dave Sanders

Absolutely awestruck, I fixed my gaze on Michelangelo's statue of David in Florence's Galleria dell'Accademia. Other admiring tourists stood, observed, chatted, and walked on. I gawked for over an hour, enthralled at the humanity of this chiseled stone. Inch by inch, I traversed the full circle around this astounding, lifelike sculpture of an adolescent David with a sling over his left shoulder and a stone in his right hand. With profound admiration, I pondered the artistic journey of this divinely talented sculptor, and I began to wonder: "Who taught Michelangelo to sculpt?"

Isn't there always a "someone" behind the one more famous? Looking at the Scriptures, for example, do you know who taught Moses about leadership, or mentored Ruth in cultural engagement, or poured wisdom into a young John Mark who later wrote one of the Gospel accounts? The principles of intergenerational influence, mentoring, and leadership were abundantly at play in the Jethro-Moses, Naomi-Ruth, and Barnabas-John Mark relationships. In light of these examples of intergenerational influence, and knowing that the next twenty years of youth ministry will be about the screener[1] generation with millennials as their primary leaders, it seems crucial for churches and youth ministry organizations to implement an intergenerational strategy for mentoring and leadership development. This chapter investigates what screeners and millennials need, want, and offer, and why millennials as young leaders require intergenerational influence as they spearhead ministry to the youngest generation, the screeners.

Millennials constitute America's largest generation ever recorded at eighty-three million, which includes seventy-eight million U.S. births and roughly five million cohort members who are immigrants.[2] Together, they represent roughly one-third of the American population. Their sheer size draws an inordinate amount of attention from marketers, educators, municipalities, politicians, and church leaders. Everyone is anxious to connect with the millennials, and these groups are clamoring for strategies and methods to make that connection successful. While the focus remains squarely fixated on millennials, the generation in their wake is methodically populating our middle schools and high schools. For the next twenty years, youth ministry will be primarily about screeners.[3] While educators, youth workers, and churches have barely glanced at this new generation, an understanding of generational theory may provide a beneficial lens through which we identify and strategize our engagement of intergenerational influence with screeners as the next youth generation and millennials as their leaders.

Generational Theory Defined

William Strauss and Neil Howe are the gurus of generational theory who—in 1991—introduced the concept of generational theory through their seminal work, *Generations: The History of America's Future, 1584 to 2069*.[4] According to Strauss and Howe, a generational cohort is defined as "everyone who is 'brought into being' at the same historical moment" and therefore share similar generational characteristics with the other members of their cohort.[5] They all come from the same "special history" and share a unique "peer personality" that shapes the way their generation characteristically behaves throughout their lifetime.[6]

While great effort is given to the historical naming and sequencing of generations in basic twenty-year cycles, attention is also devoted to understanding the persona of each generation, which is influenced by the cyclical nature of the repeating archetypes in every eighty-year phase (four twenty-year cycles) called a *saeculum*. Strauss and Howe define *peer personality* as a "generational persona recognized and determined by 1) common age location, 2) common beliefs and behavior, and 3) perceived membership in a common generation."[7] A generation is composed of people whose common location in history lends them a collective persona, and generations come in four cyclical archetypes, always in the same order—Artist, Prophet, Nomad, and Hero.[8] At the end of the eighty-year saeculum, the four basic archetypes repeat themselves. *This basic understanding of the repeating archetypes allows us to project characteristics of the screeners, even though there are yet unborn members of this generation.*

Generational Typologies and Characteristics

Describing the generational personas of the three older generations will provide a context by which we can begin to grasp how both appreciation and frustration develop between the cohorts. Consider the implications of the following similarities/differences and likes/dislikes in this abbreviated glimpse of traditionalists, boomers, and Gen Xers.

1. Traditionalists (artist archetype) were born between 1925 and 42. They are also known as the silent generation and appreciate such things as being polite, formal, respectful, and friendly, as well as hierarchical structures.[9] This generation dislikes being overly casual, cold, rude, and indifferent ("whatever" is not their go-to phrase).

2. Baby boomers (prophet archetype) were born between 1943 and 1960. There were seventy-six million born into this behemoth cohort, which is how they got their name. Boomers like recognition, caring, being knowledgeable and personal, and they like things focused on them. Boomers typically dislike distracted, defensive, and briskly efficient types.[10] Because of their current life stage—having moved through the success phase gaining knowledge and experience, and now desiring significance in life—boomers make excellent mentors. This cohort is a natural match for millennials, who strongly desire mentoring and who

value the experience boomers exude. Gen Xers and boomers are more at odds when it comes to mentoring because their values and worldviews are constructed from quite different historical contexts and social environments.[11]

3. Gen Xers (nomad archetype) were born between 1961 and 1981. They only total about forty-eight million and have been characterized as "latchkey kids" who are entrepreneurial and enjoy working on their own. This generation likes things straightforward, brief, efficient, and focused on outcome or product. Gen Xers dislike things that are overly perky, chatty, dumb, and anything involving overselling.[12] As we compare the generational personas, it becomes clear that areas for potential clashes with other generational cohorts exist. Because Gen Xers are located in the center of the lifespan development of most churches, it is important that they buy in to any discussion of intergenerational expressions within the church, particularly youth ministry, as they are typically the parents of screeners in current youth groups.

Who Are Millennials?

Millennials (hero archetype) were born between 1982 and 2004. This generational cohort is the largest generation at eighty-three million strong with five million of the ranks being immigrants, which represents a significant increase over any previous generation. They also represent the most studied and most educated generation to date.[13] A record number of people from this generation either attended or currently attend college.[14] This cohort likes things/people who are positive, cheerful, engaging, helpful, and meaningful, and dislike things/people who are snide and snippy, too formal, condescending, and slow. Diversity is the norm for this group, with over 42 percent indicating something other than "white" in surveys; millennials are quite diverse in racial and ethnic backgrounds as well as religious and lifestyle backgrounds, and millennials tend to accept and tolerate their differences quite well.[15] And, as noted earlier, this generation is enormous; it is no wonder that significant attention, effort, and resources have been expended to understand and reach this group from business, political, educational, and church sectors.

In general, millennials tend to . . .

- *be technologically fluent (or tech fluent).* They habitually use Google to seek information,[16] and they stay connected 24/7 to friends, parents, information, and entertainment.[17]
- *be cause-driven.* The millennial generation is America's newest "civic generation" (hero); [18] that is, they mirror the previous civics/heroes from four generations previous (the greatest generation) as described in the cyclical nature of archetypes by Strauss and Howe. Civics want to make a difference in their society and are thus drawn to causes that will change things. The view that millennials are usually inclined toward helping others is so widely held that companies have instituted recruiting programs for young workers involving volunteer services and helping the environment.[19]
- *be outcome-focused.* This generation is interested in the big picture (think "change the world") rather than the *details* of how to accomplish the goal. There are many paths that are acceptable as long as the outcome is achieved; it's not the process, it's the result that drives them.
- *need feedback.* This generation wants to "feel valued, respected, and rewarded for their contributions."[20] Millennials desire transparency from their coworkers and managers;[21] however, they themselves tend not to follow rules.[22]
- *desire mentors.* "Mentor me" is a cry for most millennials because they are keen to access the experience of the older, veteran generations. When millennials feel empowered, they believe they can achieve anything.[23]

Who Are Screeners?

Screeners (artist archetype, like the traditionalist/silent generation) are being born between 2005 and 2025. Projected to be fewer in numbers than the millennials, they are predicted to reflect a generational cohort persona much like the traditionalists according to the cyclical nature and the turnings of Strauss and Howe's generational theory.[24] Katy Steinmetz anticipates that screeners will be well-behaved and will develop a culture of "blanding"—playing it safe—in many ways, like the silent generation (traditionalists).[25] This ability to project artist attributes coupled with some early studies of these children and emerging adolescents allows us to begin developing a generational persona in this vastly different, technological age. Screeners will have always observed, known, and experienced life through the framework of screens—often four or five screens at a time. Nickelodeon calls this new arena "multiscreen sandboxes."[26] This cohort likes diversity, individualism, and technology, and dislikes personal reflection, old-style teaching, and any absence of technology. The generation makes up about 25 percent of the current population of the United States, and it is the most ethnically and racially diverse generation yet.[27] Screeners are also the most sexually diverse generation due to the blurring of gender roles in American culture.[28]

Tim Elmore, founder and president of the Growing Leaders organization, says that he sees the following marks in screeners:

- cautious and safety preoccupied
- green-biased
- focused on conservation
- insecure
- identity seeking
- calculated
- frugal stewards of resources
- self-reliant
- realistic and pragmatic
- issue-oriented
- globally savvy and aware[29]

Therefore, the following characteristics could inform screeners' generational persona:

- *Tech immersed.* The screeners live in a world where technology is constantly at their fingertips, and Steinmetz refers to this phenomenon as technological umbilical cords always connecting the parent and child.[30]

- *Globally savvy.* Screeners are not only more globally connected, they actually are engaged with international news and macro events and concerned about the implications for people around the world.
- *Individualistic.* Screens allow screeners to interact with each other and the world as individuals, and they like it that way. Being a smaller generational cohort, there is less of a communal identity and more of a personal interface with the world. James Steyer says, "In a world of limitless connections and hundreds or even thousands of 'friends,' many relationships are bound to be shallow and unreal."[31]
- *Averse to traditional teaching approaches.* According to Steyer, the ability for adolescents to gain information extremely quickly has shifted many of the ways in which an early adolescent screener focuses, reads, writes, and reflects.[32] In his book *Rewired,* Larry Rosen notes that "While Baby Boomer and older Gen-Xers prefer either visual or auditory modes [of receiving information], Net-Geners and iGeners learn best by touching, moving, and enjoying."[33] Rosen continues: "Literally, their minds have changed—they have been 'rewired.'"[34]
- *Extrinsically focused.* What people "out there" think of screeners becomes a driving obsession. This attitude increases the pressure placed on adolescents to succeed and achieve, but it also leads to isolation.[35]
- *Anxious.* Being isolated and always "on" in a globally perilous world brings an angst that permeates daily life for a screener. It's what Steinmetz refers to as a "highly documented life."[36]

Beginning in 2017, middle schools and youth ministries began welcoming this newest generation as 6th graders—whether they were aware of it or not. In only four or five years from that date, all of high school youth will be screeners; and soon, screeners will be entering college. This generational cohort has been born mobile, always on, building worlds (think gaming), under surveillance, homebodies, and loyal soldiers (like the traditionalists before them).

Millennials versus Screeners

The lens of generational theory can become a beneficial method for identifying and strategizing our engagement with screeners. While still in its infancy, research on screeners indicates marked differences from millennials. In a basic comparison of millennials and screeners, with a cyclical reach back into the traditionalists' persona, it is clear that the two generations bear some striking *dissimilarities*. The chart and commentary below highlight the differences:

MILLENNIALS	SCREENERS
Adventurous	Cautious and safety preoccupied
The screener world is more threatening, and screeners are more electronically observed and documented than millennials.	
Naïve	Globally savvy and aware
Screeners are interested in the news of the world and the impact of events on humankind.	
Optimistic and progressive	Realistic and pragmatic
This is a move away from "I can change the world" to "How can I affect specific change in the world."	
I want (am entitled to) it all	I seek balance and tradeoffs
This attitude of screeners is tied to being pragmatic and a bent toward conservation rather than extravagance.	
Dependent on parents/adults	Self-reliant
As a smaller generation and one prone to individualism, self-reliance is claimed as a virtue and skill.	
Secure; high self-esteem	Insecure; seeking identity
While millennials have always believed in themselves, screeners are developing insecurity due to their smaller numbers, and their individualism and external focus is creating an identity of anxiety.	
Cause-oriented	Issue-oriented
Dissatisfied with broad, encompassing causes, screeners will be fixated on issues that can be changed; it's a pragmatic approach.	

The current high school juniors and seniors are "cuspers"; the term "cusper" is used for people born in a transitional period between two generations, and they often exhibit characteristics of *both* generations. This can be observed in the events following the Parkland High School shooting in February 2018 when some students were highly engaged in school and gun safety issues, even at a national level (both *cause-* and *issue*-oriented, both *optimistic* and *realistic/pragmatic*), while other students demonstrated "blanding" by being very apprehensive, cautious, and insecure as they returned to their school with an army of police and parental protection. These various responses represent both Millennial and Screener characteristics.

Implications for Churches, Youth Ministry, and the University

Mentoring as a means of intergenerational discipleship and passing on of the faith has been a hallmark of the people of Israel in the Old Testament as well as the church from its very beginning in the book of Acts. Significant mentoring relationships are highlighted in stories such as Abraham and Lot (Gen. 12:1–9; 13; 18:22–33); Jethro and Moses (Exod. 18:13–27); Naomi and Ruth (Ruth 1:1–22; 3:1–5; 4:13–17); Moses and Joshua (Exod. 33:11; Num. 27:15–23; Deut. 34:9); Deborah and Barak (Judg. 4:4–16); Eli and Samuel (1 Sam. 3:1–10); Elijah and Elisha (1 Kings 19:19–21; 2 Kings 2:1–15); Barnabas and John Mark (Acts 12:25; 15:37–39; 2 Tim. 4:11); and Paul and Timothy (Acts 16:1–3; 1 Tim. 1:1–3, 18–19; 2 Tim. 1:1–6; 4:1–5).

Over and over, the Scriptures demonstrate influence through an *intergenerational* approach to building leadership and faith into the lives of others. This relationally based transference of values and lifestyle typically followed an *older/younger* model, a model that seems underutilized in many local churches of today. This de-emphasis has arisen perhaps because we have separated teens from congregational life for decades, or because the older generations have lost an understanding of this vital role, or because these older generations believe they are unable to connect to today's youth. Regardless of the reason for its decline, the intergenerational prototype offered to us in the Scriptures must be recaptured for the benefit of all.

This practice of intergenerational mentoring falls squarely with the three older generations, the traditionalists (1925–1942), the boomers (1943–1960), and Gen Xers (1961–1981). While boomers and millennials have some natural generational affinity and can make great mentoring pairs, it is incumbent on all three older generations to apply themselves to the biblical task of intergenerational leadership/discipleship, specifically with millennials and screeners. Transference of values and biblical lifestyles rarely just happen. The multitude of examples from Scripture demonstrates the distinctive relational nature of such faith development in the context of faith communities.

As we emphasize a cross-generational approach to mentoring and leadership, we can utilize our knowledge and understanding of the current generational differences and similarities, and then (1) look for creative intergenerational options to engage with the upcoming screener generation over the next twenty years while (2) building biblical leadership characteristics into the staff and volunteers (primarily millennials) in our ministries to youth. In a mentoring conversation, a twenty-five-year-old millennial put it this way: "We're young, impulsive, idealistic, passionate, and in need of direction, mentorship, patience, and grace (lots of grace). We need help; we have no idea what we're doing!"

As educators and church practitioners, generational theory informs us. Along with pedagogical and developmental understandings, we can add insights from generational theory to our ministry toolkits as a means of frontline engagement with each generational cohort in order to increase our mentoring and leadership effectiveness. It will take every generation in the church—so let's all be in this together! Mentor, mentor, mentor—get every generation involved and engaged in it at every level, whether personally or programmatically.

So, let me ask you: Who poured their influence into you so that you have become the person you are today? Does a name (or several) come to mind? Most likely, you can identify your inspirations fairly easily. Influential relationships play a crucial part in how humans grow; therefore, the more intergenerational influencers we can gather and train and employ into mentoring relationships, the better prepared our millennial youth ministers will be to lead and mentor our screeners in the development of a lasting Christian faith. When our faith communities exhibit the principles of intergenerational influence, mentoring, and leadership, we become a people who are biblically pouring our lives and faith into the younger generations with significant effectiveness.

And, oh yes, along with other influencers, it was Bertoldo di Giovanni (who studied under Donatello) who taught the adolescent Michelangelo while he was a sculpture student in Florence.

Notes

[1] I have termed this generation screeners because they are embedded in a technological world where they will extensively mediate life through screens. I prefer the term screener over the nondescript moniker of Gen Z.

[2] Tom Rainer and Jess Rainer, *The Millennials: Connecting to America's Largest Generation* (Nashville: B&H Publishing, 2011), 2.

[3] Called "Homelanders" by William Strauss and Neil Howe. The signature name came about through a naming contest in 2006 hosted by Strauss and Howe. Once the White House's report "15 Economic Facts about Millennials" used the moniker, "Homelanders" began to be widely used.

[4] William Strauss and Neil Howe, *Generations: The History of America's Future, 1584 to 2069* (New York: William Morrow, 1991).

[5] Strauss and Howe, *Generations*, 436.

[6] Strauss and Howe, *Generations*, 437.

[7] Strauss and Howe, *Generations*, 429.

[8] William Strauss and Neil Howe, *The Fourth Turning: An American Prophecy—What the Cycles of History Tell Us about America's Next Rendezvous with Destiny* (New York: Broadway Books, 1997), 74. Utilizing the concept of the cyclical nature of historical societal change, Strauss and Howe describe four generations (roughly eighty years) as a saeculum. One saeculum represents four turnings, always in the same order: High, Awakening, Unraveling, and Crisis. Within this saeculum, each generation plays a specific role in the societal development, which is where the labels "Artist," "Prophet," "Nomad," and "Hero" come into play. The Artist represents the High Turning, the Prophet exemplifies the Awakening, the Nomad symbolizes the Unraveling, and the Hero generation characterizes the Crisis.

[9] Ron Zemke, Claire Raines, and Bob Filipczak, *Generations at Work: Managing the Clash of Boomers, Gen Xers, and Gen Yers in the Workplace,* 2nd ed. (New York: Amacom, 2013).

[10] Zemke, Raines, and Filipczak, *Generations at Work.*

[11] Zemke, Raines, and Filipczak, *Generations at Work*; Strauss and Howe, *Generations.*

[12] Zemke, Raines, and Filipczak, *Generations at Work*; Strauss and Howe, *Generations.*

[13] Cheryl Dupont, "The Millennial Generation of Parents," *Choral Journal* 55, no. 3 (October, 2014): 75.

[14] Jackie L. Hartman and Jim McCambridge, "Optimizing Millennials' Communication Styles," *Business Communication Quarterly* 74, no. 1 (March 2011).

[15] Rainer and Rainer, *The Millennials,* 34.

[16]David H. Roberts, Lori R. Newman, and Richard M. Schwartzstein, "Twelve Tips for Facilitating Millennials Learning," *Medical Teacher* 34, no. 4 (January 2012).

[17]Zemke, Raines, and Filipczak, *Generations at Work*.

[18]Eric H. Greenberg with Karl Weber, *Generation We: How Millennial Youth Are Taking Over America and Changing Our World Forever* (Emeryville, CA: Pachatusan, 2008).

[19]Jean M. Twenge, Elise C. Freeman, and W. Keith Campbell, "Generational Differences in Young Adults' Life Goals, Concern for Others, and Civic Orientation, 1966–2009," *Journal of Personality and Social Psychology* 102, no. 5 (2012), doi: 10.1037 /a0027408.

[20]Zemke, Raines, and Filipczak, *Generations at Work*, 139.

[21]Jan Ferri-Reed, "Leading a Multigenerational Workforce: Millennializing the Workplace," *Journal for Quality and Participation* 37, no. 1 (January 2014).

[22]Nancy Sutton Bell and Harry F. Griffin, "Recruiting College Graduates: Results of a Survey on Upperclassmen's Life and Work Priorities," *Culture & Religion Review Journal* 2010, no. 3 (September 2010).

[23]Eddy S. W. Ng and Charles W. Gossett, "Career Choice in Canadian Public Service: An Exploration of Fit with the Millennial Generation," *Public Personal Management* 42, no. 3 (August 2013).

[24]Strauss and Howe, *The Fourth Turning*, 74.

[25]Katy Steinmetz, "Move Over Millennials," *Time*, December 28, 2015, 134.

[26]Thomas R. Umstead, "Millennials Are So Yesterday," *Multichannel News*, April 1, 2013, 9.

[27]Anthony Turner, "Generation Z: Technology and Social Interest," *Journal of Individual Psychology* 7, no. 2 (2015): 104.

[28]"Meet Generation Z: Forget Everything You Learned about Millennials," *Sparks and Honey Marketing Agency*, June 17, 2014, www.slideshare.net/sparksandhoney/generation -z-final-june-17.

[29]Tim Elmore, "Homelanders: The Next Generation," *Psychology Today*, February 7, 2014, www.psychologytoday.com/blog/artificial-maturity/201402/homelanders-the -next-generation.

[30]Steinmetz, "Help!"

[31]James Steyer, *Talking Back to Facebook: The Common Sense Guide to Raising Kids in the Digital Age* (New York: Scribner, 2012), 25.

[32]Steyer, *Talking Back to Facebook*.

[33]Larry D. Rosen, *Rewired: Understanding the iGeneration and the Way They Learn* (New York: Palgrave Macmillan, 2010), 45–46. "Net-Geners" and "iGeners" are other names for millennials and screeners/homelanders.

[34]Rosen, *Rewired*, 226.

[35]Patricia M. Greenfield, "Linking Social Change and Developmental Change: Shifting Pathways of Human Development," *Developmental Psychology* 45, no. 2 (2009): 403.

[36]Steinmetz, "Help!" 42.

Chapter Fourteen

Welcoming Emerging Adults

Holly Catterton Allen

E merging adults are navigating a culture that finds Christianity too narrow and judgmental. For this reason (as well as others), many eighteen- to thirty-year-olds are walking away from church—though not necessarily their faith. Our task is to find ways to join twentysomethings during these crucial formative years, as they enter the work force, forge adult identities, revisit childhood beliefs, and re-story their lives.

Emerging adults often desire authentic intergenerational relationships as they enter adulthood; they need those who are older and wiser to listen as they voice doubts and fears, negotiate peer and hierarchical relationships, and integrate who they were with who they are becoming. As we facilitate these differentiation and individuation processes, we are living out the commitment to connectedness and community to which Christ calls us.

A couple of years ago, I conducted some research with emerging adults and their spiritual journeys for Taylor University's Higher Education Symposium called A Faith for the Generations. I created a brief survey which I sent, using a snowball sample technique, to the friends of my two millennial children who then sent it to *their* friends, and to my friends' adult children who sent it to *their* friends. Beyond the basic demographic questions, here are the questions of the survey:

1. Looking back on your college years, how are your college experiences still impacting your faith and/or spiritual development? Please include both *positive* and *negative* trajectories.
2. How would you describe your arc of faith since you left college?
3. How would you describe where you are now in your faith/spiritual journey? (e.g., Spiritual life? Involved with a church? Participating in social justice/benevolent/ministry?)

I received a few dozen completed surveys; I include below the responses from two twentysomethings raised in Christian homes who are currently struggling to find a church home. Emma,[1] twenty-eight, who attended a private Christian university, wrote,

> In college, as I studied the radical life Christ called his followers to, it became clear that this was not what I or most others I knew were living out daily. I also became much more aware of the severe and overwhelming needs of so many people in the world. Many church activities I had spent so much of my life doing seemed unrelated to helping others. All of these conflicting thoughts contributed to me not attending church for the first time in my life my junior and senior years of college. I felt too hypocritical attending church when I did not understand so much of the Bible; and the passages I did understand, I felt I was too poorly representing in my life. I graduated and a few months later began attending church again. When I chose to return to church, I still did not understand how to live a Christian life or understand much of the Bible. I still do not. I never lost my faith in God, but felt conflicted about my life and the lives of other Christians not being able to live out the way of Christ. I decided to attend church again because I believed I should try.

Josh, twenty-five, attended a private, nonreligious university. Josh wrote,

Most of my friends in college were nonreligious, so I suppose that still impacts the way that I experience faith and spirituality. Namely, I don't think there's much of a place for it in the public sphere (this is probably compounded by my coursework in political science). During college, I developed a lot more skepticism, and since leaving have been trying to move back into the faith; it has not been easy, though, as I haven't found any communities that I feel like I belong in. Young adult programs and Bible studies are either filled with people that I can't relate to or who don't have the time to commit to really getting to know each other. Groups for older adults don't seem to want to accept me because I'm much younger, don't have kids, etc. It's very lonely; and as a result, I think my faith has been generally eroding since leaving school. I don't see a lot of people like me who have strong faith.

I will return to these stories later.

Crucial Place

The college and post-college years are a critical period in the life cycle of human beings. This is the period when "one begins to care for oneself, deal with one's own and others' sexuality, search for meaningful work, and negotiate and renegotiate relationships to parents, peers and communities."[2]

Much has been said on the unique characteristics of this particular generation of twentysomethings since Jeffrey Arnett's book, *Emerging Adulthood*,[3] came out in 2004. Two of the most common insights are:

1. they are taking longer to grow up and embrace the typical tasks of adulthood—work, marriage, and children—than generations before them; and
2. they are leaving the church in higher numbers than the generations preceding them.

Current twentysomethings are definitely marrying later: the average age of men at first marriage is now twenty-nine, and of women is twenty-seven—up from twenty-six for men, and twenty-three for women in 1990, and twenty-two and twenty in 1960.[4]

The second generalization is that current emerging adults are leaving organized religion in higher numbers than in the past. In the General Social Surveys (GSS) conducted since 2000, nearly one-quarter of people ages eighteen to twenty-nine have described their religion as "none." By comparison, only about half as many young adults were unaffiliated in the 1970s and 1980s.[5]

In the last fifteen years, the Barna Group has focused some of its resources and energies on understanding the "departure of young adults from church life when they leave home for college or enter the workforce after high school or college."[6] Barna and Kinnaman frame the discussion about emerging adults differently from the GSS; they say that seven out of ten drop out of church life. Some—four out of ten—are "nomads," that is, they are "trying on various worldviews, lifestyles, and pathways open to them—majoring on experiences and relationships rather than on truth and restraint."[7] Two out of ten are "exiles," that is, they are "lost between church culture and wider culture [they feel] called to inhabit and influence."[8] They want to follow Jesus *and* be relevant to the wider cultural marketplace. Nomads and exiles still identify for the most part as Christian, though they may not attend a church. "Prodigals" have not only left the church, they have left their faith; about one out of nine young adults who grew up Christian are currently prodigal according to Kinnaman's research.[9]

How can we create good places for these wandering twentysomethings to reconnect, to once again choose what we call the abundant life in Christ?

Who Are Emerging Adults?

Christian Smith's recent work with Patricia Snell, *Souls in Transition: The Religious and Spiritual Lives of Emerging Adults,*[10] offers an in-depth look at the worlds of younger emerging adults.[11] Smith describes the eighteen- to twenty-three-year-old participants in his study as quite optimistic. Reflecting this optimistic outlook, Jeffrey Arnett says that when emerging adults describe their future, they see "lifelong, harmonious happy marriage; happy, thriving children; and satisfying and lucrative work."[12] Sharon Parks adds another dimension to this optimism, saying that young adults want their faith communities to be ideal, that is "pure, consistent, authentic, and congruent."[13] If emerging adults seek and cannot find this authentic and pure faith community, "they may become disillusioned and abandon church or faith or both."[14] This particular dynamic is reflected in both Emma's and Josh's responses to the survey.

This new generation also values tolerance. In fact, tolerance may be the most monolithic descriptor of this generation. Smith notes several common characteristics of emerging adults that capture various facets of tolerance, including "everybody's different," "it's up to the individual," "more open-minded," and "all cultures are relative."[15] Closely related to the value of tolerance is the idea that choice (in and of itself) is good; that is, "if I chose it, it is good," or "if you chose it, it is good [for you]."

Other common characteristics of emerging adults that impact, intersect with, or influence their spiritual journeys are that they typically seek mentors, love story/narrative, and express deep interest in social justice issues. Relationships are particularly important to them, as well as community, with the added stipulation that they desire *authentic* relationships and *authentic* community.[16]

According to Barna and Kinnaman, nomads and exiles have not left their faith—they have just left the church.[17] Can we make a compelling case for the value of church life to these wanderers? Most seasoned believers recognize that transformation from nonbeliever to new believer, and new believer to mature believer, happens best in community. Is it possible to make a persuasive case to emerging adults for the value of life in community?

The biggest challenge we face is that it is difficult to impact twentysomethings since (1) *they* are rarely among us in our churches, and (2) *we* are rarely with them—in *any* venue.

Something New

I have experienced something in the last few years that contradicts the pervasive message that twentysomethings are dropping out of church in unprecedented numbers. My husband and I moved to Nashville, Tennessee, in 2014; since we arrived, we have observed that several churches are attracting *hundreds* of twentysomethings. For several months, we visited two of these fresh, amazing, and vibrant faith communities, Ethos and Midtown. Over the several weeks that we were visiting these various venues, I took the opportunity to ask some specific questions of those who worship with Ethos and Midtown. Week after week, I asked the young men and women who sat near me, "Why are you a part of this faith community? What draws you here?" And I asked the ministry staff, "What draws these students and twentysomethings here? What are they looking for? What are they finding?"

Elliot, a staff member at Midtown offered,

> Our authenticity; there is no religiosity. We speak and talk like this all the time; we're accessible. It's life conversation, not Sunday conversation. We are the opposite of Christian Smith's moralistic, therapeutic deism. There is no show. And humility; this is the real me, and I have stuff. We are on the same level.

Dave, another Midtown staff member, added,

> A safe place to ask questions and to doubt. We don't appear to be a particular denomination—that is, not connected to the religious establishment, where everything is over-professionalized. They see that we are not pastor-centric—they aren't attracted to the superstar model of a pastor. And our worship is not a performance—there is no stage; we call no attention to those who facilitate our singing.

Finally, a female college student at Midtown had this perspective:

> The preaching is honest, gripping, real. I sense that the ministers struggle with real issues just like all of us. And I can tell that the ministry team looks out for each other.

I heard similar things at Ethos; Rachel, a staff member there, said,

> Freedom to find—or help create—ministry. A very simple church structure—Sunday worship and small groups. Around that, room to initiate and create and experiment.

And Cyrus, another member of the Ethos staff, answered,

They feel welcome and received where they are. Don't have to fit a mold. Don't have to be at some particular place, socially, morally, or theologically. And they value our authenticity. We are pretty real here. No BS.

Lastly, a male college student at Ethos shared what drew him there:

I feel safe here. I can just be me. I can ask any question I want, and no one will be shocked. It's okay to ask questions—even if you are not sure you believe.

Key themes were repeated in almost every conversation: authenticity, simplicity, humility; a sense of empowerment; "real" relationships. Perhaps most importantly, participants felt welcome and received where they were, even with their doubts. To this last point, the mission statement on the Ethos website reads,

Whether you are a devoted follower of Jesus, a skeptic giving this whole church thing a shot, or somewhere in between—you are welcome here. At Ethos we will never assume that you have your life together, if you won't make that assumption about us. We are a group of imperfect people, loved by a perfect God. . . . We hope Ethos will become a place where you find life in Jesus Christ.[18]

One Conviction, One Observation: Two Choices

One conviction and one observation have led me to two viable choices. The *conviction* is that the generations need to be together—infants to octogenarians, and *this includes twentysomethings*. The *observation* is that twentysomethings are sparsely represented in traditional churches. In light of this conviction and this observation, I find that I have two choices.

The first is to go where twentysomethings are; in my case, that means Ethos or Midtown. My husband and I have committed to doing exactly that in Nashville. The reason is that we know these young adults need older people to walk with them.

The problem with this choice for others with similar convictions is that many communities do not have an Ethos or a Midtown. The twentysomethings may not be attending traditional churches, and indeed they may not be part of a faith community at all. Thus, the second choice is to discover ways to welcome these wandering young adults into our more traditional churches. Both Josh and Emma (in the earlier-mentioned surveys) indicated that they had made some effort to visit various churches, but had not felt welcomed, or had not found what they were looking for. We must ask: "How can we welcome them? How can we offer twentysomethings some of what they are seeking in our less edgy faith communities?" I submit a few suggestions below:

Welcome

Explicitly welcome emerging adults at each gathering, saying, for example, "We are particularly blessed to have among us our twentysomethings. We want to bless you as you move through these challenging years, and we are glad you are here to worship with us today."

Acknowledge

Voice acknowledgment of the unique challenges of this crucial stage of life. For example, offer opportunities to discuss issues of differentiation and individuation that many emerging adults are experiencing, helping them see that differentiating from family and church of origin doesn't have to be done alone; it can be accomplished in connection with others, in community. Other conversations could acknowledge the overwhelming nature of emerging adulthood, and the willingness of this community to offer wisdom and discernment to aid twentysomethings as they adjust to the adult work world, cope with financial responsibility, and navigate a sexually charged environment.

Invite

Invite emerging adults to serve on leadership teams, and then *listen* to them. Let these twentysomethings know that you seek their ideas, their input, and that you want to hear their voices. Empower them to start ministries. Emerging adults have amazing amounts of energy and countless ideas; traditional churches need that energy and those ideas. Listen. Empower. Invite.

Be Authentic; Be Transparent

This young generation craves authenticity. Of course, older generations have witnessed the damage too much transparency can cause, but that should not hinder us from sharing more openly (but wisely) with those coming along behind. This generation is actually interested in the stories of older people; they are also actively seeking mentors. Hearing our stories will build connecting bridges by which these mentoring relationships can form.

Be a Safe Place

Make it known that this church is a safe place to discuss doubts, real doubts about God, his existence, his role in the world, the exclusivity of Jesus's claim, the problem of evil in the world. (Of course, *becoming* a safe place for these questions is part of the journey.) There are other adults—not just young adults—who have questions and will be grateful to know that their questions can be addressed in an atmosphere of love and acceptance—even if there is disagreement.

Lean into God's Presence

Barna and Kinnaman close their book *Churchless* with a moving piece about what faith communities offer that no other community can. They indicate that young adults can meet most of their needs in any number of venues, but only faith communities offer the very presence of God. In fact, when twentysomethings decide to visit a new faith community, they are not really looking for a church; they are "looking for an encounter with God, or if not that explicitly—they are looking for his essence which is love."[19] It will not matter if we welcome them, listen to them, and invite their questions, and it will not matter if we are authentic and can discuss young adult faith development articulately if the powerful presence of God is not among us. Acknowledging God's empowering presence among us and confessing our utter dependence on God draws *all* the generations together into the centrifuge of God's grace.

Notes

[1] *Emma* is a pseudonym, as is *Josh* from the next survey data.

[2] Bonnie Cushing and Monica McGoldrick, "The Differentiation of Self and Faith in Young Adulthood: Launching, Coupling, and Becoming Parents," in *Human Development and Faith: Life Cycle Stages of Body, Mind, and Soul,* ed. Felicity B. Kelcourse (St. Louis, MO: Chalice Press, 2004), 249.

[3] Jeffrey Jensen Arnett, *Emerging Adulthood: The Winding Road from the Late Teens through the Twenties* (New York: Oxford University Press, 2004).

[4] Eleanor Barkhorn, "Getting Married Later Is Great for College-Educated Women," March 15, 2013, www.theatlantic.com/sexes/archive/2013/03/getting-married-later-is-great -for-college-educated-women/274040/.

[5] "Religion among the Millennials," *Pew Research Center,* February 17, 2010, www .pewforum.org/2010/02/17/religion-among-the-millennials/.

[6] George Barna and David Kinnaman, *Churchless: Understanding Today's Unchurched and How to Connect with Them* (Carol Stream, IL: Tyndale Momentum, 2014), 98.

[7] Barna and Kinnaman, *Churchless,* 97.

[8] Barna and Kinnaman, *Churchless,* 97.

[9] David Kinnaman, *You Lost Me: Why Young Christians Are Leaving Church . . . And Rethinking Faith* (Grand Rapids: Baker Books, 2011).

[10] Christian Smith with Patricia Snell, *Souls in Transition: The Religious and Spiritual Lives of Emerging Adults* (New York: Oxford University Press, 2009).

[11] Smith, who directs the National Study of Youth and Religion (NSYR), has been conducting longitudinal qualitative and quantitative research since 2003, following the same cohort of 3,000–3,500 young people who were thirteen to seventeen during the first wave of the research project; sixteen to twenty-one during the second wave; eighteen to twenty-three in the third. Several major books have resulted from this research; the most relevant for our purposes are (with Melinda Lundquist Denton) *Soul Searching: The Religious and Spiritual Lives of American Teenagers* (New York: Oxford University Press, 2005), and *Souls in Transition: The Religious and Spiritual Lives of Emerging Adults.*

[12] Arnett, *Emerging Adulthood,* 222.

[13] Sharon Daloz Parks, *The Critical Years: Young Adults and the Search for Meaning, Faith, and Commitment* (San Francisco: HarperCollins, 1986), 96.

[14] Brian Simmons, *Wandering in the Wilderness: Changes and Challenges to Emerging Adults' Christian Faith* (Abilene, TX: Abilene Christian University Press, 2011), 31.

[15] Smith, *Souls in Transition,* 48–51.

[16] See, for example, Smith, *Souls in Transition;* Simmons, *Wandering in the Wilderness.*

[17] Barna and Kinnaman, *Churchless.*

[18] www.ethoschurch.org/about/.

[19] Barna and Kinnaman, *Churchless,* 193.

Chapter Fifteen

Engaging the Elders among Us

Diane E. Shallue

Vernon, age seventy-eight, enjoyed participating in a day services program for children and older adults created by a Lutheran congregation in Minneapolis, Minnesota, in 1995. Vernon told me,

> The kids are the best thing about this place. I prefer children to older adults, believe it or not, because I enjoy them more. That is the reason I came here—because they have children. Putting younger people with older people keeps the older people young. . . . If you live with just older people, you get withdrawn. (Personal interview, October 12, 2001)

From 2000 to 2002, I volunteered, observed, and interviewed participants and staff at a facility, which I will call Hilltop Day Services, for my doctoral dissertation. As a result of that research and my twenty-five years of experience serving in congregations, I have come to the conclusion that more interactions between older adults and children need to be intentionally fostered for the sake of the mental and spiritual health of older adults. In this chapter, I will explore how these intergenerational interactions help older adults create meaning and purpose, and how congregations can play a role in fostering these interactions.

An *Intergenerational* Day Care

Hilltop Day Services was built as an intergenerational day care with separate wings for the children and older adults with a common entrance. The staff created a lively, upbeat program while attempting to reproduce a home-like place where the older adults could play the role of a respected elder. The energy of the children contributed to the lively atmosphere, adding fun for the older adults as well as the staff. The older adults took on the role of elder as wise, valued, and respected adults, restaged with benefits for all involved.

Ageism

Ageism is an issue in American culture. Competent adults go to work, are independently mobile, and have good memories. Older adults lose these abilities and have to adjust to a negative view of themselves, a view encompassed in the term "elderly." The term "ageism" was penned by Robert Butler, director of the National Institute on Aging, in 1975. Butler defines ageism as "a process of systematic stereotyping of and discrimination against people because they are old, just as racism and sexism accomplish this with skin color and gender. Old people are categorized as senile, rigid in thought and manner, old-fashioned in morality and skills."[1] Because of ageism, older adults are often viewed in a negative way and not valued. Petunia, a sixty-nine-year-old participant, told me about her experience of not being valued:

> I told you about that one place that was a church, and I knew that I would not stay there. They led us to the place where they keep people like myself. They led us to the *basement*—like they were having coal delivered and they did not want anyone to see it. I did not think it was very appropriate at all, and I knew that was not the place for me. Like I said, I came . . . here and saw that playroom there with kids playing in it. I said to my daughter, "This is the place for me." (personal interview, October 8, 2001)

Older adults want to be respected and have worthwhile tasks. Many of the older adults told me that they came to Hilltop to be volunteers, to help with the children, or as their "day out." They did not self-identify as dependent adults who could not be home alone during the day; here they could be *elders*, not the *elderly*.

Elder vs. Elderly

At the day care facility, I talked to the directors of both the adult side and the child side about the difference between the concepts of *elder* and *elderly*. The director of the adult side explained,

> When you say *elder*, it has a connotation of respect—people who are wiser, who . . . have done lots of things. There is pride, success, achievement. When you say *elderly*, it has a connotation that means weak, frail, needy, and dependent. (personal interview, September 26, 2002)

The director of the child side gave me very similar definitions of the two words:

> An *elder* is someone who is older than you are, like a mentor—someone you look up to, to give you information about something that they have experienced from their own life. *Elderly* has a connotation of being old and feeble. (personal interview, September 26, 2002)

The directors modeled the respectful behaviors that they wanted the staff to display with the adult participants. As a result, the staff members consistently interacted with the adult participants in attentive and respectful ways that promoted a self-image as a valued elder.

Aging and Meaning

Aging is a journey that all of us travel. In the last century, the West has seen aging as a problem to be solved through science and technology. Science asks, "What can we do about it?" rather than asking, "What does it mean?" Medical technology has lengthened the period of old age, but drained it of meaning or purpose.

Sharon Kaufman, in her research, found that social interactions play an important part in the process of making meaning. Older people create a coherent picture of their past and a purposeful integrated present by picking and choosing which stories and memories fit with their present interpretation of themselves.[2] Kaufman found that three sources of meaning for older adults were their life stories, historical events, and their experiences and values. Leo Missinne, who also studied meaning-making in aging adults, reports,

> The search of a life that matters for us and for our fellow human beings is the most important part of human life. . . . The question "What is the meaning of my life?" will become more tragic and more urgent when one is in a period of crisis; when one suffers a loss such as the death of a spouse; or when a person feels that the end of life is near—when we are becoming older.[3]

People create a sense of who they are in the present by telling stories of the past, recalling their values, and constructing a coherent picture of themselves in the present.

Vernon is an example of a participant using intergenerational interactions to create meaning out of his memories. Vernon lost a daughter at age five to acute leukemia, but he still talked about her with joy. In this interview, he shared his view of children.

> Children are much more willing to share. They are more willing to forgive. They think entirely different. Like the Bible says, you will see heaven through the eyes of a child. That is true—just watch children closely. We had a man who lived down the block from us. He hated children, even his own. I never knew [my daughter] had done this until she passed away; she loved everybody in the neighborhood. She would go and sit on his lap and just listen and never say a word. And then she would tell him, "I have to go now." Children have a knack for getting people to like them, and they forgive very easily, which most adults don't. . . . So the children keep you young and they are also like teachers.

They teach you that the world is not cruel. (personal interview,
October 12, 2001)

The value Vernon placed on his own daughter and how he interpreted her
loving nature influenced how he perceived and interacted with the children, making meaning out of those experiences.

Benefits of Intergenerational Interactions

The benefits of intergenerational programs for older adults have been
shown through numerous research studies. Carmen Hernandez and Marta
Gonzalez used service-learning pedagogy to engage elders and college
youth, finding a reduction of stereotypes and improvement in their well-
being.[4] Margaret Skropete, Alf Colvin, and Shannon Sladen,[5] as well as
Morita Kumiko and Kobayashi Minako,[6] discovered when older adults
interacted with children and shared stories, the older adults increased
their feelings of dignity. The interactions provided meaningful engagement for all.

The staff at the day care facility where I did my research recognized
these benefits. One of the staff in the Adult Day Services program said this:

> I think the program is so important for the grandmas and
> grandpas as well as the children. Grandpa Jacob started volun-
> teering one day a week on Wednesdays in a child room. At first
> he just sat in a chair and the children would come up to him.
> Now he has no time to sit—he is so busy with the children. It
> has made a changed man of him. . . . One morning, one girl was
> being dropped off by her grandmother and did not want to stay
> and was crying. Then the little girl saw Grandpa Jacob coming
> in the door and she said "down" and ran over to Grandpa Jacob.
> He picked her up and she was fine. The grandmother left feeling
> better and Grandpa Jacob felt really good that the little girl was
> happy to see him. (personal interview, January 14, 2001)

I observed many times that interactions with the children improved the
well-being of the older adults, even those with dementia.

Creating Caring Communities in Congregations

Older adults possess a foundation of faith with deep connections to God and a strong sense of spirituality. They can teach others about the finality of life, the value of contemplation, and the joy of relationships. Yet, many congregations struggle to create respectful intergenerational interactions with their aging members.

As valued elders, older adults are strong branches, nourishing the vine that is the church, part of a caring community that connects all ages. Janet Ramsey and Rosemary Blieszer, in their research, found this to be true. They state,

> Young and old persons need each other, to be community together. In our contemporary life, age groups are too often seg- regated, but intentional intergenerational activities can enrich our lives, in families, in congregations, in civic organization. They help to mitigate isolation and celebrate experiential differ- ences across generations. Older adults bring history to life—they are the holders of stories for the community, thus they help it to know its roots, even while they join younger persons to enliven life together. . . . It is a community joy and challenge to accom- pany older adults. For elders who are sick in mind or body, contacts with a caring community should be included in all pre- scriptions for health.[7]

The benefits go both ways—to the elders and back to younger adults. Elders can teach how to experience loss in a compassionate way. Losses come gradually or suddenly, but are usually unanticipated and difficult to deal with. Elders can teach younger generations how to (a) accept loss, (b) main- tain one's sense of identity in the face of loss, (c) create a caring community that can support a person in the midst of loss, and (d) show compassionate care for others. These valuable lessons are going to be needed for a whole generation of aging Boomers.

Implications for Congregations

Most congregations are *multi*generational, but they may focus on only one or two age groups. How can leaders in congregations model the types of behaviors that promote valuable *inter*generational interactions? How can their ministry with older adults go deeper, beyond socialization to improving their mental and spiritual well-being? How can older adults be connected to younger families in intentional ways?

Engaging older adults in conversation with younger members can be a beneficial process. Missinne says, "In order to discover the meaning of my life, I need to express myself, to talk about it with someone."[8] Through discussion and willingness to listen, younger and older people can define their values to help each other find meaning and purpose. Ramsey and Blieszner share, "As human beings, we appear to be compelled to enter a meaning-making process almost immediately after a crisis, telling others the story of our emotional suffering."[9] When a person is badly shaken, telling stories about the event can facilitate healing.

Lois Knutson found that careful listening to older adults was beneficial for the whole family. She states, "As senior adults and their families discern the spiritual meaning of their lives, pastoral care helps them to remember that God who was with them in the past continues to be with them in the present and promises to be with them in the future."[10] This is another way that conversation between the generations can be healthy for all ages. Although meaning cannot be given, spiritual guides can assist older adults and their families to find purpose in life through listening, sharing of insights, and framing their reflections with the love of God.

Knutson goes on to suggest some elements of these types of visits.

- Approach this visit with prayer, attention, and sensitivity
- Use active listening to create a sacred space
- Follow the agenda of the senior adult
- Include rituals of the faith tradition such as scriptural readings and/or prayer
- Give them time to gather their thoughts and feelings
- Speak slowly and distinctly to those with health challenges
- Use symbolic items and pictures such as a cross or a picture of Jesus as the Good Shepherd[11]

Congregations might assign families with children to visit older adults monthly to foster these types of conversations.

In addition to listening, congregations can create rituals to affirm and connect older adults to the community. Dayle Friedman says, "Ritual can serve as an orienting anchor in the midst of confusing, alienating losses, changes and stresses."[12] He continues,

> Sadly, elders in our society have little ritual to mark or frame their experiences. The great transitions of older adulthood go largely unmarked. Between retirement, which might be acknowledged in a social way, and death, there is no normative or even common ceremony. . . . Infusing old age with rituals can teach old and young the meaning of their existence and the justification for their continued being.[13]

Rituals could be created for transitions such as retirement, becoming a grandparent, or moving to assisted living. Active older adults could participate in the ritual of baptism, become mentors and encouragers for younger families, and help congregations integrate all generations.

More significant than programing, congregations could help older adults do a life review. This type of sacred remembrance would be beneficial to them, their personal family, and the faith community. A sacred remembrance is searching one's memories for the presence and purpose of God and then sharing those memories in community. A congregation is an ideal place for this type of remembrance. Remembering the mighty acts of God sustains faith and provides a witness to the presence of God. This is storytelling at a deep and meaningful level, of value to all ages but especially to older adults to enhance their mental and spiritual health.

Congregations who are intentional about connecting the generations will find the lives of their elders enhanced, helping them create a sense of meaning and purpose through visits, conversations, rituals, and life review. Tapping into the wisdom of older adults regarding how to deal with loss and how to create meaning from memories creates elders who can witness to the work of God, building a stronger faith community.

Notes

[1]Robert N. Butler, MD, *Why Survive? Being Old in America* (New York: Harper & Row, 1975), 12.

[2]Sharon R. Kaufman, *The Ageless Self: Sources of Meaning in Late Life* (Madison: University of Wisconsin Press, 1986), 150.

[3]Leo Missinne, "The Search of Meaning of Life in Older Age," *Ageing, Spirituality and Well-Being*, ed. Albert Jewell (London: Jessica Kingsley Publishers, 2004), 115.

[4]Carmen Requena Hernandez and Marta Zubiaur Gonzalez, "Effects of Intergenerational Interactions on Aging," *Educational Gerontology* 34, no. 4 (2008): 303.

[5]Margaret Skropete, Alf Colvin, and Shannon Sladen, "An Evaluative Study of the Benefits of Participating in Intergenerational Playgroups in Aged Care for Older People," *BMC Geriatrics* 14 (October 2014): 109.

[6]Morita Kumiko and Kobayashi Minako, "Interactive Programs with Preschool Children Bring Smiles and Conversation to Older Adults: Time-Sampling Study," *BMC Geriatrics* 13 (March 2013): 111.

[7]Janet L. Ramsey and Rosemary Blieszner, *Spiritual Resiliency and Aging: Hope, Relationality, and the Creative Self* (Amityville, NY: Baywood Publishing, 2012), 65.

[8]Missinne, "The Search of Meaning," 118.

[9]Ramsey and Blieszner, *Spiritual Resiliency and Aging*, 100.

[10]Lois D. Knutson, "Pastoral Care of Elders and Their Families," *Aging, Spirituality, and Religion: A Handbook*, vol. 2, eds. Melvin A. Kimble and Susan H. McFadden (Minneapolis: Fortress Press, 2003), 208.

[11]Knutson, "Pastoral Care of Elders," 209–10.

[12]Dayle S. Friedman, "An Anchor amidst Anomie: Ritual and Aging," *Aging, Spirituality and Religion*, vol. 2, eds. Melvin A. Kimble and Susan H. McFadden (Minneapolis: Fortress Press, 2003), 135.

[13]Friedman, "An Anchor amidst Anomie," 136.

Part Five

UNIQUE MINISTRIES AND APPROACHES

Chapter Sixteen

Exploring Intentionally Intergenerational Environments

Tammy Tolman

"If you want to go fast, go alone. If you want to go far, go together."
—African Proverb

It was a simple Passover meal in a home where all ages gathered to eat, drink, laugh, and be together—but mostly to remember. Over the past ten years, in our intergenerational faith community, an intentional environment has been created where there is genuine love and acceptance. After the simple meal, we huddled into a smaller space, comfortable to be close together. With forty candles ablaze, we recounted the things Jesus said on the night he ate with his friends, two thousand years ago.

As all ages shared a truth of Jesus, there was a special silence when Sophie, one of our youngest, stood to read softly and seriously, "I am the way and the truth and the life," before extinguishing one of the candles. Then one of our older participants stood to read her statement. She couldn't help but do a little skip of pure joy as she said, "Praise God," and God's love oozed from her. On we went until there was one candle left. All focused and centered on that candle as we remembered the thirty-nine lashes. We remembered, we prayed, we worshiped as we huddled together in a room two thousand years later.

As we concluded, I expected many would leave, considering the range of young families, older couples, teenagers, and empty nesters there on that eve of the Easter weekend. Surely once the formalities were over, it would be time for them to go—but no one left. In fact, the talking was so loud at times I could hardly hear myself speak. All ages were laughing and telling stories together; it wasn't men in one corner, women in another, and teens on their devices in another corner. It was real conversation, across all ages. An environment was created where all ages could *collide*.[1] It was beautiful. It was a night to remember, an experience to anchor us all to each other and to Jesus.

Doing Life Together on a Sunday

But what does doing life together on a typical Sunday look like? Admittedly, it is a challenge to draw all generations together on a Sunday morning in a 9:30–11:00 time slot.

This particular morning was a very wet morning; we expected that many would just stay at home, but the room was full of people of all ages ready for this particular intergenerational experience where everyone was encouraged to mix around the tables. We began by worshiping in song; then we prayed around the tables. Then there were visuals, some stories, and a drama from the front to help us explore the fundamental truth that we are created for community and that we are better together (even though it is challenging). The stories brought laughter and tears and helped connect all ages at the same time. Through drama, story, and an interactive experience with Play-doh, we discovered that as we press into each other, we can choose to appreciate, teach, and love each other, and that this is God's desire for a faith community.

One mother I spoke with afterward said she had really wanted to sit quietly in church today without her kids, but then admitted that she had thoroughly enjoyed the environment that was created which allowed her to spend time with God *and* her children.

Another mother with three children under the age of three said, "Normally my husband is in the nursery with one of our children, I am in the cry room with the other, but today we were able to REALLY be here, all in together. It was a nice change."

An older man said he "walked in, saw the tables set up, and thought . . . *oh, no.*" But he made the effort to come over to me and say that he had really engaged in the morning and had ultimately loved the opportunity.

For the concluding event of the morning, I had asked all table participants to combine their Play-Doh and create something together, experiencing how we are transformed by being together.

All the members of one family were sitting at a table making their own things from Play-doh; but when they joined it all together, they made a scene that they couldn't have made individually. It was unique and intriguing.

An older woman from another table shared that God had given her a specific insight with regard to the Play-doh combination. She described how she had fashioned the various Play-doh balls at her table in a way that allowed every color to still be vibrantly displayed, demonstrating visually that we can be "all together but with our personalities intact." It was a beautiful way to see the body of Christ.

A Lifelong, Intentional, Relational, Holistic Environment

The following key words/phrases have given us language and a foundation to rethink and change the way we do church, in order to draw closer to God and to each other. Those who are willing to walk this journey together are being transformed by the experience.

We are a "lifelong, intentional, relational, holistic environment where all generations do life together."

- Lifelong: We are never meant to stop learning. The best time to start is when we are born; the best time to stop is when we die. It is important to see discipleship as a lifelong learning journey for everyone at every age.
- Intentional: We need to be focused with the end in mind, and to be intentional about making every moment matter, always

leading toward the final goal. If we practice *intentionality*, we might be surprised how often God can be a part of every aspect of life. If we are not intentional about drawing close to God and to others, other things will distract us from what is important; and of course, there is an enemy who is very intentional in distracting us all (John 10:10).

- Relational: Deep, authentic relationships take love, acceptance, listening, and sharing over *time*—lots of time. Lack of time is often an excuse for not being able to have deep relationships. We have no less time today than in any other era. What is important is where we spend our time. Relationships with God and each other are the only things that last beyond eternity; surely the best way to use our time is in deep, authentic relationships.

- Holistic: We need to reconsider the silos in our lives. In every aspect of life, our tendency is to segment, isolate, and specialize. We were created for community with all parts of ourselves (physically, emotionally, socially, intellectually, psychologically) as well as with other people.

- Environments: When we change our language from "programs" to "environments," we start to reconsider how to use time and resources to create spaces where faith formation can occur. What environments can we create that will help people of all ages connect, worship, serve, and grow together?

- All generations: Our story becomes more authentic and valid when we are intersecting with all generations, when we understand that we are part of a much *bigger* story. This understanding comes about in two ways:
  - Knowing we are part of God's story that has always been and always is.
  - Walking with those who are further down the track than we are and helping those on the track behind us.

- Do life together: Life is a journey with others, a joint passion, a story shared. Our faith and lives need to interconnect in the things we do every day.

Part five of this book offers half a dozen *lifelong, intentional, relational, holistic environments where all generations have opportunities to do life together,* specific environments where the generations collide. There are endless ways to create environments when we *intentionally* gather to be *relational* and *holistic* in places where the *generations* can *do life together* their whole *life long,* with a core desire to draw closer to God.

Note

[1]*Collide* is the title of a book Tammy has written focusing on intergenerational ministry.

Chapter Seventeen

Faith Storytelling with All Ages

Karen DeBoer

A professor shared his story as part of "This Month's Psalm," a three-minute storytelling time held during worship in which anyone could offer to read all or part of a Psalm and describe how it connected to his or her life.

The 60ish professor settled himself in front of the microphone, opened his Bible, and announced, "Psalm 13, a psalm of David:"

How long, LORD? Will you forget me forever? How long will you hide your face from me? How long must I wrestle with my thoughts and day after day have sorrow in my heart? How long will my enemy triumph over me?

Look on me and answer, LORD my God. Give light to my eyes, or I will sleep in death, and my enemy will say, "I have overcome him," and my foes will rejoice when I fall.

But I trust in your unfailing love; my heart rejoices in your salvation. I will sing the LORD's praise, for he has been good to me.

The professor closed the Bible, took a deep breath, looked over the congregation, and said, "This psalm is my life story.

"I have struggled with depression for the past twenty-five years," he continued. "It comes and goes with greater and lesser intensity. At the moment, I feel quite strong. But there have been many deep valleys along the way.

"David's opening phrase, 'How long, LORD? Will you forget me forever?' whispers in my heart every day in some form. But I know I need to travel with him to the end of the psalm where he declares, 'But I trust in your unfailing love. . . . I will sing the LORD's praise, for he has been good to me.' This psalm—and others like it—are my lifeline."[1]

Author and congregation member Syd Hielema says those stories had a ripple effect on his community: "All of us who are gathered for worship— from the 5-year-old to the 95-year-old—realize in a deeper way that we are all redeemed sinners, loved by Jesus, shaped by grace, struggling with our own 'thorns in the flesh,' longing for wholeness. We all stand together at the cross with open hands."

Developing an intergenerational storytelling culture in which sharing faith stories becomes a rich, natural pathway to growing together in Christ doesn't require multiple hours of strategic planning or extra committee meetings. What it does require is a commitment to making space for faith stories in your congregation's life together, and then taking steps to share stories together.

Begin with a conversation about the value of making space for faith storytelling using the following talking points.

Stories Shape Our Identity

In a *New York Times* article called "The Stories That Bind Us," author Bruce Feiler described the results of research conducted by Emory University psychologists Marshall Duke and Robyn Fivush.[2] The researchers developed a test called "Do You Know?" which contained twenty questions about family history and asked children to answer the questions.[3] Comparing the results of the test with results of other psychological tests the children had taken and then reassessing the children again after the events of September 11, 2001, revealed that the more children knew about their family history, the greater their sense of self-worth. As Feiler reports, "Dr. Duke said that children who have the most self-confidence have what he and Dr. Fivush call a strong 'intergenerational self.' They know they belong to something bigger than themselves."[4]

Sharing with each other stories of God's faithfulness shapes our identities as children of God. Those stories remind us to whom we belong, and sharing them in intergenerational contexts reminds us that we *all* belong.

Stories Nurture Faith

Telling the stories of God at work in our lives reminds us of God's faithfulness, brings to life the stories and promises found in Scripture, and nurtures our faith.

About ten years ago, the church I attend did a summer series on the Lord's Prayer, selecting a different phrase for our focus each week. The worship planning team printed the words of the prayer in permanent marker along the top of a twenty-five-foot banner of laminated butcher paper and hung it from the stage in front of the worship area.

Each week after the message, all ages were invited to come forward and add something to the banner under the phrase that had been that day's focus: words of praise written in colored marker under "Our Father in heaven, hallowed be your name," descriptions of the ways and places we see God at work under "your kingdom come, your will be done, on earth as it is in heaven," post-it notes of supplication under "Give us today our daily bread," and so on. By the end of the summer, we had created a giant visual of all we had learned. It was really something.

One service in particular stands out in my memory. On the day we were learning about the phrase "Forgive us our sins, as we have forgiven those who sin against us," our pastor invited Josephine to come forward and share her story. Josephine and her two boys had come to Canada from Rwanda. During the genocide, members of her family had been murdered by people she and her family had known all their lives. Josephine described how those events had impacted her understanding of what it means to forgive and the deep pain she experienced as she lived out of and lived into forgiveness.

I'm reminded of Josephine's testimony every time I pray the Lord's Prayer. I imagine anyone who heard her story that day does the same.[5] Stories of God at work in the lives of others bring the words of Scripture to life in ways that nurture our own faith.

Stories Bless and Strengthen the Body

Space is made for faith storytelling at my colleague Syd's church (yes, same Syd). One Sunday, a mother whose baby was being baptized read a letter she had written to the congregation. She herself had been baptized as a baby in that same church and had experienced some rebellious, difficult years as a teenager and young adult. In her letter, she thanked the congregation for fulfilling the vow they had made when she was baptized there as a baby, for not giving up on her, for continuing to pray for her, and for extending grace and love to her. She added, "Thank you for being our family, for loving us, and for raising our son up in your prayers even before he was born."

Syd says, "It's easy for a baptism to become a family event with spectators like a hockey game: family members are the players on the ice and the church members are the fans in the stands."[6] Understanding baptism as being a congregational event impacts the way it is celebrated.

How might the inclusion of storytelling transform celebrations in your congregation from hockey games with spectators to congregational events in which all of God's family is blessed and strengthened?

Stories Invite Grace

We respond to opinions differently than we do to stories.

> Opinions tend to be black and white. Stories are multi-colored.
> Opinions can become walls to hide behind. Stories render
>   us vulnerable.
> Opinions divide people into us and them. Stories bring
>   people together.

Opinions can generate negative emotions. Stories often generate
more loving emotions.[7]

In a North American culture where opinions are more likely to be posted than discussed, and where the responses involve "liking," "disliking," "unfriending," and "retweeting," stories invite a more radical response—they provide us with the opportunity to reflect the presence of Jesus living in us through the Holy Spirit and they invite us to live into and out of grace.

Four Things to Keep in Mind When Making Space for Faith Storytelling

1. *Stories are a gift.* Handle with care. Steven Covey says, "Most people don't listen with the intent to understand; they listen with the intent to reply."[8] Listen well.
2. *Not all stories are yours to tell.* Stories belong to the owner. Respect privacy and obtain permission prior to telling a story.
3. *Stories can be ordinary.* Tish Harrison Warren says, "I often want to skip the boring, daily stuff to get to the thrill of an edgy faith. But it's in the dailiness of the Christian faith—the making the bed, the doing the dishes, the praying for our enemies, the reading the Bible, the quiet, the small—that God's transformation takes root and grows."[9] Stories help us see God in the ordinary details of our lives. They don't need to be about dramatic life-changing events in order to have value.
4. *Storytellers need varying supports.* Not everyone feels comfortable telling their story. Some may prefer to write it down and read it or to be interviewed while seated. Holding a visual aid or other link to the story can be helpful, as can offering to film the story-teller and play the video rather than having them tell the story in person. Frameworks such as a template for storytelling and a time limit may also be appreciated.

Where to Begin

Wondering where to begin faith storytelling with all ages? Start where you are.

- List all the places within your church where faith formation (both in large groups and small groups) is already happening. Some examples: worship, midweek ministry, service, children's ministry programs, intergenerational small groups, adult Bible study.
- Note one to three places where you would like to build upon what is already happening by making space for storytelling.
- Add some of the ideas that have already been bubbling up in your mind around what you might do.
- Visit the online toolkits on *Faith Storytelling* and *The Intergenerational Church*[10] for a variety of ideas to try and to jumpstart your own thinking.
- Try and try again!

When I was gathering resources for *The Intergenerational Church* toolkit, I had the pleasure of interviewing several members of intergenerational small groups. Rebekah, a group member from Winnipeg, told me that what keeps the group members coming back are the life-altering moments they've shared together—moments like the time a couple arrived with their newly adopted baby because they wanted the first people to meet the baby to be the ones who had walked the journey of adoption with them; and the time when one of the group leaders died suddenly and everyone gathered on the scheduled date anyway, eating and mourning and remembering with each other and with the teens who didn't normally come anymore but showed up on that day and as the children wandered in and out of the kitchen.

God's story, intertwined with their own stories, is what binds Rebekah's group together and shapes their identities as members of God's big family. As Rebekah says,

> In the Bible, we have [the stories of] Daniel, Moses, and others to show us God's faithfulness, but we also have those stories of God's faithfulness in the people sitting next to us. You can know and have hope and understand God's relationship with you through your relationship with others.
>
> That's what it's all about.[11]

I couldn't agree more.

Notes

[1]Syd Hielema, "Faith Storytelling Kit: A User's Guide" (Grand Rapids: Faith Formation Ministries, 2016), 4–5, www.crcna.org/FaithFormation/toolkits/.

[2]Bruce Feiler, "The Stories That Bind Us," *The New York Times*, March 15, 2013, www .nytimes.com/2013/03/17/fashion/the-family-stories-that-bind-us-this-life.html.

[3]Questions included: Do you know where your grandparents grew up? Do you know where your mom and dad went to high school? Do you know where your parents met? Do you know an illness or something really terrible that happened in your family? Do you know the story of your birth?

[4]Feiler, "The Stories That Bind Us."

[5]The story of Josephine and the Lord's Prayer was previously published by Karen DeBoer as a blog post titled "Learn the Lord's Prayer with All Ages" on *The Network* on February 15, 2017, network.crcna.org/intergenerational-ministry/learn-lords-prayer -all-ages/.

[6]Syd Hielema, "Frequently Asked Questions," *The Banner,* April 19, 2013, www .thebanner.org/departments/2013/04/frequently-asked-questions.

[7]Syd Hielema, "Where Does Jesus Live in Your Church (Part 3)," *The Network*, November 8, 2016, network.crcna.org/faith-nurture/where-does-jesus-live-your -church-part-3.

[8]Steven Covey, *Seven Habits of Highly Effective People* (New York: Free Press, 1989), 239.

[9]Tish Harrison Warren, *Liturgy of the Ordinary* (Downers Grove , IL: Intervarsity Press, 2016), 35–36.

[10]Participants of this workshop at InterGenerate 2017 explored a variety of faith storytelling resources and tools, all of which can be found online in the *Faith Storytelling* toolkit and *The Intergenerational Church* toolkit. The kits have been curated by Faith Formation Ministries of the Christian Reformed Church in North America and will provide you with an abundance of ideas. You may access them at www.crcna.org /FaithFormation.

[11]Karen DeBoer, "Sticking Together: Profile of an Intergenerational Small Group," accessed March 1, 2018, www.crcna.org/FaithFormation/toolkits/intergenerational -church-toolkit/sticking-together-profile-intergenerational-group/.

Chapter Eighteen

Walking beside Each Other

Linda Staats

"The principles that describe the gospel's transmission across cultures could just as easily describe the way we ferry faith across generations."[1]

I am continually in awe of the Holy Spirit's stirring when generations are brought together. At a recent "Glocal" (a combination of global and local) Gathering hosted by my national denomination, youth and adults gathered for forty-five minutes of interaction in the Cross†Generational Engagement workshop[2] I was facilitating. When the adults and youth reflected on their experience and conversations with one another, there were tears—tears of appreciation, tears at the newly found understandings. There were also smiles—smiles inspired by the power of face-to-face authentic exchanges between generations. This was the result of a mere forty-five minutes together.

In 2009, I began leading workshops on intergenerational ministry as one expression of the newly created Glocal Gatherings.[3] The focus of a Glocal Gathering is introducing the concept of "accompaniment," a lens and foundation for ministry and mission. Accompaniment is the practice of "walking beside the other," as Christ walks beside us, for the purpose of restoration and reconciliation within our communities (local) and the world (global) (2 Cor. 5:11–21).

Cross†Generational Foundation

Too often our image of mission is of youth going on a mission trip or a small group of adults, often consisting of one or two generations, traveling somewhere, "over there," to serve. Ministry seen through the lens of accompaniment offers a new perspective and means to be the full body of Christ.

Ministry viewed through the lens of accompaniment encourages us to crisscross and connect the borders of age and stage that separate us—right here and right now, within our churches. In doing so, our congregations and households become infused with a new perspective, a deepened sense of urgency and connection with one another, locally and globally. A congregation's potential to bring the generations together is tapped as they accompany and engage one another in the ministry and mission of sharing the good news of Jesus Christ.

Ministry and mission are strengthened at all levels when the gifts of every generation are woven into the very fabric of a faith community. Through engagement of all generations, a congregation has an opportunity to introduce individuals and households to a healthy perspective of what it means to be a disciple. The outcome is a ministry that meaningfully engages children, youth, young adults, adults, and elders into its very life and witness. When we practice accompaniment across the borders and boundaries of age that exist in our own congregation, then we are better equipped to go beyond the walls of our church to walk alongside others, as Christ walks beside us.

Accompaniment: Values and Action

The journey of accompanying one another across generations begins when we recognize and commit to five intertwined *values* in our relationships:

- Vulnerability
- Mutuality
- Inclusivity

- Sustainability
- Empowerment

The ministry of accompaniment bears fruit when our *actions* are based on

- Mutual decision-making
- Sharing resources
- Recognizing expertise
- Telling stories
- Building networks across borders of age and stage in life

Derived from my conversations facilitated between youth and adults at ELCA-hosted Glocal Gatherings in the United States and Puerto Rico, the descriptions and questions for the *values* and *actions* that follow are meant to stimulate rich and meaningful conversations. Engaging in these conversations in mixed age groups will give insight into the generational culture within one's congregation, community, and household.

Following your reflection and discussion of each *value* and *action* ask:

- What are we able to celebrate in our cross†generational ministry that is in alignment with accompaniment values and actions?
- What existing ministry can we simply tweak to become more effective?
- Is there an action we need to add to our ministry to more effectively accompany one another across the generations?

Utilize these questions when planning and evaluating one's cross†generational ministry through a lens of accompaniment.

Values

The following values ground, support, and guide cross†generational relationships and our work in God's world.

Vulnerability

Vulnerability is opening ourselves up to God's reconciliation in our relationships. Being vulnerable helps us face our suspicions and stereotypes of "the other." In our culture, vulnerability often means weakness, but Jesus shows us that vulnerability is an openness to giving up control and power.

- What are examples in my community of faith of one group or generation giving up power or control for another?
- Do people play together, enjoying silly, safe games? Are laughter and tears shared?
- Are there explicit guidelines for appropriate roles, boundaries, and safe relationships between generations?
- How can being vulnerable open one up to a deepening, authentic relationship with people of another generation? With those across the street or around the globe?

Mutuality

Mutuality is built upon trust with one another. Mutuality is offering thoughtful care and working toward deeper relationships because we value another's well-being, just as we value our own. Proclaiming and living out the gospel of Christ requires time and patience as we make plans and decisions—together.

- How does each generation show concern for the well-being of others in my congregation?
- What are examples of generations making decisions together and working toward deeper trusted relationships?
- How is this value reflected in our congregation's ministry outside our walls?

Inclusivity

In accompanying one another, we look to see who is excluded, why, and by whom. All communities exclude someone. Inclusivity means we commit to including those who are being left out. We ask ourselves, "Who is a part of our community? Who is absent? Why?"

- Think of a time when you were excluded because you were too old or too young. How did you feel?
- When has an individual or a group of people been excluded by our church because of age, intentionally or unintentionally?
- What needs to change in the physical environment in our church for all ages to feel included? Even if our congregation consists

of primarily one or two generations, how can we walk alongside those of another generation in our community?

Sustainability

In cross†generational ministry, sustainability means establishing long-term, authentic relationships between individuals of different generations or ages. Sustainability means we recognize that any given relationship will require tending to sustain it.

- How is the word *sustainability* used in our society and world?
- How does our congregation continue to sustain and maintain vibrant, caring relationships with
  - The frail?
  - The immobile?
  - Students away at college?
  - The newly married?
  - Those serving in the military?
  - Young adults?
  - Those with spouses or family members not engaged in the life of the congregation?

Empowerment

We engage in empowerment when we recognize that relationships often have an imbalance of power and when we struggle to balance and correct those asymmetries. Sometimes empowerment will mean that the person or ministry partner with the most power steps back so that the less powerful one has a chance to shine; or that the more powerful person will work to increase the influence and authority of the less powerful.

Timothy was still a young person, possibly a teenager, when Paul recognized his gifts and encouraged him to lead. Timothy learned by experience and with guidance from a wise elder who empowered him and mentored him. It was accompaniment at its best.[4]

- Share a time when you felt empowered by someone older than you. Younger than you.

- Share a time when you deliberately let go of your authority and equipped and encouraged someone else to lead.

Actions

As we accompany one another across the borders of generations, our *actions* will bear more fruit when they are based around the following approaches.

Resource Sharing

To truly be the body of Christ, one needs to think carefully about how to share resources and receive resources in a way that respects every age and doesn't limit the contributions and gifts of the other. Resources include opportunities, access to decision-makers, education, family connections, property, facilities, time, money, knowledge, and life experience.

- How are resources shared and received in our congregation so it doesn't undermine or limit the contributions of another generation?
- Does every generation in our congregation have access to decision-makers, property, facilities, time, and funds?
- How do the various generations and age-related ministries share space within the church building?
- What are the resources and gifts that each generation has to share in the life of our faith community?

Expertise Recognition

Regardless of age, everyone is a teacher and learner. Every believer is gifted by virtue of their baptism and being one of God's creations. Expertise recognition across generations can be as simple as asking everyone—from age three to one hundred and three—"What is something you are able to do or knowledge you have that you can teach or share with another?" Follow this question with, "What is something you want to learn how to do or to learn more about?" How could this question and exercise give birth to new collaborative, cross†generational ministries?

In the story of David and Goliath, we learn from King Saul's attempt to be supportive of this young person that God had already given David everything he needed to answer God's call and fulfill God's mission. We are fellow workers and servants in the kingdom.

- How is "expertise recognition" practiced across generations in our congregation? Youth ministry? Older adult ministry?
- Is our congregation open to people's gifts, ideas, and opportunities that are not listed on the time and talent sheet?

Storytelling

Storytelling means recognizing God's story is already present—in the other and in their story. Storytelling means creating time and space for sharing and receiving one another's stories. Storytelling across generations is recognizing that each individual's story is shaped by one's life experience and by his or her time and place in history. Accompaniment happens when we exchange stories, expecting our perception of "the other" to change and for respect to grow. Exchanging stories contributes to a community's shared identity.

- When in the life of our faith community and within our household do we hear the daily stories and life-stories of one another?
- How do the faith stories of another generation shape the story of our congregation? Our household?
- How does the Christian narrative shape my own story?

Network Building

Network building is creating trusted relationships across generations. Network building breaks down segregation and division created by age. This is critical if we are to nurture and pass on our faith and build a sustainable faith community.

- Do the majority of adults in our congregation know the names of at least five children or youth?
- Do youth know the names of at least five adults other than those of relatives?

- Give examples of "networking" across generations in our congregation and neighborhood.
- What are examples of mentoring one another across the life span?
- Is there an age group that is excluded and lacks voice and influence in our congregation?
- How can one age group advocate for another?

Thoughtful Decision-Making

We practice thoughtful decision-making when we take seriously the needs of all who will be affected—when we work to hear all voices, paying special attention to the voices of those who are frail, vulnerable, or unable to be "at" church, are home-bound, in college, at work, in prison, or committed care-givers to another generation.

- Are there at least three generations represented on our congregation's boards and teams?
- Which generation makes most of the decisions in our congregation?
- Which generations do these decisions effect?
- Are decisions sometimes made without involving the age group who will be most affected?
- Is there disconnect between the generations represented inside the walls of our church and those represented in the surrounding community?

A Cross†Formed Blessing

May you be blessed this day by viewing one another through God's eyes—in a "cross†formed," grace-filled way of life that goes beyond boundaries of age or stage, familial relationships, bloodlines, and household. And like the characters in the Wizard of Oz, may we be our best because we are journeying together, rather than apart.

Notes

[1]Kenda Creasy Dean, *Almost Christian* (New York: Oxford University Press, 2010), 98.

[2]The Cross†Generational Engagement workshop is based on the ministry of the Global Mission Unit, Evangelical Lutheran Church in America (ELCA) and its concept of "accompaniment." See www.elca.org/en/Our-Work/Global-Church/Global-Mission.

[3]I was asked to lead these gatherings by Rev. Sunitha Mortha, Director of Mission Formation for the Global Mission Unit, ELCA.

[4]Tim. 4:7b–8.

Chapter Nineteen

The Art of Christian Relationships

Liz Perraud

> *You don't need to know much about generational theory to recognize that Mabel (in her eighties) and Fred (in his twenties) might approach life with different worldviews. Mabel and Fred's relationship was ruined over a baseball cap. You can be right or you can be in relationship, and they both wanted to be right. One strongly believed it is okay for a man to wear a hat in a church building, and one strongly believed it is not. Plenty of other people shared each opinion.*
>
> *A disagreement about a hat became about respect or saving face. Each was approached by well-meaning people who asked, "You can understand Mabel/Fred's opinion, can't you? Can you give in a little to smooth things over?" Neither budged. The issue was avoided and an unhealthy atmosphere festered. The children and youth at LOGOS on Wednesday nights probably noticed. There was concern with losing both of these adults, and yet no one had a workable solution.*

As followers of Christ, we have an advantage in knowing how to live in community. Christ taught and modeled the way we are to think about one another, care for one another, and decide to treat one another. We can create glimpses of kingdom-of-God living when we commit to treating one another as children of God. Our responsibility and calling is to work toward this kind of living.

To create such an arena, we first learn *about* God's love for God's people and God's desire for people to love one another. Then we *practice* loving God and loving others until it's second nature—so familiar that it can be done without thinking about it. We practice our faith in a safe environment and then carry that faith to the wider community: the whole salt and light thing.

A weekly LOGOS ministry is an environment to learn and practice loving God and loving others.

Logos is Greek for "word"; and in the first chapter of the book of John, Christ is identified as "the Word" incarnated, or made flesh. LOGOS (the ministry) helps churches bring "the Word" to young people through intergenerational relationships. LOGOS provides the setting for regular, intentional community modeled after the early church as described in Acts 2:42 where "they devoted themselves to the apostles' teaching and to fellowship, to the breaking of bread and to prayer."

> LOGOS offered the solution to Mabel and Fred's broken relationship. They were both at LOGOS every week because they both believed they had been called to serve a specific and purposeful role. Mabel was head cook for dinner, and Fred was a recreation leader and ate with middle schoolers.
>
> Mabel said her life was saved when she was asked to help cook at LOGOS after her husband passed away. It was a step into a loving, intergenerational, consistent community where she had a place to serve—for over fifteen years. Fred, who grew up attending LOGOS, asked to serve in whatever capacity was needed so that he could give back to the ministry and the people who had supported him through some rocky teen years. For him, it was also a step into a loving, intergenerational, consistent community where he had a place to serve.

We each have our own stories—messy, painful, and complicated—and we each can glimpse kingdom-of-God living on our own. But when we bring our stories together, with all the messiness of being right, taking risks, learning to trust, and exposing our vulnerable selves to one another, kingdom building takes off. A foundational belief of GenOn Ministries[1] is that an abundant, life-giving relationship with God through Jesus Christ is the most important thing and that nurturing that relationship is the most important thing the church does. Opportunities for kingdom-of-God living at LOGOS provide the context for nurturing, life-giving relationships with Christ.

With regular, intentional community, it's harder to walk away when life gets messy. Though we live in a culture that generally doesn't commit to much, in LOGOS we commit to being together. Commitment comes not only through the registration of children and youth, but also as parents, grandparents, and other adults in the church find ways to serve based on their gifts and interests. Joyful serving as a calling rather than recruitment out of guilt or obligation makes all the difference in the world. The peer-to-peer and generation-to-generation relationships created through spending time together provide the "stickiness" of the faith, compelling us to return for more.

Tara Dew, Director of Children and Youth Ministry at First Christian Church in El Reno, Oklahoma, says, "LOGOS is the church being the church in a tangible way in a world that often doesn't slow down to even say more than hello to one another. Adults and children in LOGOS have relationships that last beyond their teen years. Some of our best success stories have been how adults have been transformed as they served in ministry."

GenOn Ministries defines LOGOS as a ministry that lives out "the theology and practice of growing intergenerational Christian relationships in a planned and purposeful setting." This approach . . .

- is designed to work in all Christian churches, all sizes, all locations
- engages young people in the life of the church, providing opportunities to build Christian relationships with each other and with mature Christian adults
- teaches churches how to invite adults into ministry using their gifts and talents which provides the staffing to run LOGOS

- gives children and youth the opportunity to learn and practice what it means to be a disciple of Christ
- means regularly scheduled gatherings that create a balanced approach to ministry, nurturing the body, mind, and spirit that include some combination of:
  - Bible Study (apostles' teaching)
  - Recreation (fellowship)
  - Family Time (breaking of bread)
  - Worship Arts (prayers)

The purpose of *Bible Study* at LOGOS is to understand the Bible as the model for Christ-centered living where young people become knowledge-able about the Bible, stories of faith, and Scripture's relationship to their lives. They learn that our relationship with God changes our relationships with others because we are each made in the image of God and so is everyone else.

The purpose of *Recreation* at LOGOS is to experience great fun at the expense of no one else. Recreation provides opportunities to gather for fellowship, to affirm, and to try new things in a noncompetitive atmosphere. Relationships are built in fun settings that model unconditional love and acceptance.

The purpose of *Family Time* at LOGOS is to experience being part of God's family over a shared meal. "Table families" eat together each week for a program year (about six to eight months). The time together is not merely about eating, but about relationships, sharing, and celebration with one another.

The purpose of *Worship Arts* at LOGOS is to learn and practice ways to serve God through worship. Relationships develop and deepen through working together to create artistic expressions to share in corporate worship.

Through over fifty years of working with churches of a variety of sizes, settings, and denominations, GenOn Ministries believes that the best practices of LOGOS include investment by parents or grandparents; leadership in congregational worship; invitation to adults to hear a call to serve; involvement and support by clergy; participation of youth (middle school and high school age); equipped and trained leaders; midweek bridge to faith formation; and most importantly, authentic Christian relationships modeled.

> *Mabel and Fred made it through the LOGOS program year. Each stayed committed to being there, to serving in their roles, and to being part of the community. Healing began to happen even as they basically avoided one another. On the final evening, the relationship won. One apologized to the other in a quiet and meaningful way. The other smiled, acknowledged acceptance, and offered an appreciation for the apology. There was hugging too.*
>
> *A few days later, Mabel posted a message on Facebook explaining why she needed to retire from cooking at LOGOS. She wrote that she was unable to say this on Wednesday night because she would have cried. She explained that it had nothing to do with not loving to cook for the young people, but that her body was giving out, unable to stand and lift like she used to. But she wasn't going away—just doing something different. Next fall, she would be at the welcome table at LOGOS to greet them, check them in, and hand out their nametags. She reminded the children and youth that no matter what, Jesus always loves them and so does she.*
>
> *Many responses acknowledged how perfect her new role would be and offered thanks for her years of cooking and loving the kids. The best comment was from Fred: "Thank you for feeding the generations. I know the kids have a place in their hearts for you."*

God loves you and so do I. Regular, intentional Christian community reminds us of both.

Understanding the "why" of LOGOS is critical—to God, relationships are everything. The "how" is flexible and adaptable. Most churches start LOGOS slow and small. The regular, intentional community provides the time and arena to see one another through God's eyes and to practice treating one another as beloved children of God. We live best that way, even when we don't feel like it, even when we think it's undeserved.

Tara from El Reno also shared, "LOGOS has changed our church completely. We began LOGOS fifteen years ago and had only seven youth at that time. We began with just youth that first semester and then added elementary in the fall. We now have over fifty children and youth here on a Wednesday evening, and the church is alive."

God loves you and so do I. Learned and practiced by young and old and everyone in between week after week, year after year, until it becomes nearly second nature to believe it, live it, and be transformed by it.[2]

Notes

[1]GenOn Ministries is a nonprofit organization that equips Christian communities for discipleship through intergenerational relationships, including training and resources for a LOGOS ministry.

[2]For more information about LOGOS or other intergenerational resources, go to GenOnMinistries.org.

Chapter Twenty

Connecting the Generations through Visual Faith

Nancy S. Going

Imagine a scene at your church where grey heads, well-groomed dad hair, spikey blue adolescent locks, and tousled towheaded preschoolers are angled close together in deep, reflective spiritual conversation. There are smiles and nods as they talk and listen.

Would this be an uncommon scene in your church?

As we think about the daunting task of reconnecting the generations of the church in the first decades of the twenty-first century, three things stand out:

- First, people are living very different lives than in the past where intergenerational relationships happened more naturally in family, neighborhood, and church.
- Second, people of all ages are engaging God's Word less and less,[1] though Scripture remains essential for all spiritual formation.
- Finally, how we deeply link life and Scripture within the hearts and minds of people of all ages is the formidable challenge we face as we seek to return the church to its powerfully effective intergenerational roots.

The Power of Images

Quite simply, images now have power that words do not. The unalterable reality is that images are constantly swirling all around us in the globally accessible world we live in. It is estimated that we are exposed to three thousand advertising images daily, but have the time to process fewer than three hundred of them.[2] No matter our age, we are ingesting them in mass doses and interpreting them in ways that impact our daily lives.

The forces that shaped people who are now over forty, forces that socialized them into members of a culture, included parents, schools, churches, and peers. These influencers relied on *words* in real-time life to convey the values, morals, and human identity that lead to thriving. Today, that process of socialization is unquestionably driven by images as well as words. But these images are absorbed more often individually or with peers rather than explored in community or between generations. Delivery systems like television, the Internet, and smart phones have become primary socializing realities for the younger generations.

Having noted these generational differences however, we must acknowledge that images influence people *of all ages*. The business and marketing world has this figured out, and spends incalculable dollars advertising products and services using images. Images sear messages into our memories. They create emotional links to concrete products.

Two keenly relevant questions for churches addressed in this chapter are how can images of today's world be used to reflect and engage the biblical narrative? And, how can these images work to naturally connect people across generations?

The Process of Visual Faith

Enter the Visual Faith Project, an action research project of Vibrant Faith.[3] Our exploration of what happens when Scripture is paired with images flows from our organization's goal of helping people live a vibrant faith in Jesus Christ. Visuals have been used in a variety of ways throughout church history: to tell the story, to gain attention, to entertain, and to provide Christian education—all good purposes. Pushing deeper here, the goal of the Visual Faith Project is *spiritual transformation* for people of all ages.

Images and the Brain

Through this work, we are reclaiming the biological element in the process of spiritual transformation. That God has "fearfully and wonderfully" wired us has been documented by the nascent field of brain studies, with compelling discoveries about how our brains work as we process our learning, emotions, and experiences—essential aspects of the formation of faith. In his book *Brain Rules,* John Medina makes it clear that vision is by far the most dominant of the five senses, and that what we *see* almost always trumps the data gathered by our other senses.[4] Interestingly enough for this work, the brain's manner of processing the visual is far more complex than originally imagined; it engages not only emotion but *experiences* in the simple process of seeing. Not surprisingly, Medina makes a strong case for pictures as a powerful tool in education and for learning.

As the global population is increasingly learning from images, we need to adjust our teaching and discipling—our transmission of meanings—to embrace all styles of learning. There is no right and wrong about these different modes of processing information. The reality is that much is at stake if we fail to make this significant shift; for example, connecting the message of Jesus with those who desperately need him may be more difficult. Images can be a significant aspect of our transmission of meanings.

Human Longings

In addition, the richness of both our desires and our giftedness lies at the center of the Christian story. As humans, we simply long for Eden—perfect and abundant love, ample resources, excitement, silence, knowledge, power, peace, and intimate relationship with our Creator. The reality of life in our broken world, this less-than-Eden place, leaves us longing for more. Our longings are at the heart of the process of spiritual transformation; but often, the church has tried to disciple people of all ages without engaging human longings.

Longings are God-given reminders that we are dependent beings—we are simply not self-sufficient; we aren't like God. Ultimately, our longings are fulfilled only by the grace and presence of God in our lives.

Our longings and our gifts or strengths are interconnected as well. We may be gifted in various arenas and feel compelled to contribute with those strengths. We want to make a difference—seeking to fulfill our deeply human longings to be needed and to belong.

Engaging life's longings with images is a means of influencing our life journeys. We can employ images that touch hearts. We can unpack those images to shape our view of life. We can engage Scripture with these images, thus allowing the biblical story to live in and through the power of the emotional connections made visible by the image.

The Visual Faith Process

The methodology of the Visual Faith Project is disarmingly simple.

- Choose an image and read Scripture (or conversely, read Scripture and choose an image)
- Ask questions about God, self, and others
- Listen to one another and ask follow-up questions

Or in greater detail:

1. Spread fifty or more printed images in a random fashion on a table. Invite people to select an image they are drawn to.
2. Read Scripture. (Note: the image and Scripture-reading steps can be interchanged so that people choose an image after hearing the section of the Bible.)
3. Ask questions. These questions are offered as suggestions to guide you:
   - What about this image most grabs your attention?
   - What story does this image tell?
   - What story does this section of the Bible tell?
   - Does the Scripture passage relate to your image?
   - Where is God in your image? In the passage?
   - As you listen to responses, other questions may follow. Ask your own questions as you carefully listen to questions and responses. Often these tangents can be the most fruitful parts of a conversation.

Intergenerational Visual Faith

Through Vibrant Faith's research on the process of visual faith, we have discovered that there is especially rich engagement for people when using images with Scripture *intergenerationally*:

- **It evens the playing field.** Centering conversations, Scripture reflection, and learning around images allows the stories of people of all ages to carry equal weight and to be received with equal value.

- **It creates space for the Spirit to move.** The conversations and stories that result from pairing images with Scripture tap into people's memories and emotion in powerful ways. The God whose story is told in Scripture suddenly becomes evident in everyday photographs, and people of all ages are able to see God as active in their own lives and stories.

- **It creates space for connecting.** People of all ages are much more easily drawn in to deep conversations with one another when they are using images to center their conversations. We have frequently heard ministry leaders say: "The images helped my people find words for things that they had just carried inside." This outcome is common in the young and the old, and all those in between.

- **Affective engagement happens very naturally.** Not only is vision by far the strongest of our senses, but brain studies assert that we actually "see" in the memory and emotional centers of our brains.[5] This means that as we engage our memory and emotional centers together, everyday images help us make quite natural emotional connections to one another, to God, and to God's Word.

- **Both males and females are drawn in.** When churches work to create intergenerational activity and conversations, we quite often default to structured conversations or crafts to provide traction for learning. Males especially report a sense of awkwardness with those activities. In our experience, a wide breadth of everyday images to choose from encourages natural conversations and frees all people to actively engage with others.

Visual Faith is above all a "taste and see" experience.

"Come to me, all you who are weary and burdened,
and I will give you rest" (Matt. 11:28).

- Which of these photos reminds you of a time when you were weary?
- Which of these photos connects with your "heavy burdens"?
- Is the "rest" God promises us present in any of these photos?
- What "rest" might God be trying to give you today?

Notes

[1]George Barna, "The Bible in America: 6-Year Trends," *Barna*, June 15, 2016, www.barna.com/research/the-bible-in-america-6-year-trends/.

[2]David Lamoureux, "Advertising: How Many Marketing Messages Do We See in a Day?" *Fluid Drive Media*, February 23, 2012, www.fluiddrivemedia.com/advertising/marketing-messages/.

[3]Find out more about the Visual Faith Project at www.vibrantfaith.org/visualfaith.

[4]John Medina, *Brain Rules: 12 Principles for Surviving and Thriving at Work, Home, and School* (Seattle: Pear Press, 2008), 224.

[5]Medina, *Brain Rules*, 224.

Chapter Twenty-One

All-Age Worship

Olivia B. Updegrove

Most church members know the routine. The children grab an activity at the beginning of worship. They finish it before church has even begun. Worship begins. A few words are said, a song is sung, and the children plow forward to hear the "Children's Sermon/Message/Time/Moment." The adults admire the cute kids. Some are paying attention and ready to answer, "Jesus," when the question comes. Others are upside down on the stairs. An adult finishes the "lesson," and the children then leave the sanctuary and return at the end of worship to whomever is taking them home.

When children are older, they are typically invited to stay in worship. These older children, however, are not often given tools regarding how to participate in their new place. Most churches do not have an intentional process for welcoming children and preparing them to engage in worship, and thus children and their families may be set up for failure. Without important conversations for the entire worshiping community, a child may never feel welcomed as an active participant in Sunday morning worship. Children may get bored, restless, and want to leave, with their family following—because being "cute" is not the same as being treated as a sacred part of Christ's worshiping body.

Children and Worship

Sonja Stewart and Jerome Berryman,[1] who wrote *Young Children and Worship*,[2] believe that children already know God and are able to worship fully. The Children and Worship[3] approach helps guide children in how to live into what they already are able to do. In a conversation with Rev. Olivia Stewart, executive director of Children and Worship Institute, in August 2017, Rev. Stewart said:

> Children and Worship is a multisensory storytelling worship
> approach for children that follows the same order of worship
> that adult church does. Children are invited to enter into a time
> of singing; hearing and watching a Bible story being told; won-
> dering; praying; and finally, a sending or blessing.

The unique and special concepts and activities of Children and Worship are based around the primary elements of worship: gathering in God's name, proclaiming God's Word, responding to the Word, and going in God's name:

- Gathering in God's name: Typically, the children are greeted in a special space. The children come to enter into God's story, to encounter God, to be still with God, and to listen to God.
- Proclaiming God's Word: As children gather around in a circle sitting on the floor, a Bible story is told quietly and slowly using textured two- and three-dimensional materials that children with a variety of learning styles can enjoy. After the story, the children are invited to enter into a time of wonder about the story. The "wondering questions" are designed not primarily to elicit discussion, but rather to provide opportunity for children to wonder internally.
- Responding to the Word: Just as adults in typical worship gatherings respond to the Word in prayer, song, offering, or celebrating the Eucharist and baptisms, the children have the chance to

respond to the Word as well. This is their "work." They may retell the story they just heard; they may paint or use other craft materials to respond to the story; they may pray at the prayer table; or they may tell their own story.

- Going in God's name: As they leave the gathering space, each child is given a special blessing as they go out to be God's disciples in their homes, schools, and communities.[4]

By following the published guidelines of Children and Worship along with ongoing conversations with Rev. Olivia Stewart and her trainers, I have begun integrating this unique approach into our corporate worship on Sunday mornings where all ages worship together.

There are no short cuts. The process matters for both the children and the adults. The primary elements that make Children and Worship a success work only when those in leadership consistently make sure they are staying true to its foundational processes and understandings.

Orientation Matters

A four-week orientation process is offered once a year for the children participating in the Children and Worship programs. For some, this process can seem tedious. However, this process is the foundation that prepares the children with tools to engage in the worship experience most fully. The orientation sets up expectations for the children to successfully engage in worship. As all ages begin to worship together, the orientation process can also prepare those who are older to experience worship more fully.

Adults who are now a part of this Children and Worship process need to become oriented to this way of experiencing worship; they need to understand the language and methods behind how to listen, talk, and hear God as our children learn.

The Story Is Enough

Every time I have introduced stories into a corporate worship experience, pushback comes from adults who are not prepared and oriented to sit and hear the stories. Their comments include, "It is too slow for me"; "I get bored"; "It takes too long"; or even, "How do the kids sit there and listen?"

Understanding the methods and intentions behind Children and Worship can help—thus the orientation. In orientation, participants learn that each story has gone through an intense process to eliminate what does not need to be in the story to make it "enough" to experience. In addition to being oriented to this unique approach, transferring Children and Worship into a larger, all-age worship setting will require some accommodations in order for worshipers to experience the intimacy that makes the stories powerful in both their words and their silence.

1. Everyone must be able to hear and see the story. It is important to invest financial resources to make sure that all are able to actively engage in the story together. The storyteller is not the focus of the story; it is the story that matters. Creating visual ways of focusing—like screens or televisions where a camera can be focused on the hands of the storyteller and the figures—is ideal for those adults who are more comfortable in their pews. If a person is struggling to listen to the story, I always encourage them to come forward and be close to the story as it is told. This is still the ideal way to experience the stories. My church has chairs ready for those who may not be able to sit on the floor.

2. The storytellers, in training, are encouraged to "talk more softly." This way of speaking is still possible in an all-age worship gathering, but a microphone is necessary. Having the microphone allows everyone to hear; the soft voice is more about the tone and less about the actual volume.

3. The children and adults who choose to come to the front are received by a greeter prior to moving into the space where the story is being told. They are asked if they are ready to enter into the story space. We review some of the best ways to be in the space for new people or on days when the kids and adults need more time to prepare. If a child is not ready to worship, they are invited to stay on the front pew with a parent and watch the story with those who have remained seated. As the children and adults prepare to hear the story, a greeting is extended and a song is sung.

The adults are not "watching" the children enter the story. *All* are hearing one of God's special stories together. Adults do not need to enter the story as children. They can come with childlike wonder, but everyone can hear the stories in a place that is authentic to them at that moment. The stories, even when heard over and over, can always provide new insight and connection for every age that is open to trusting the experience. We trust that the story is enough.

Due to initial resistance, some storytellers may seek to make the story more "entertaining"—louder, more dramatic, flashier—to accommodate the larger audience. Do not. *Do not.* Do not. Instead, *trust the process.* Trust that some of the discomfort in the beginning is planting the seeds for faithful growth.

Trust that the story is enough. Trust that worship is enough. Trust that the kids bring enough. Help adults remember that they are enough. Let us all know that God is always enough.

Leaders

In the past, pastors have typically supported my call to minister with children. They have even been supportive of introducing elements of these worship programs into worship. However, ultimately, *support* is not enough; a senior pastor and/or primary leader must be *fully engaged* (especially in the first few years) in the process of implementing an inter-generational version of Children and Worship or other ways of promoting all-age worship. If a senior pastor does not see herself or himself as one of the primary influences for children and youth, then they need to begin another type of conversation before moving into this important step.

Once I had moved into the role of the primary preaching pastor, I was able to enter more deeply and rest more fully in the holistic worship that Children and Worship can be. I use the understandings of Children and Worship in many messages as we all seek to slow down, trust the stories, talk to God, pray to God, worship God, and be in community with one another as God's beloved.

Children and Worship is not a quick-fix endeavor. It is an established approach that is worth the time and money for those who want to engage in an experience that can transform an entire faith community. Like any change, however, it must have leaders who are intentionally part of the paradigm shift.

Shifting from *Children* Worshiping Together to *All* Ages Worshiping Together

This integrated approach to Children and Worship, like all worship, is constantly in process. Some of the primary changes from a children's experience to a corporate worship experience have been discussed: preparing children and adults to enter the storytelling space; making sure everyone can see and hear the story; recognizing the process must make room for both children and adults in a space together; ensuring that senior leadership is intentionally involved. Another piece is deciding how much of the entire worship experience will be Children and Worship, and how much will consist of more traditional adult-oriented worship, and if the children will stay with the adults at that point, or if they will move to another space for their response/work time.

There are other shifts that will need to be made based on a church's size, finances, space, and resources. For example, children are invited to work with the stories they have heard during their wondering and response time; in our setting, there was no way to get the fifty-pound desert box (sand box needed for telling the Old Testament desert stories) down the stairs after a story was told, so until those stories ended, we had brown kinetic sand that was ready for children to use.

The one key element that I am still working to transfer is the blessing received by the children at the end of the service. While there is a "Sending Forth" for the congregation as a whole, this individual blessing of the child can be life giving. I am sure adults could use that personal blessing as they prepare to go back and face the world as people of faith who are truly loved. Even as I write this, my mind is percolating possibilities.

Children and Worship is much more than just stories. It is more than just ways for children to engage. It provides an intentional way for the whole body of Christ to assemble, proclaim, and learn to be God's people with songs, prayers, offerings, and stories. We all need to know that we are in a beloved relationship with God. Each of us is enough, just as the stories are enough. We can create sacred places and engage in worship, prayer, and conversations with God that include all people at "all places at all times."

Notes

[1]Over the past three decades, Jerome Berryman has built on his work with Sonja Stewart creating another form of Children and Worship that he calls *Godly Play*. The concepts discussed in this chapter can be used with Godly Play as well as Children and Worship.

[2]Sonja Stewart and Jerome Berryman, *Young Children and Worship* (Louisville: Westminster John Knox Press, 1989).

[3]"Children and Worship," accessed March 1, 2018, www.childrenandworship.org/.

[4]These descriptions are drawn from the Children and Worship website: www .childrenandworship.org/about.

The Intergenerationally Sticky Church

Cory Seibel

The process of becoming a vibrant intergenerational church can be compared to baking a cake. In order to bake a cake successfully, one must take a number of factors into consideration. However, combining the correct ingredients is essential. If the necessary ingredients are not mixed well, there is a good chance the cake will not hold together properly. One only needs to do an Internet search for images of "cake fails" to see how unfortunate a thing that can be.

Similar observations can be made about multigenerational churches today. Many of us are eager to see our churches become characterized by a strong sense of cohesion between people of different generations. There are immense benefits that accompany the strengthening of intergenerational cohesion within the church. Nonetheless, the sad reality is that the experience of many churches in recent decades has been painfully similar to "cake fails." In far too many cases, the generations have not held together well. Against the backdrop of this recent history, despite our best intentions, many of us have been left feeling unsure of how to foster cohesion among the generations within our churches.

As I have contemplated this challenge, I have found benefit in the theory of *intergenerational solidarity* developed by Vern Bengston, now Professor Emeritus of gerontology and sociology at the University of Southern California. Over the course of roughly forty years, Bengston worked with a series of collaborators to conduct the largest longitudinal study of families ever undertaken, one that involved more than 350 multigenerational families and more than 3,500 individuals. The concept of intergenerational solidarity, which focuses upon issues of cohesion within families, occupied a central place in this longitudinal study.[1] The big question at the heart of Benston's research was basically this: "What factors help to strengthen the bonds of cohesion within multigenerational families?" Bengston came to identify six distinct, interrelated dimensions of family solidarity.[2]

While Bengston's work was concerned solely with the experience of intergenerational solidarity within families, a chorus of observers has suggested that his theory has immense implications for other intergenerational contexts beyond the family. For example, in their book *Generational Intelligence*, Simon Biggs and Ariela Lowenstein argue, "Bengston's domains of familial intergenerational solidarity . . . also serve as powerful indicators of solidarity between generations in the larger community."[3] Similarly, in *Intergenerational Relations*, Roma Stovall Hanks and James Ponzetti make the following observation: "Too little has been done to apply his research questions and methods to non-family groups. . . . The work of Bengston and his colleagues is rich with questions about intergenerational relationships that need to be answered for non-family as well as family groups."[4]

This closing chapter represents an effort to undertake the sort of engagement with Bengston's work for which these authors advocate. It is an initial attempt at sketching out how the domains identified by Bengston could be used as a framework for discussing intergenerational cohesion within churches. In this chapter, I will appropriate Bengston's work in new ways. For example, while Bengston's writings on intergenerational solidarity remained largely *descriptive,* I endeavor to extrapolate from his research insights that are *prescriptive* in nature. In other words, I am interested in investigating the practical implications that can be drawn from his empirical work. In addition, because my intent is to explore the implications of his sociological research for the life of the church, I will bring his categories into conversation with concepts from the Christian tradition. I also will translate Bengston's terminology into language intended to be more accessible to church leaders. As I take these steps, I hope to do so in a manner that honors his valuable contribution by accurately representing his work.

As we consider the relevance of Bengston's theory of intergenerational solidarity for the life of the church today, I will suggest that every multi-generational congregation can strengthen intergenerational cohesion, or *stickiness*, by fostering a blend of six key ingredients. Together, these six ingredients form the acrostic COHERE.

I am convinced that the secret to strengthening stickiness between people of different generations within the church is not so much a strategy as it is a recipe. It is less about implementing specific programs and more a matter of attending to a mix of essential ingredients. Fortunately, these are not really "secret ingredients." They are already present in every church to varying degrees. The key is to be intentional in working with these ingredients.

Connecting: Crossing Relational Lines

According to Bengston, the extent to which people of different generations actively associate with one another is an important dimension of intergenerational cohesion. Within families, he and his team saw this reflected in how much "family members share activities with other family members."[5] Contact between family members can be formal or informal, face-to-face, or fostered from afar with the use of technology. However, a basic tenet of Bengston's research is that "more contact implies a greater degree of solidarity in the family."

This may sound fairly obvious. However, as we contemplate the relevance of Bengston's observation about the importance of "contact" for the life of the church, we can recognize that its implications are quite profound. In Western societies, we have been socialized in an environment that encourages us to associate largely with peers from within our own age groups. As a result, contact with people of other generations outside of our families is often quite limited. This pattern has been all too commonly—and all too uncritically—reflected within the church. Bengston's attention to the importance of contact helps us consider that when churchgoers of different generations fail to associate with one another relationally, the strength of intergenerational cohesion within the church is hampered.

Jurgen Moltmann notes that to the residents of our modern world, it seems natural that "birds of a feather flock together." In Christ, however, we are provided "a new orientation," one that calls us to move beyond friendship "within a closed circle" toward "open friendship" with those who are different from us.[6] This call to open friendship has important implications for intergenerational relations within the church. As Paul Hill poignantly expresses, "The business of the body of Christ is to build bridges between the generations, and the wood used for the bridge is the cross of Christ."[7]

Helping people cross the lines that keep them from associating with the members of other generations is a key ingredient of intergenerational cohesion within churches. Intergenerationally sticky churches are those that strive to encourage and enable people of all ages to connect with one another relationally.

Organizing: Creating Opportunity Structures

Bengston found "family structure" to be another factor influencing intergenerational cohesion within families. For Bengston, "structure" describes the impact that "spatial constraints" have upon intergenerational family relationships.[8] For example, when family members live far apart, this often limits how much contact they can have with one another. Family structure therefore serves an "opportunity function" within intergenerational families. It determines "the difficulty, in terms of distance, time, or cost" of interaction between family members.

Structure also has significant bearing on intergenerational dynamics within the church. Every congregation must decide how to structure its ministries to accomplish its mission. However, the structures we employ are never value-neutral. They bear the shaping influence of underlying values, priorities, and assumptions. In recent decades, the priorities that have guided the structural choices of many churches have tended to assume the necessity of separating the generations. As a result, opportunities for connections to be formed between people of different generations have been greatly limited.

"We shape our spaces and then they shape us."[9] These words, spoken by Sir Winston Churchill, are true not only of buildings, but of all human structures, including organizational structures. If we apply this principle to the life of the church, we can see that the ministry structures employed in recent decades have shaped us in profound ways. As Jaquelle Crowe expresses, our participation in these ministry structures tends to form us to believe "that our friends should exclusively be from our generation."[10] In essence, many church members have been shaped not to expect, or even seek, opportunities for engagement with people of generations outside their own.

In their book, *Intergenerational Space*, Robert Vanderbeck and Nancy Worth highlight the need for spaces that have been designed "for the purpose of facilitating and promoting interaction between members of different generational groups."[11] In essence, these authors are calling for opportunity structures that encourage and enable people of different generations to connect. This is an enormously important consideration for any church that strives to foster cohesion among the generations. Intergenerationally sticky churches employ structures that provide opportunities for people of different generations to foster relationships with one another.

Harmonizing: Sharing Core Convictions

Bengston found that cohesion within families also is impacted by "the degree of agreement on values, attitudes, and beliefs among family members."[12] As two of Bengston's collaborators explain, "similar views promote solidarity among family members and . . . dissimilar views contribute to dissension."[13] However, family cohesion is impacted not only by the actual differences between family members, but also by the assumptions that they make about one another's beliefs.[14]

Since Bengston began his research around 1970, a multitude of books, articles, and seminars has been dedicated to exploring differences in perspective across the generations and the impact of those different perspectives at home, in the workplace, and in a number of other contexts. The local church has certainly been one context in which the power of these differences has been felt. Ronald Sider and Ben Lowe note that churchgoers of different generations often "don't see eye to eye on many things, whether it's about stylistic issues such as worship music or Sunday attire, or about doctrinal or ethical issues such as sexuality or social justice."[15] Some of these differences are fairly inconsequential; others have contributed to considerable heartache and perplexity within churches.

While emphasis is often placed on the differences between generations, we have more in common than is often acknowledged. Because of our shared identity in Christ, this is especially true within the church. Intergenerationally sticky churches strive to help Christians of all ages recognize the core values and beliefs that they hold in common. Through liturgy, learning activities, and leadership processes, people of different generations can be helped to discover that they are "singing the same song."

At the same time, very real differences do exist between the generations. If we are not careful, these differences can cause us to adopt negative assumptions about one another's beliefs and motivations. Providing opportunities for intentional intergenerational conversations to take place can help foster understanding.[16] As people of faith, we may discover that some of our differences are not as dissonant as we assumed, but rather diverse contributions to the same song. In other words, through intentional dialogue, intergenerationally sticky congregations learn to help the generations "harmonize" their differences in ways that strengthen cohesion within the church.

Empathizing: Transforming Limited Perceptions

Another dimension of intergenerational cohesion identified by Bengston addresses the nature and intensity of family members' attitudes and emotions toward one another, or *affect*. All relationships have an *affective* dimension, "whether positive, neutral, or negative."[17] The sentiments that individuals attach to their relationships with other family members often are complex. They can be influenced by their perceptions of the quality of communication in their relationships, as well as by their evaluations of the level of trust, understanding, and closeness that they experience in these relationships.[18]

The level of cohesion between people of different generations within the church also is impacted by how they feel toward one another. Because of the distance that often exists between members of older and younger generations in the church, their perceptions and evaluations of one another are frequently influenced by age-based stereotypes that they may hold. These stereotypes often are overly simplistic, "erroneous, unrepresentative of reality, and resistant to modification."[19] Left unchecked, stereotypes cause us to amplify the differences between generational groups and to evaluate members of other groups in a less favorable light.

Churches that desire to strengthen intergenerational cohesion must attend to this affective dimension of relations between people of different generations. Encouraging young and old to develop empathy toward one another is perhaps one of the most transformative ways that a church can address this. Empathy is the capacity to understand and *feel with* the emotions of others. It has been described as putting oneself in the place of the other or trying to consider what it is like "to walk in their shoes."

Practices like storytelling can be powerful means of helping people of different generations learn to empathize with one another. As young and old share about their lives, this can foster understanding between them and lead them to recognize the ways in which some of the assumptions they have made about one another have been biased and limited.[20]

Intergenerationally sticky churches are committed to paying attention to this affective dimension and to finding ways to encourage people of different generations to develop empathy toward one another, thereby helping limited perceptions be transformed.

Recognizing: Acknowledging Mutual Responsibilities

Intergenerational cohesion in families is also influenced by the degree to which family members have a shared understanding of the *norms* that should guide their relationships.[21] Norms can be defined as standards of behavior that govern how family members interact with one another and what they expect from one another.[22] In essence, they address the responsibilities that family members have toward one another.[23] This is an especially important facet of intergenerational cohesion, one that requires ongoing attention, because norms change over time.[24]

Over the last several decades, Western societies have journeyed through a period of pronounced change. As a result, in many contexts, members of older and younger generations no longer share a common understanding of their responsibilities and obligations to one another. The absence of shared expectations between young and old can lead to disappointment, disillusionment, or outright discord. This loss of clear norms is felt within many churches as people of different ages struggle to understand what responsibilities, if any, they have to one another. The resulting disorientation leads to weakened ties of cohesion between the generations.

Scripture provides valuable insight into the responsibilities that people of different generations have toward one another within the community of faith. For example, we find these instructions to a young pastor in 1 Timothy 5:1–2: "Do not rebuke an older man harshly, but exhort him as if he were your father. Treat younger men as brothers, older women as mothers, and younger women as sisters, with absolute purity." Numerous other passages speak to the responsibilities of older generations toward children and of young people toward their elders.[25]

While we must exercise care in how we apply these ancient texts to our contemporary context, they do provide us the opportunity to develop biblically informed norms that can guide our relationships with one another as younger and older persons within the church. In a world in which intergenerational relations have undergone immense change, this may very well be a crucial aspect of biblical literacy today. Intergenerationally sticky churches help people of all ages engage with Scripture to discover a guiding vision of the responsibilities that they have to one another.

Exchanging: Honoring Diverse Gifts

The final dimension of intergenerational cohesion identified by Bengston is "the degree to which family members exchange services or assistance."[26] Exchanges can consist of things like gifts, shelter, services, advice, and money. According to Bengston's team, these exchanges within families reflect "issues of power, dependency, and justice."[27] Intergenerational cohesion is impacted by family members' perceptions of who has power within the family, the degree to which exchanges within the family are characterized by reciprocity or dependency, and whether the distribution of these exchanges is fair.

Exchange dynamics also have significant bearing on the experience of intergenerational cohesion within the church. The New Testament pictures the church as a body in which all members have been empowered and gifted by the Holy Spirit to make an essential contribution. Within this biblical vision, all members are called to exercise their gifts with a shared commitment to humility, mutuality, and equity.

The intergenerational dynamics within many churches in recent decades have fallen sadly short of this biblical vision. In many cases, power struggles have arisen between younger and older generations, leading to "win/loss" battles for control. In some situations, older generations have refused to make room for younger people to exercise their gifts. At times, the members of younger generations have adopted dismissive attitudes toward the contributions of older adults. Each of these scenarios exposes the struggles of multigenerational churches to foster exchange dynamics consistent with the biblical vision of mutuality and equity.

God's design has never been for older members of the community to share exclusively with other elders or for younger members to benefit only from the Spirit's work among their peers. Rather, the Holy Spirit desires to use people of all ages to serve "the common good" within the body of Christ (1 Cor. 12:7). Because of this "common good" principle, we cannot afford to say to one another, "I don't need you" (1 Cor. 12:21–22). We are all connected in Christ's Spirit, and all are needed.

Intergenerationally sticky churches encourage people of different generations to value, honor, and receive one another's gifts. They recognize the need to foster dynamics of power, mutuality, and equity that strengthen, rather than undermine, cohesion between the generations within the church.

Conclusion

In this chapter, I have explored six key ingredients that can help every church strengthen cohesion between people of diverse generations. While much more can be done to explore the interplay between Bengston's theories and the life of multigenerational churches, this chapter has provided an initial investigation into the potential value that his work holds for churches today.

Within churches today, the six ingredients explored in this chapter are greatly needed. In order for us to receive the benefit of these ingredients, however, they must be *kneaded*. In other words, we must be intentional about working with this blend of essential ingredients and mixing them together to help the generations in our churches learn to COHERE. As we do so, we are likely to grow together as intergenerationally sticky communities of faith.

Notes

[1]Vern L. Bengston and David J. Mangen, "Generations, Families, and Interactions: An Overview of the Research Program," in *Measurement of Intergenerational Relations*, eds. David J. Mangen, Vern L. Bengston, and Pierre H. Landry, Jr. (Newbury Park, CA: SAGE Publications, Inc., 1988), 10.

[2]This model entails six key dimensions: (1) Affectual Solidarity: the sentiments and evaluations family members express about their relationship with other members; (2) Associational Solidarity: the type and frequency of contact between intergenerational family members; (3) Consensual Solidarity: agreement in opinions, values, and orientations between generations; (4) Functional Solidarity: the giving and receiving of support across generations; (5) Normative Solidarity: expectations regarding filial obligations and parental obligations as well as norms about the importance of family; (6) Structural Solidarity: the "opportunity structure" for cross-generational interaction reflecting geographic proximity between family members.

[3]Simon Biggs and Ariela Lowenstein, *Generational Intelligence: A Critical Approach to Age Relations* (New York: Routledge, 2011), 128.

[4]Roma Stovall Hanks and James J. Ponzetti, Jr., "Family Studies and Intergenerational Studies: Intersections and Opportunities," in *Intergenerational Relations: Conversations on Practice and Research Across Cultures*, eds. Elizabeth Larkin, Dov Friedlander, Sally Newman, and Richard Goff (Binghampton, NY: Haworth Press, 2004), 15.

[5]David J. Mangen and Richard B. Miller, "Measuring Intergenerational Contact in the Family," in *Measurement of Intergenerational Relations*, eds. David J. Mangen, Vern L. Bengston, and Pierre H. Landry, Jr., 99.

[6]Jurgen Moltmann, *The Open Church: Invitation to a Messianic Life-style* (London: SCM Press, 1978), 30–31, 60–61.

[7]Paul G. Hill, "Youth and Family Ministry as Congregational and Community Renewal," in *The Difficult but Indispensable Church*, ed. Norma Cook Everist (Minneapolis: Fortress Press, 2002), 162.

[8]Kay Young McChesney, "Measuring Family Structure," in *Measurement of Intergenerational Relations*, ed. David J. Mangen, Vern L. Bengston, and Pierre H. Landry, Jr., 56.

[9]Robert Allan Hill, *Renewal: Thought, Word, and Deed* (Lanham, MD: Hamilton Books, 2009), 96.

[10]Jaquelle Crowe, "Friends Your Age Are Not Enough," *Desiring God*, January 5, 2017, www.desiringgod.org/articles/friends-your-age-are-not-enough.

[11]Robert M. Vanderbeck and Nancy Worth, *Intergenerational Space* (Abingdon, UK: Routledge, 2015), 1.

[12] Kay Young McChesney and Vern L. Bengston, "Solidarity, Integration, and Cohesion in Families: Concepts and Theories," in *Measurement of Intergenerational Relations*, eds. David J. Mangen, Vern L. Bengston, and Pierre H. Landry, Jr., 23.

[13] Pierre H. Landry, Jr. and Mary E. Martin, "Measuring Intergenerational Consensus," in *Measurement of Intergenerational Relations*, eds. David J. Mangen, Vern L. Bengston, and Pierre H. Landry, Jr., 126.

[14] Landry and Martin, "Measuring Intergenerational Consensus," 128.

[15] Ronald J. Sider and Ben Lowe, *Future of Our Faith: An Intergenerational Conversation on Critical Issues Facing the Church* (Grand Rapids: Brazos Press, 2016), 1.

[16] Some helpful resources have been created to assist churches in facilitating these sorts of intentional discussions. A prime example is James Gambone, *All Are Welcome: A Primer for Intentional Intergenerational Ministry and Dialogue* (Crystal Bay, MN: Elder Eye Press, 1998).

[17] Rebecca L. Gronvold, "Measuring Affectual Solidarity," in *Measurement of Intergenerational Relations*, eds. David J. Mangen, Vern L. Bengston, and Pierre H. Landry, Jr., 74.

[18] Gronvold, "Measuring Affectual Solidarity," 78.

[19] Fay Lomax Cook, "Age Stereotypes," in *The Encyclopedia of Aging: A Comprehensive Resource in Gerontology and Geriatrics*, ed. George L. Maddox, 3rd ed., vol. 1 (New York: Springer, 2001), 45.

[20] Mary Price-Mitchell, "Storytelling Is a Conduit for Intergenerational Learning," *Psychology Today*, September 19, 2016, www.psychologytoday.com/blog/the-moment -youth/201609/storytelling-is-conduit-intergenerational-learning/.

[21] McChesney and Bengston, "Solidarity, Integration, and Cohesion in Families," 23.

[22] Vern L. Bengston and David J. Mangen, "Family Intergenerational Solidarity Revisited: Suggestions for Future Management," in *Measurement of Intergenerational Relations*, eds. David J. Mangen, Vern L. Bengston, and Pierre H. Landry, Jr., 229.

[23] David J. Mangen and Gerald Jay Westbrook, "Measuring Intergenerational Norms," in *Measurement of Intergenerational Relations*, eds. David J. Mangen, Vern L. Bengston, and Pierre H. Landry, Jr., 188.

[24] Mangen and Westbrook, "Measuring Intergenerational Norms," 189.

[25] A key verse in the biblical witness regarding how younger generations are meant to respond to their elders is Leviticus 19:32: "Stand up in the presence of the aged, show respect for the elderly." God's concern toward the treatment of seniors is also evident in the passages that express concern for widows. In Deuteronomy, for example, God's people are encouraged to be intentional about including widows in their sacred feasts (e.g., Deut. 14:29, 16:11, 14). This concern is reinforced in the New Testament, as well (Acts 6:1; James 1:27). A few key passages that speak to the responsibilities of older generations toward children include the following: Deuteronomy 4:9–10, 11:18–19; Psalm 71:17–18, 78:4–6, and Mark 10:13–15.

[26] McChesney and Bengston, "Solidarity, Integration, and Cohesion in Families," 23.

[27] Paula Hancock, David J. Mangen, and Kay Young McChesney, "The Exchange Dimension of Solidarity: Measuring Intergenerational Exchange and Functional Solidarity," in *Measurement of Intergenerational Relations*, eds. David J. Mangen, Vern L. Bengston, and Pierre H. Landry, Jr., 159.

Selected Bibliography

Allen, Holly Catterton, and Christine Lawton Ross. *Intergenerational Christian Formation: Bringing the Whole Church Together in Ministry, Community, and Worship.* Downers Grove, IL: InterVarsity Press, 2012.

Amidei, Kathie, John Roberto, and Jim Merhaut. *Generations Together: Caring, Praying, Learning, Celebrating, and Serving Faithfully.* Naugatuck, CT: Lifelong Faith Associates, 2014.

Barna, George, and David Kinnaman. *Churchless: Understanding Today's Unchurched and How to Connect with Them.* Carol Stream, IL: Tyndale Momentum, 2014.

Bengston, Vern L., and David J. Mangen. "Family Intergenerational Solidarity Revisited: Suggestions for Future Management." In *Measurement of Intergenerational Relations*, edited by David J. Mangen, Vern L. Bengston, and Pierre H. Landry, Jr., 222–38. Newbury Park, CA: Sage Publications, 1988.

Clark, Chap, ed. *Adoptive Youth Ministry: Integrating Emerging Generations into the Family of Faith.* Grand Rapids: Baker Academic, 2011.

Csinos, David M., and Ivy Beckwith. *Children's Ministry in the Way of Jesus.* Downers Grove, IL: InterVarsity Press, 2013.

Dean, Kenda Creasy. *Almost Christian: What the Faith of Our Teenagers is Telling the American Church.* New York: Oxford University Press, 2010.

Fraze, David. "Friends, Mentors, Heroes: Connecting with Other Generations." In *Owning Faith: Reimagining the Role of Church and Family in the Faith Journey of Teenagers*, edited by Ron Bruner and Dudley Chancey, 219–40. Abilene, TX: Leafwood Publishers, 2017.

Gambone, James. *All Are Welcome: A Primer for Intentional Intergenerational Ministry and Dialogue.* Crystal Bay, MN: Elder Eye Press, 1998.

Glassford, Darwin, and Lynn Barger Elliot. "Toward Intergenerational Ministry in a Post-Christian Era." *Christian Education Journal* 8, no. 2 (2011): 364–78.

Harkness, Allan G. "Intergenerationality: Biblical and Theological Foundations." *Christian Education Journal* 9, no. 1 (2012): 129–32.

Kinnaman, David. *You Lost Me: Why Young Christians Are Leaving the Church . . . And Rethinking Faith.* Grand Rapids: Baker Books, 2011.

Lave, Jean, and Etienne Wenger. *Situated Learning: Legitimate Peripheral Participation.* Cambridge: Cambridge University Press, 1991.

Martineau, Mariette, Leif Kehrwald, and Joan Weber. *Intergenerational Faith Formation: Learning the Way We Live.* New London, CT: Twenty-Third Publications, 2008.

May, Scottie, Beth Posterski, Catherine Stonehouse, and Linda Cannell. *Children Matter: Celebrating Their Place in the Church, Family, and Community.* Grand Rapids: Eerdmans, 2005.

McIntosh, Gary L. *One Church, Four Generations: Understanding and Reaching All Ages in Your Church.* Grand Rapids: Baker Books, 2002.

Powell, Kara, Jake Mulder, and Brad Griffin. *Growing Young: Six Essential Strategies to Help Young People Discover and Love Your Church.* Grand Rapids: Baker Books, 2016.

Powell, Kara, and Chap Clark. *Sticky Faith: Everyday Ideas to Build Lasting Faith in Your Kids.* Grand Rapids: Zondervan, 2011.

Roberto, John. "Our Future Is Intergenerational." *Christian Education Journal* 9, no. 1 (2012): 105–20.

———.*Becoming a Church of Lifelong Learners: The Generations of Faith Sourcebook.* New London, CT: Twenty-Third Publications, 2006.

Ross, Christine. "Four Congregations that Practice Intergenerationality," *Christian Education Journal* 9, no. 1 (2012): 135–47.

Smith, Christian, and Melinda Lundquist Denton, *Soul Searching: The Religious and Spiritual Lives of American Teenagers.* Oxford: Oxford University Press, 2005.

Smith, Christian, with Patricia Snell. *Souls in Transition: The Religious and Spiritual Lives of Emerging Adults.* Oxford: Oxford University Press, 2009.

Snailum, Brenda. "Implementing Intergenerational Youth Ministry within Existing Evangelical Church Congregations: What Have We Learned?" *Christian Education Journal* 9, no. 1 (2012): 165-81.

Strauss, William, and Neil Howe, *The Fourth Turning: An American Prophecy—What the Cycles of History Tell Us about America's Next Rendezvous with Destiny.* New York: Broadway Books, 1997.

———. *Generations: The History of America's Future, 1584 to 2069.* New York: William Morrow, 1991.

Vanderwell, Howard, ed. *The Church of All Ages: Generations Worshiping Together.* Herndon, VA: Alban Institute, 2008.

White, James W. *Intergenerational Religious Education: Models, Theories, and Prescription for Interage Life and Learning in the Faith Community.* Birmingham, AL: Religious Education Press, 1988.

Whitesel, Bob, and Kent R. Hunter. *House Divided: Bridging the Generation Gaps in Your Church.* Nashville: Abingdon Press, 2000.

Williams, Angie, and Jon F. Nussbaum. *Intergenerational Communication across the Life Span.* Mahwah, NJ: Routledge, 2001.

Wuthnow, Robert. *After the Baby Boomers: How Twenty- and Thirty-Somethings Are Shaping the Future of American Religion.* Princeton, NJ: Princeton University Press, 2007.

Zahn, Drew. "Connecting the Generations." *Leadership Journal* 23, no. 2 (April 2002). http://www.ctlibrary.com/le/2002/spring/3.37.html.

Zirschky, Andrew D. *Beyond the Screen: Youth Ministry for the Connected but Alone Generation.* Nashville: Abingdon Press, 2015.

About the Contributors

Holly Catterton Allen, PhD, is Professor of Family Science and Christian Ministries at Lipscomb University in Nashville, Tennessee. Holly's areas of academic interest are children's spirituality and intergenerational ministry. Her passion for cross-age ministry emerged during the four years that her family worshiped with a church that met in homes on Sunday evenings in intergenerational small groups. Holly's doctorate is from Talbot School of Theology in La Mirada, California, and her dissertation focused on children's spirituality and intergenerational Christian experiences. Her most recent book (with Christine Ross) is *Intergenerational Christian Formation: Bringing the Whole Church Together in Ministry, Community, and Worship*. Holly is the chair of the task force that convened the InterGenerate Conference.

Joseph Azzopardi is a PhD candidate at Avondale College of Higher Education in New South Wales, Australia. He has completed a master's degree in Youth and Young Adult Ministry from Andrews University in Berrien Springs, Michigan. Joe spent ten years as a teacher, with classes ranging from kindergarten to high school; he also served as a school chaplain. He has pastored rural senior congregations as well as an urban young adult congregation. This broad background with various age groups, combined with his passion for practical Christianity, has led Joe to research the intersection of discipleship, well-being, and intergenerational relationships. With this research, Joe's mission is to equip Christian leaders to cultivate disciples, rather than only members, in their churches.

Chris Barnett serves at the Centre for Theology and Ministry in Melbourne, Australia, and is responsible for intergenerational ministry across the Uniting Church Synod of Victoria and Tasmania. His role includes a focus on consultancy, advocacy, resourcing, and training in relation to ministry with children and their families, with a strong emphasis on intergenerational engagement. Though originally trained as a pharmacist, Chris has extensive experience in congregational, regional, and denominational ministry, even acquiring a graduate degree in Bible and Ministry at Ridley College, Melbourne, along the way. He has a passion for assisting leaders, congregations, and regional groups in developing and implementing their vision for ministering to families with children.

Joseph P. Conway, DMin, has served since 2011 as the senior minister with the Acklen Avenue Church of Christ in Nashville, Tennessee, an intentionally intergenerational congregation. He also worked as a youth minister for over ten years with churches in Connecticut and Tennessee. His doctoral work focused on the ways churches can serve their local communities through the combined engagement of every generation. In his ministry, he seeks to stem the tide of loneliness and spiritual immaturity caused by age separation through a consistent, holistic intergenerational culture. Joseph holds degrees from Abilene Christian University, Gordon-Conwell Theological Seminary, and Fuller Theological Seminary and is an adjunct professor at Lipscomb University in Nashville, teaching Bible, theology, and ministry courses.

Rev. Melissa Cooper is an ordained deacon in the United Methodist Church and an associate with Vibrant Faith, providing ministry coaching services in intergenerational ministry, cross-generational communication, and camp and retreat ministry. She received her Master of Theological Studies degree from Boston University School of Theology. Melissa served for eight years in camp and retreat ministries in North Carolina and Florida, spending much of her career developing a model for intergenerational camping. She has spoken at various regional and national gatherings for the United Methodist Church, the United Church of Christ, and the Evangelical Lutheran Church in America on the topics of intergenerational ministry and cross-generational communication. She has also written curriculum for youth and children for Sparkhouse.

Gareth Crispin is the minister for youth, children, and families at an Anglican church in Cheshire, United Kingdom. He is studying for a PhD in Family Ministry and Intergenerational Church at Cliff College, UK, where he is an adjunct lecturer for undergraduate and postgraduate courses. He is the coauthor of *Together with God: An Introduction to Family Worship*, and he copresents the monthly podcast *Together with God*, a series of conversations on faith, family, and today's church. Gareth is especially interested in the relationship between church and family in the development of faith in youth and children.

Karen DeBoer serves as Creative Resource Developer for Faith Formation Ministries. In that role, she creates and curates resources for topical toolkits on the intergenerational church, welcoming children to the Lord's Supper, and children's ministry. Her love for children led her to pursue an Early Childhood Education degree from Dordt College, and her love of words prompted her to pursue a Bachelor of Arts in English degree from the University of Waterloo. Karen shapes her work around the conviction that faith is nurtured when people of all ages feel certain they belong to God and experience that belonging within God's family, the church.

Lynn Barger Elliott, MDiv, is the associate pastor at Mayflower Congregational Church and an instructor in the Congregational and Ministry Studies Department at Calvin College. As a pastor, preacher, and professor, she strives to equip leaders to create environments where God's people of all ages can learn from each other about living into their faith. She holds a degree in Philosophy from Wheaton College and an MDiv from Princeton Theological Seminary. Lynn, an ordained Presbyterian pastor, and her husband, Mark, have served intergenerational church communities for more than two decades across Pennsylvania, New Jersey, Michigan, and Illinois.

Darwin K. Glassford, PhD, is the executive pastor at Harderwyk Ministries and Director of Graduate Programs and Online Learning at Kuyper College. As a former professor at Montreat College and Calvin Theological Seminary, his research focused on integrating young people in the worship life of the church. His current focus involves helping churches take intentional steps to enhance their intergenerational ministry strategies. This focus is informed by his studies in educational ministries at Wheaton College and theological studies at Trinity Evangelical Divinity School. His doctoral research at Marquette University focused on the philosophical, historical, and theological foundations of education, with additional study at Covenant Seminary on the relationship between Christianity and contemporary culture.

Nancy Going currently serves as Executive Director of Vibrant Faith Ministries, an organization with a twenty-five-year history of work with churches to recreate transformative Christian formation. She is involved with the Visual Faith Project, a research and praxis initiative of Vibrant Faith that allows leaders and churches to access the power of images for spiritual transformation. Nancy holds a Master of Arts in Counseling from Covenant Seminary and a PhD from Luther Seminary, where she studied adolescent spiritual development. Prior to Vibrant Faith, Nancy served on the Children, Youth, and Family team at Luther Seminary. In addition, she is a twenty-year veteran of youth ministry and has written curriculum and articles on faith development.

Amy Kippen is a Resource Specialist and a FAITH5 Coach with Faith Inkubators. She is also a full-time student at Luther Seminary, pursuing both a Master of Divinity and ordination in the Evangelical Lutheran Church in America. Amy's fifteen years of experience in family ministry include leading a change from the "drop-off norm" to parent involvement every week at church and every night at home. Amy is a contributing author to the book *Let's Kill Sunday School before It Kills the Church.* In both her congregational work and her role with Faith Inkubators, she has seen the power of visionary church leaders equipping and challenging parents to be the primary faith teachers for their children.

Rev. Aqueelah Ligonde, an ordained clergywoman for the Presbyterian Church (USA), is an enthusiastic speaker and leader with a passion for today's generation of youth, women, and leaders. She has worked with numerous organizations such as the Princeton Seminary Institute for Youth Ministry and Youth Specialties, and she serves on the Executive Board of GenOn Ministries, an organization dedicated to intergenerational relationships. Aqueelah holds a Master of Divinity from McCormick Theological Seminary. She is currently pursuing a Doctor of Ministry from Louisville Theological Seminary, and she is a Staff Consultant with Ministry Architects. For over a decade, Aqueelah served as the Associate Pastor at the First Presbyterian Church in Jamaica, Queens, New York.

Wilson McCoy, DMin, has served since 2010 as the Associate Minister at College Hills Church of Christ in Lebanon, Tennessee. His responsibilities include working with young professionals, preaching and teaching, adult formation, and small groups. Before College Hills, Wilson served churches in Tennessee, Texas, and Brisbane,

Australia. Wilson received an undergraduate degree in Bible from Lipscomb University and a Master of Divinity from Abilene Christian University. Wilson completed his Doctorate of Ministry at Lipscomb University, focusing on intergenerational spiritual formation. He endeavors to develop intergenerational rhythms in the life of his local congregation while training other ministers to do the same.

Jim Merhaut is the Founder and Director of Coaching to Connect, a training and coaching service offered to individuals, organizations, and couples. Jim is a professional executive and life coach, as well as a leadership consultant and trainer, writer, retreat leader, and national speaker. He holds a Master of Science in Religious Education from Duquesne University. He has authored and coauthored nine books and dozens of other publications, including the Lifelong Faith book, *Generations Together*, and *Families on a Mission*. Jim has over three decades of church ministry leadership experience and specializes in intergenerational faith formation. He is also a professional musician and recording artist with singer and songwriter J. D. Eicher.

Liz Perraud is the Executive Director of GenOn Ministries, a nonprofit organization that equips Christian communities for discipleship through intergenerational relationships. Liz has led training workshops, consulted, and preached throughout the United States and Canada for over fifteen years with GenOn. She holds a Bachelor of Business Administration from The College of William and Mary in Williamsburg, Virginia, and is an ordained elder in the Presbyterian Church (USA). Liz has written articles on intergenerational relationships and ministry for *Presbyterians Today*, *The Presbyterian Outlook*, Princeton Theological Seminary's *The Thread*, *Building Faith* and *NEXT Church* blogs, and *What Matters Now in Children's Ministry*.

John Roberto serves as the Coordinator of Training Services and Project Coordinator for the Vibrant Faith Institute and holds a master's degree in religious education from Fordham University. He works as a consultant to churches and national organizations, teaches courses and conducts workshops in faith formation, and has authored numerous books and program manuals on faith formation. His latest publications include *Families at the Center of Faith Formation* and *Seasons of Adult Faith Formation*. John is the founder of LifelongFaith Associates and the Center for Ministry Development. He was also the creator and project coordinator of the Generations of Faith Project, a project funded by the Lilly Endowment to develop intergenerational faith formation in Catholic parishes across the United States.

Dawn Rundman, PhD, is the Director of Development for Faith Formation Resources at Augsburg Fortress, where she also serves as the Assistant Director for Evangelical Lutheran Church of America Relations. She holds a doctoral degree in Developmental Psychology from the University of Oregon. After six years teaching psychology at Concordia University, she pivoted to a career in church publishing at Augsburg Fortress. She has developed over 20,000 pages of curriculum and five Bibles for kids. She has also authored three children's books and has written the "Preschooler Age-Level Insights" column for *Children's Ministry Magazine*. She encourages parents, grandparents, and church leaders to embrace research on early childhood in order to help them nurture faith in babies, toddlers, and preschoolers.

Dave Sanders earned a DMin in Youth, Family, and Culture from Fuller Seminary. As a tenured professor in the Christian Ministries Department at Judson University, he teaches courses on youth ministry and adolescent studies, as well as mentoring, intergenerational leadership, evangelism, spiritual formation, and intercultural missions. For over thirty years, Dave has engaged with church and parachurch youth ministry, specifically through involvement with Young Life staff positions. He served for fifteen years with Military Community Youth Ministries (MCYM) Club Beyond, ministering to military teens on NATO bases across Europe. Dave also directed two partnership projects between the American Bible Society and MCYM, a web-based engagement tool called RezLife.com and the *I AM Military Teen Bible*.

Rev. Jason Brian Santos, PhD, is the Mission Coordinator for Christian Formation at the Presbyterian Mission Agency. In this role, he focuses on Christian education, camps and conferences, and ministering to children, youth, college students, and young adults. He also serves as the National Director of UKirk Collegiate Ministries. Jason is an ordained teaching elder in the Presbyterian Church (USA) and holds a Doctor in Practical Theology from Princeton Theological Seminary. He is the author of *A Community Called Taizé* and *After Paradise* (forthcoming).

Cory Seibel, PhD, is Pastor of Lifelong Faith Formation at Central Baptist Church in Edmonton, Alberta. Cory has devoted nearly two decades to exploring generational dynamics in the church and society. He earned his MTh degree in Applied Theology through Spurgeon's College, London, and a PhD in Practical Theology from the University of Pretoria, South Africa. His doctoral research was supervised by Malan Nel, an internationally recognized intergenerational youth ministry specialist. Prior to joining the pastoral team at Central Baptist Church, Cory served churches in Virginia and North Dakota and taught at seminaries in South Dakota and California.

Diane E. Shallue, EdD, is a deacon in the Evangelical Lutheran Church in America with twenty-five years of service in congregational ministry in the Minneapolis area. Diane's focus is Christian education with a particular passion for intergenerational ministry. Diane was an Adjunct Instructor at Luther Seminary for fourteen years. Although now retired from congregational ministry, she is currently an Adjunct Professor at United Lutheran Seminary in Philadelphia and Gettysburg.

Tori Bennett Smit, DEdMin, is the Regional Minister for Faith Formation for the Synod of Central, Northeastern Ontario and Bermuda with the Presbyterian Church in Canada. Throughout thirty-five years of ministry, Tori has advocated for children's and youth ministries that prioritize intergenerational relationships in faith formation. In response to the present realities of the congregations she serves, Tori's doctoral dissertation with Columbia Theological Seminary focused on specific forms of ministry that would best serve congregations with ten or fewer children. Tori uncovered five intentional practices of intergenerational ministry as the answer to this issue. She has written leader guides for Montreat Conference Center, Canada Youth, and Kergyma Bible Studies and serves as a trainer for GenOn Ministries.

Linda Staats describes her foundation for nurturing faith across generations as being shaped first by parents, grandparents, and mentors who modeled a Christian faith, and second by a master's degree in Human Development and the Family with a specialty in Marriage and Family Enrichment from the University of Nebraska. Linda brings a lifespan approach to discipleship, stewardship, and global mission through her service in the Evangelical Lutheran Church in America. She is a national speaker, workshop facilitator, curriculum writer, consultant, and congregational coach; she is also the developer of HomeGrown Faith (www.homegrownfaith.net). Linda's career reflects her desire to connect people's own holy stories with God's story and to empower all generations to serve like Jesus.

Jessica Stollings is a national speaker, author, and the President of ReGenerations, an organization that bridges generational gaps to build a better future (re-generations .org). Pastors, ministries, and churches across the country have built solutions around her ideas. Jessica's passion for intergenerational connections grew out of her leadership roles in talent development and corporate communications for Alpha Natural Resources (a former Fortune 500 company) and out of her role as a nationally syndicated news reporter and producer for a Focus on the Family radio show. Jessica graduated from King University with degrees in English and Communication.

Tammy Tolman is the founding pastor of an Intergenerational Creative Arts community in Australia, called "ICentral316," among the Churches of Christ in Australia. Tammy has been actively involved in ministry to children and their families for three decades. She is the author of *Piece by Piece* and *Exploring Intergenerational Ministry*, and her "Discovery Learning Series" curriculum and worship music impacts children and youth around the world (www.discoverylearningseries.com). Tammy speaks and trains at conferences across all denominations throughout the world, and for thirty years, she has directed camps for kids and families. Tammy is passionate to see the family of God be empowered to grow and walk the lifelong journey of faith together. Follow her blog at tammytolman.blogspot.com.au.

Rev. Dr. Olivia B. Updegrove is Minister of Family and Children's Ministries at Disciples Home Mission in Indianapolis, Indiana, and part-time pastor at Independence Christian Church in Independence, Kentucky. Olivia is an ordained minister in the Christian Church (Disciples of Christ). She attended seminary at Lexington Theological Seminary and completed her doctoral work at Claremont School of Theology with an emphasis in preaching. She has worked with children, youth, and young adults at various stages of her ministry, and she has a deep passion for biblical education for all ages as a foundation for deeper spiritual growth. She has published three children's books—*What Is God?*, *Who Is Jesus?*, and *Where Is Holy?*